**WITHDRAWN
UTSA Libraries**

COMPETITION AND THE REGULATION OF UTILITIES

Topics in Regulatory Economics and Policy Series

Michael A. Crew, Editor
Graduate School of Management
Rutgers University
Newark, New Jersey, U.S.A.

Previously published books in the series:

Rowley, C., R. Tollison, and G. Tullock:
Political Economy of Rent-Seeking

Frantz, R.:
X-Efficiency: Theory, Evidence and Applications

Crew, M.:
Deregulation and Diversification of Utilities

Shogren, J.:
The Political Economy of Government Regulation

Hillman, J., and R. Braeutigam:
Price Level Regulation for Diversified Public Utilities

Einhorn, M.:
Price Caps and Incentive Regulation in Telecommunications

COMPETITION AND THE REGULATION OF UTILITIES

edited by
Michael A. Crew
Graduate School of Management
Rutgers University
Newark, New Jersey

Kluwer Academic Publishers
Boston/Dordrecht/London

Distributors for North America:
Kluwer Academic Publishers
101 Philip Drive
Assinippi Park
Norwell, Massachusetts 02061 USA

Distributors for all other countries:
Kluwer Academic Publishers Group
Distribution Centre
Post Office Box 322
3300 AH Dordrecht, THE NETHERLANDS

Library of Congress Cataloging-in-Publication Data

Competition and the regulation of utilities / edited by Michael A.
  Crew.
      p.   cm. — (Topics in regulatory economics and policy series ;
  7)
    ISBN 0-7923-9083-0
    1. Public utilities—Government policy—United States—Congresses.
  2. Telecommunication—Government policy—United States—Congresses.
  3. Competition—United States—Congresses.   I. Crew, Michael A.
  II. Series.
  HD2766.C677   1990
  363.6'0973—dc20   90-45770
                                                                    CIP

Copyright © 1991 by Kluwer Academic Publishers

Printed on acid-free paper.

All rights reserved. No part of this publication may be reproduced, stored in a retrieval system or transmitted in any form or by any means, mechanical, photocopying, recording, or otherwise, without the prior written permission of the publisher, Kluwer Academic Publishers, 101 Philip Drive, Assinippi Park, Norwell, Massachusetts 02061.

Printed in the United States of America.

CONTENTS

Authors and Discussants — vii

Preface and Acknowledgments — ix

1 Introduction to Competition and the Regulation of Utilities — 1
  Michael A. Crew

2 The Law and Economics of IntraLATA Competition: 1+ Issues and Access Charge Imputation — 7
  Mark Sievers

3 Diversification and Regulated Monopoly — 33
  Michael A. Crew and Keith J. Crocker

4 Predatory Pricing Safeguards and Telecommunications Regulation — 51
  Alexander C. Larson

5 Oil Pipeline Rates: A Case for Yardstick Regulation — 71
  Jordan Jay Hillman

6 Telecommunications Services as a Strategic Industry: Implications for United States Public Policy — 97
  Robert G. Harris

7 Productivity Growth and Technological Change in the United States Telecommunications Equipment Manufacturing Industries — 121
  Show-Ling Jang and J.R. Norsworthy

8 Entry and Welfare Loss in Regulated Industries   141
   Timothy J. Brennan

9 Information Economics and New Forms of   157
   Regulation
   Michael A. Crew and Michael R. Frierman

10 Franchise Bidding for Public Utilities Revisited   173
   Michael A. Crew and Mark A. Zupan

11 Privatization of Electricity in the United States   189
   Douglas A. Houston

AUTHORS AND DISCUSSANTS

Thomas A. Abbott, III, Assistant Professor of Economics, Graduate School of Management, Rutgers University

Timothy J. Brennan, Associate Professor, Graduate School, University of Maryland, Baltimore

Pat Chirico, Director—Utility Industry Relations, New Jersey Bell Telephone

Michael A. Crew, Professor of Economics and Director of the Center for Research in Regulated Industries, Graduate School of Management, Rutgers University

Keith J. Crocker, Associate Professor of Economics, Pennsylvania State University

Robert A. Dansby, Division Manager, Bell Communications Research

Michael R. Frierman, Assistant Professor of Economics, Graduate School of Management, Rutgers University

Joseph P. Gatto, Staff Manager—Demand Analysis, AT&T Communications

Sharon Gifford, Assistant Professor of Economics, Graduate School of Management, Rutgers University

David J. Goodman, Professor and Chair, Electrical and Computer Engineering, and Director, Rutgers Wireless Information Network Lab, Rutgers University

James Green, Division Staff Manager, Southern New England Telephone

Robert G. Harris, Associate Professor, School of Business Administration, University of California at Berkeley

Malcolm C. Harris, Sr., Associate Professor of Finance, College of Business Administration, St. John's University

Jordan Jay Hillman, Professor Emeritus of Law & Research Counsel, The Transportation Center, Northwestern University Law School

Douglas A. Houston, Associate Professor of Economics, School of Business, University of Kansas

Show-Ling Jang, Economist/Expert Witness, Public Service Commission of Washington, DC

Alexander C. Larson, District Manager, Southwestern Bell Telephone

Son Lin Lai, Senior Policy Advisor, New Jersey Board of Public Utilities

Raymond Makul, Director, New Jersey Office of Rate Counsel

Eileen Moran, Vice President—Investments, Public Service Resources Corporation

J.R. Norsworthy, Professor of Economics, School of Humanities & Social Sciences, Rensselaer Polytechnic Institute

Carl Pechman, Principal Economist, Office of Research, New York State Department of Public Service

Michael F. Riccardelli, Partner, Riccardelli and Rosa

David Salant, Senior Member—Technical Staff, GTE Laboratories

Joseph C. Schuh, Director—Economics, Orange and Rockland Utilities

Richard Simnett, District Manager, Bell Communications Research

Mark Sievers, State Regulatory Policy Director, US Sprint

Charlotte Twight, Associate Professor of Economics, Boise State University

Dennis Weller, Manager—Industry Policy, GTE

Mark A. Zupan, Associate Professor, Department of Finance & Business Economics, School of Business Administration, University of Southern California

PREFACE AND ACKNOWLEDGMENTS

This book is a result of two seminars held at Rutgers—The State University of New Jersey on October 27, 1989, and May 4, 1990, entitled "Competition and the Regulation of Utilities." Twelve previous seminars in the same series resulted in *Problems in Public Utility Economics and Regulation* (Lexington Books, 1979), *Issues in Public Utility Pricing and Regulation* (Lexington Books, 1980), *Regulatory Reform and Public Utilities (Lexington Books, 1982), Analyzing the Impact of Regulatory Change* (Lexington Books, 1985), *Regulating Utilities in and Era of Deregulation* (Macmillan Press, 1987), and *Deregulation and Diversification of Utilities* (Kluwer Academic Publishers, 1989).

Like the previous seminars, these seminars received financial support from leading utilities. The views expressed, of course, are those of the authors and do not necessarily reflect the views of the sponsoring companies. AT&T, Atlantic Electric Company, Elizabethtown Gas Company, Garden State Water Company, GTE Service Company, Hackensack Water Company, Jersey Central Power & Light Company, New Jersey Bell Telephone Company, New Jersey Natural Gas Company, New Jersey-American Water Company, New York Telephone Company, NYNEX Service Company, Public Service Electric and Gas Company, Rockland Electric Company, Shorelands Water Company, and United Telephone Company of New Jersey provided funding for both seminars. Niagara Mohawk Power Corporation and South Jersey Gas Company provided funding for the first seminar. The support went far beyond financial assistance. Company managers freely gave their time and advice and, on several occasions, provided information about their industries. I especially thank George Baulig, Bill Cobb, Lawrence Cole, Frank Delany, Theresa Flaim, Robert Iacullo, Edward Jones, Patricia Keefe, Alfred Koeppe, Brian Lane, James Lees, Elmer Martin, Russell Mayer, Charles Morgan, Glenn Phillips, Don Schlenger, Joseph Schuh, Robert Thompson, Michael Walsh, and Bill Wiginton. Alfred E. Koeppe, Vice President of Public Affairs, New Jersey Bell, provided the introduction to the Seminar on October 27, and Everett Morris, Senior Executive Vice President, Public Service Electric and Gas Company, introduced the May 4 Seminar. I would like to thank them for their interest in the program.

Many thanks are owed to the distinguished speakers and discussants, listed on pages vii and viii, for their cooperation making the seminars and this book possible.

They all worked very hard in achieving deadlines, without which the speedy publication of this book would have been impossible. I would especially like to thank Linda Brennan, Administrative Assistant in the Center for Research in Regulated Industries. Not only did she provide able editorial and research program assistance, but she also mastered *Xerox Ventura Publisher*, the pc-based typesetting program used to provide the camera-ready copy for this book. The usual disclaimers are applicable. None of the people named here is responsible for any errors. The views expressed are the views of the authors and not of the sponsoring companies.

MICHAEL A. CREW

COMPETITION AND THE REGULATION OF UTILITIES

1
INTRODUCTION TO COMPETITION AND THE REGULATION OF UTILITIES
Michael A. Crew

Traditionally, the very idea of competition having any impact on the regulation of utilities was antithetical to the basic philosophy of utility regulation. The institution of regulation had developed because there was a problem with competition. Because of overwhelming scale economies in traditional utilities, monopoly was the natural order of things. Natural monopoly was a considered a classic example of market failure—where the free interplay of market forces did not yield the efficient outcome associated with competition. Thus, the failure of the free market outcome resulted in (natural) monopoly, with the resultant inefficiency and inequity. From an economist's point of view, regulation was seen as a way of resolving the pricing or allocative inefficiency resulting from natural monopoly.[1] Regulation apparently served not only to protect the interests of consumers but also to provide guarantees to the regulated monopolist. In this vein, regulation was perceived as an efficient governance structure, at least when compared with alternatives like franchise bidding (Williamson 1976).

Implicit in this simplified tradition view of competition and regulation of utilities was the notion that regulation was performed in some sense in the public interest. This was not without its challenges.[2] The notion that regulation might be used as a device for cartel management, or that regulatory commissions might get captured by industry interests, has been around for a long time. More recently, regulation has been under attack for a number of regulatory-induced inefficiencies.

Rate-of-return regulation was attacked by Averch and Johnson (1962) for providing incentives for excessive capital relative to labor. In addition, it has been criticized for its lack of incentives for cost minimizing behavior generally. As essentially a cost-plus system with gross revenues based directly on costs, the argument was that it provided very few incentives for cost minimization, and more likely resulted in higher costs. With an increase in this kind of concern about higher costs being induced by regulation, there was a demand for different forms of regulation, such as price caps[3] and even deregulation. Thus, the notion that, like oil and water, competition and regulation did not mix, was abandoned for the prospects of large efficiency gains from regulatory reform and deregulation.[4]

The papers in this volume are related in varying degrees to the general theme of how regulation and competition will interact in traditionally regulated monopolies. In view of the fact that most progress in competition and most innovations in regulation have taken place in telecommunications, especially long distance, many of the examples provided involve telecommunications. However, much of the analysis may be extended to other regulated industries to the extent that competitive forces increase there.

The paper, "The Law and Economics of IntraLATA Competition: 1+ Issues and Access Charge Imputation," by Sievers deals with an extension of the kind of competition found in long-distance telecommunications to within the Local Access and Transforation Area (intraLATA).[5] Sievers reviews the status of intraLATA competition. Jurisdictions vary as to their treatment of intraLATA competition: some permit competition; others allow the local company to block calls made on the long distance carriers within the LATA; and others require that the local company get compensated for calls carried by them within the LATA. The tide of events seems to be running with Sievers. Engineering cost arguments against intraLATA competition, on the grounds that it may cause duplication of facilities and higher costs, are unlikely to gain much credence compared to arguments on the benefits of vigorous competition. However, if competition is to succeed, the local companies need to become and to be permitted to become strong competitors. Currently, they are restricted in how they may compete. Changes in intraLATA competition should not be undertaken piecemeal but should form part of a comprehensive review of the restrictions on competition by local companies.

Crew and Crocker, "Diversification and Regulated Monopoly," and Larson, "Predatory Pricing Safeguards and Telecommunications Regulation," deal with two aspects of a major issue in the regulation natural monopoly, namely, regulation of a multi product firm which operates in both competitive and traditionally regulated markets. Crew and Crocker deal with problems such as the allocation of costs between regulated and non-regulated ventures. Larson deals with the issue of predatory pricing. Crew and Crocker's models provide some support for allowing regulated companies into unregulated markets, provided scope economies are present. Their results imply that scope economies from diversification will normally benefit the regulated customers, provided that the company does not have considerable discretion in choosing its technology and tilting production toward the unregulated market at the expense of regulated output. Larson provides a survey of the law and economics of predatory pricing as applied to telecommunications. His discussion supports the notion that regulatory safeguards on predatory pricing are likely to create more costs than benefits. He argues that they impede the ability of telephone companies to respond quickly and effectively. Given the increasing competition in telecommunications and the antitrust safeguards against predatory pricing, the concern of regulation with predatory pricing appears redundant. While considerable further work needs to be done in this area, both Crew and Crocker and Larson's arguments suggest that the benefits of allowing regulated companies to diversify may outweigh the costs of doing so, and that some traditional regulatory concerns may be excessively restrictive.

The papers by Hillman, Harris, and Jang and Norsworthy, while all relating to individual industries, have lessons for other regulated industries. Hillman's paper, "Oil Pipeline Rates: A Case for Yardstick Regulation," deals with the important topic of yardstick regulation for oil pipelines. While his application is highly specific, the potential application of yardstick regulation goes beyond oil pipelines. He reviews the evolution in the law regulating oil pipelines. While showing that some progress has been made in introducing economic efficiency considerations into regulation, he provides a careful critique of the operation of existing regulation and suggests an alternative based upon a yardstick approach. His approach seeks to use competitive market prices as the yardstick, with administration of price discrimination limited to dealing with possible "favoritism" to subsidiaries and affiliates.

"Telecommunications Services as a Strategic Industry: Implications for United States Public Policy" by Harris and "Productivity Growth and Technical Change in the United States Telecommunications Equipment Manufacturing Industries" by Jang and Norsworthy provide important insights for telecommunications. Harris is concerned with the prospect and the reality of the displacement of the United States as the world leader in telecommunications. He argues that regulatory structures and the Modified Final Judgement may impede the introduction into the network of the many innovations in telecommunications. For example, the low penetration of local measured service provides little or no benefits to local telephone companies of fostering the development of terminals and computers in residences. This stands out in contrast to France, where the publicly-owned telephone system has made great advances in getting its Minitel terminals in residences, providing widespread access to the benefits of its vastly improved network.[6]

Jang and Norsworthy's examination of productivity in telecommunications equipment provides a number of novel features. They produce an estimate of the price index for semiconductors. Over the period 1978-86, they show a drop of over 50 percent in the prices of semiconductors, adjusted for quality, compared to a small increase in the respective component of the Producer Price Index. In addition, they show productivity growth to be rather modest—2.5 percent was at the high end of the range. In industries where there is strong technological change, their approach is an important first step in devising improved measurements of productivity by incorporating quality improvements. It is potentially highly relevant to price-cap schemes being proposed in local telecommunications, as price-cap schemes incorporate deductions for productivity. It raises the issue, not only of whether local telephone companies will be able to achieve the targets set for productivity, but also the need for measuring productivity more accurately.

The papers by Brennan, Crew and Frierman, and Crew and Zupan are concerned in varying degrees with proposals for regulatory reform. In his paper, "Entry and Welfare Loss in Regulated Industries," following a brief critique of existing regulation, Brennan discusses how regulation might respond to entry. One response is laissez-faire. At the other extreme, there is the traditional protection from entry offered by the regulator. Protection against entry may have the familiar bad effects on cost minimization. However, allowing entry may result in an increase in price in the monopoly market and a decline in price in the market with entry. Brennan provides a first step in evaluating the welfare tradeoff with a simple test comparing the effects of price and quantity ratios in the markets concerned.

In "Information Economics and New Forms of Regulation," Crew and Frierman examine the contribution of information economics, particularly principal-agent theory, in regulatory economics. They provide a brief primer on information economics and its role in regulation. Their analysis is concerned particularly with employing information economics to evaluate the efficiency of price caps versus rate-of-return regulation. Information economics highlights the difficulties of regulation. Because of information asymmetries, the regulator has to pay a rent to the monopolist. The challenge is to minimize the rent payment that is needed to get the monopolist to reveal his private information. Too low a payment will not induce truthful revelation. Moreover, the payment alone will not induce truthful revelation. It has to be accompanied by a scheme that will do so. Information economics provides a new and rigorous means of examining some regulatory problems.

In "Franchise Bidding for Public Utilities Revisited," Crew and Zupan reexamine franchise bidding as a means of regulating utilities. The considerable experience of franchise bidding and the changed regulatory climate make this an opportune time to review franchise bidding. The incentives provided for innovation and minimum-cost operation provide a strong basis for its consideration. Experience of CATV franchising supports the notion that the problems in the transfer of sunk investments may not be as significant in practice as argued by Williamson (1976). Franchise bidding provides incentives for efficiency at the bidding stage and by reintroducing, at least partially, the discipline of asset transfer into utility markets. This is currently almost entirely absent and may be at least as great a barrier to efficiency as lack of competition in the product market. Following a review of the role of franchise bidding, Crew and Zupan examine how franchise bidding might operate in world of price-cap regulation and how it might be applied to all utilities, especially telecommunications.

Finally, Houston's paper, "Privatization of Electricity in the United States," deals with an extreme form of deregulation-privatization. Public ownership may be seen as the most extreme form of regulation. Privatization is itself an extreme response to this form of regulation. While Houston is mainly concern with privatization of federal electric power supply, his analysis does have implications for the privatization of municipal electric utilities in the United States. Currently municipal utilities are beneficiaries of subsidies. Removal of subsidies would be a major efficiency effect of privatization.[7]

While the contents of this volume is idiosyncratic rather than comprehensive in its coverage of the problem of competition and regulation of utilities, it does provide

INTRODUCTION

a starting point for the further discussion of some of the major issues. In addition, it provides a few pointers as to where we go from here. Currently, while there is competitive entry into traditional utility markets, regulation is far from dead. Indeed, there may be a tendency to replace one form of regulation, rate-of-return regulation, with another, price-cap regulation. Indeed, it seems that regulation will continue for the indefinite future. Regulation seems unlikely to disappear.[8] Much more likely regulation will take differ forms. Hence, this book examines new regulatory forms as a means of making regulation more efficient. One hopeful sign is the better understanding of economic principles and a willingness to apply them toward more efficient regulation.

Notes

1. Goldberg 1976 provides perceptive insights into regulation when viewed as an administered contract. He saw the regulatory contract, as administered by a commission, as protecting the customer's right to be served and the company's right to serve.
2. Posner (1974) states the issue in his own inimicable way. "One assumption was that economic markets are extremely fragile and apt to operate very inefficiently (or inequitably) if left alone; the other was that government regulation was virtually costless."
3. For example, Vogelsang (1989, 21) provides arguments that price caps are likely to promote efficiency. "... it should provide incentives for the regulated firm to produce efficiently, and still protect customers from monopoly exploitation."
4. This is something of an oversimplification and probably much too optimistic a view of the world, since it implies an extremely powerful role for economic argument in bringing about reforms that promise efficiency. A more realistic analysis might be much more complicated, employing rent-seeking arguments. For an introductory discussion of rent seeking and regulation, see Crew and Rowley (1989).
5. The LATA refers to the territory within which the local telephone company carries calls, whether local or toll. Recall that the local company is not permitted to carry calls between LATA's (inter LATA).
6. Almarin Phillips (1989) provided a warning similar to Harris about the risk of United States telecommunications losing its leadership role. He provides information on the French system.
7. Crew and Kleindorfer (1990) examine the performance of publicly and privately owned utilities. Their survey of the evidence shows that private utilities are usually less inefficient than publicly owned utilities.
8. Some have argued that it might grow even in unlikely places such as telecommunications, the cradle of utility deregulation. See Phillips (1984) for an early cautionary tale on expecting too much from deregulation.

References

Averch, H., and L.L. Johnson. 1962. "Behavior of the Firm under Regulatory Constraint." *American Economic Review* 52 (December): 1053-1069.
Crew, Michael A., and Paul R. Kleindorfer. 1990. "Public versus Private: Alternative Ownership Scenarios for Electric Utilities." Santa Monica: Reason Foundation.
Crew, Michael A., and Charles K. Rowley. 1989. "Feasibility of Deregulation: A Public Choice Analysis." In *Deregulation and Diversification of Utilities*, edited by M.A. Crew. Boston: Kluwer Academic Publishers.
Goldberg, V.P. 1976. "Regulation and Administered Contracts." *Bell Journal of Economics* 7 (Autumn): 426-48.
Phillips, Almarin. 1989. "New Technologies and Diversified Telecommunications Services." In *Deregulation and Diversification of Utilities*, edited by M.A. Crew. Boston:

Kluwer Academic Publishers.

Phillips, C.F., Jr. 1984. *The Regulation of Public Utilities.* Arlington, VA: Public Utility Reports.

Posner, R.A. 1974. "Theories of Economic Regulation." *Bell Journal of Economics* 5 (Autumn): 335-58.

Vogelsang, Ingo. 1989. "A Price Cap Regulation of Telecommunications Services: A Long-Run Approach." In *Deregulation and Diversification of Utilities*, edited by M.A. Crew. Boston: Kluwer Academic Publishers.

Williamson, Oliver E. 1976. "Franchise Bidding for Natural Monopoly—In General and with Respect to CATV." *Bell Journal of Economics* (Spring): 73-104.

2

THE LAW AND ECONOMICS OF INTRALATA COMPETITION:
1+ Issues and Access Charge Imputation

Mark Sievers

Introduction

With the divestiture of AT&T in 1984, most states gave local exchange carriers (LECs) an exclusive franchise on 1+ intraLATA toll traffic and forbid interexchange carriers (IXCs) from providing intraLATA toll services. However, a number of states now permit facilities based intraLATA toll competition, and the market structure for intraLATA competition is a current issue in a number of jurisdictions.

This paper presents a survey and analysis of the major issues that have arisen in states that have addressed intraLATA competition. Specifically, this paper consists of the following sections:

1. *Survey of Institutions.* This section presents a description of the major regulatory institutions that impact intraLATA market structure. The intraLATA provisions of the AT&T divestiture are discussed, and the alternatives employed by state regulators to deal with intraLATA markets are described. This section also briefly describes the telecommunications technologies that impact intraLATA regulation.
2. *IntraLATA Competition.* This section discusses the economic benefits associated with intraLATA competition. This section also discusses the potential impacts of intraLATA competition on local service contribution.
3. *Recommendations.* This section suggests an intraLATA market structure that allows intraLATA competition while mitigating the potential harms of such competition. This section suggests means of dealing with 1+ intraLATA dialing and local facilities "bottleneck" problems.

Specifically, this paper concludes that the benefits of allowing intraLATA competition exceed the potential for harm. The intraLATA defaults set up by the divestiture court provide a reasonable market structure for allowing intraLATA competition. That is, Interexchange Carriers (IXCs) should be allowed to carry intraLATA traffic that originates on switched access lines when customers dial the appropriate 10XXX access code for their desired IXC. Local exchange carriers (LECs) should continue to be allowed to retain the exclusive right to carry 1+ intraLATA traffic so long as they are forbidden from entering interLATA markets. For technical reasons, LECs should not be given exclusive rights to carry 1+ intraLATA traffic that originates on dedicated access lines nor should they be given the exclusive right to carry 1+ intraLATA 800 traffic.

1. Survey of Institutions

IntraLATA competition is governed by two sets of institutions. At a basic level, intraLATA competition is the product of the provisions of the Modified Final Judgment (MFJ) that resulted in the divestiture of AT&T and the creation of LATAs (Local Access Transport Areas) throughout the United States.[1] Broadly speaking, the provisions of the MFJ forbid Bell Operating Companies (BOCs) from providing interLATA long distance services.[2] The divestiture Court left the question of whether there ought to be intraLATA, intrastate competition to state regulators. Thus, the second set of institutions that govern intraLATA competition are the provisions adopted by state regulators to deal with intraLATA competition.

1.1. Modified Final Judgment Provisions

The divestiture Court describes LATAs as follows:

> Pursuant to the decree, all Bell territory in the continental United States is divided into LATAs, generally centering upon a city or other identifiable community of interest. Most simply, a LATA marks the boundaries beyond which a Bell Operating Company may not carry telephone calls. What the Operating Companies will do in the services field after divestiture is (1) to engage in exchange telecommunications, that is, to transport traffic between telephones located within a LATA, and (2) to provide exchange access within a LATA, that is, to link a subscriber's telephone to the nearest transmission facility of AT&T or one of AT&T's long-haul competitors.
>
> Once the divestiture is completed, the Operating Companies will be allowed to transport communications only to and from telephones and other apparatuses located within the same LATA (intra-LATA traffic); because of their local monopoly position, the decree does not permit the Operating Companies to carry calls between different LATAs (inter-LATA traffic). Only AT&T and its intercity competitors—such as MCI, Sprint, and Satellite Business Systems—may carry telecommunications traffic which originates in one LATA and terminates in another.
>
> Thus, contrary to much popular and even industry understanding, the purpose of the establishment of the LATAs is only to delineate the areas in which the various telecommunications companies will operate; it is not to distinguish the area in which a telephone call will be "local" from that in which it becomes a "toll" or long distance call. ... *The distance at which a local call becomes a long distance toll call has been, and will continue to*

be, determined exclusively by the various state regulatory bodies.[3] [footnotes omitted, emphasis in original]

The divestiture Court created the interLATA restriction to prevent the BOCs from using their control of access to local facilities to impede competition in long distance markets, and recently reaffirmed the restriction.[4]

In deciding how large LATAs ought to be, the Court balanced the competitive impacts against the financial benefits that would accrue to the BOCs.[5] A large number of small LATAs would benefit interexchange carriers, but would make BOCs increasingly dependent on local service revenues rather than their historical reliance on a mixture of toll and local service revenues.[6] On the other hand, the Court observed that a smaller number of large LATAs could diminish long distance competition. The Court reasoned that larger LATAs would increase the ability of the BOCs to use their control over local facilities to the detriment of their long distance competitors, just as the Bell system had used its control over local facilities to retard competition in national long distance markets.

The divesture Court also required the BOCs to provide IXCs with interLATA access "on an unbundled, tariffed basis, that is equal in type and quality to that provided for the interexchange telecommunications services of AT&T and its affiliates." With regards to intraLATA access, the divestiture Court required that IXCs be given access "equal in technical quality to the access provided to [IXCs] for inter-LATA calls."[7] The Court also required that access for all IXCs (including AT&T) for intraLATA calls would require that the IXCs' customers dial a "10XXX" access code. The Court required that if customers just dial 1, their intraLATA calls will automatically be carried by the BOC. The Court reasoned that intraLATA presubscription, where customers could select a primary intraLATA carrier and a primary interLATA carrier, would be extremely expensive to implement ($1 billion in 1983). It also noted that intraLATA presubscription would place BOCs at a disadvantage since they are forbidden from carrying interLATA traffic, and few customers would select as their primary carrier a long distance company that could only carry intraLATA traffic.[8]

It is important, however, to emphasize two aspects of the Court's intraLATA structure. First, the Court did not grant the BOCs a monopoly on intraLATA calling to compensate them for their inability to carry interLATA traffic.[9] Indeed, the Court has observed that the "lack of competition in [the intraLATA] market would constitute an intolerable development" and that "the significant amount of the traffic that is both intrastate and intra-LATA should not be reserved to the monopoly carrier."[10] Second, the Court did not foreclose state regulators from determining the appropriate structure for and degree of intraLATA competition. Instead, the Court expressly left the determination of the appropriate degree and structure of intraLATA competition to state regulators to resolve as a matter of state policy.[11]

1.2. State Policy Alternatives

What alternatives are available to state regulators for dealing with intraLATA

traffic? Broadly speaking, there are three public policy options for dealing with IXC-carried intraLATA traffic:
1. *IntraLATA Competition*—regulators could allow IXCs to carry intraLATA traffic and simply pay access charges to the LECs just as they do for interLATA traffic;
2. *IntraLATA Compensation*—regulators could allow IXCs to carry incidental intraLATA traffic, but require compensation payments to LECs above ordinarily applicable access charges to either discourage IXC-carried intraLATA traffic or to recompense LECs for toll revenues or contribution lost as a result of the "unauthorized" intraLATA traffic; or,
3. *IntraLATA Blocking*—regulators could require that unauthorized intraLATA traffic be blocked either by the LECs or by the IXCs.

Implementation of each of these options is constrained by several network and access service considerations. Also, each option presents regulators with a number of permutations and alternatives.

Network and Access Service Considerations. There are several different types of access service arrangements between LECs and IXCs, and each access service arrangement affects the feasibility of the three policy options.[12]

When an IXC other than AT&T originates a call with Feature Group A (FGA) access arrangements, its customers must first dial a local seven digit number to access the IXC, then dial an authorization code, and then dial the long distance number that the customer wishes to reach. When an IXC other than AT&T orginates a call with Feature Group B (FGB) access arrangements, its customers must go through the same basic dialing process as with FGA access, but the local seven digit number used to access the IXC begins with 950. Because FGA and FGB use a local number as the primary means of access to the IXC, which then performs subsequent routing, LECs cannot block or screen intraLATA calls that orginate with FGA or FGB.

When calls are originated with Feature Group D (FGD) access arrangements, customers simply dial "1" to access their presubscribed long distance carrier, and then the long distance number they wish to reach ("1+ access"). FDG access is found only in "equal access" end offices. FGD access allows the LEC to automatically screen and carry any 1+ intraLATA calls. In addition to a 1+ presubscribed carrier, FGD access allows customers to select any IXC for their long distance calls by dialing "10XXX", where "XXX" represents the IXC's access code.[13] In states where IXCs may not carry intraLATA traffic, LECs may or may not block attempts to use 10XXX dialing to make intraLATA calls or divert 10XXX intraLATA call attempts to LEC networks, depending on state law.

IXCs may also employ 800 access arrangements, such as US Sprint's FON-CARD. Under such arrangements, a customer dials an 800 number, then "0" plus the long distance number s/he wishes to call, and then an authorization code. IntraLATA traffic that originates under such access arrangements cannot be blocked or diverted by LECs.

IXCs may also employ dedicated access arrangements. Under such arrangements, a dedicated line, either rented from the LEC ("special access") or owned by the customer or a third party, is used to establish a connection between the customer and its IXC. Under such arrangements, the customer need not dial any access codes to reach its IXC. Since such arrangements do not involve an LEC switching function, intraLATA traffic that originates over dedicated access facilities cannot be blocked or diverted by LECs.

Broadly speaking, FGD access arrangements allow LECs to divert and carry all 1+ intraLATA traffic, and, when required by state law, block 10XXX intraLATA traffic. IntraLATA traffic originating over FGA or FGB cannot be blocked by the LEC, and may, depending on the capacity and characteristics of the IXC's switch, be blocked by the IXC. About 95 percent of all telephone customers are served by equal access end offices, (Federal Communications Commission 1990, 14) so most customers have the ability to reach a presubscribed long distance carrier other than AT&T by 1+ dialing. Because of the customer inconvenience associated with FGA and FGB, IXCs typically use FGD for originating calls whenever possible.[14]

IntraLATA 800 traffic presents a special problem. Persons who call an 800 number have no way of knowing whether the 800 number they call is within or outside of their LATA. Thus, in an environment where intraLATA competition is allowed, it is infeasible to require that LECs carry all 1+ 800 traffic and allow IXCs to carry only 10XXX 800 traffic. Also, blocking 800 intraLATA call attempts is infeasible since 800 numbers are assigned to IXCs and the LEC passes 800 calls to the IXC based on the 800 number's first three digits (NXX). Thus, when customers dial an 800 number, the LEC may not know the terminating location of the call.

IXCs' networks are not currently configured to carry intraLATA traffic efficiently. IXCs' national networks, such as US Sprint's, are typically configured with only one point of presence (POP) in most LATAs.[15] Thus, a switched intraLATA call carried over an IXC's network would first travel to the LEC's end office, then to the LEC's toll office that serves the IXC's POP, then to the IXC's POP, then to the IXC's switch (which may not be in the POP), back to the IXC's POP, back to the same serving toll office, and then routed through various end offices to the called number. In contrast, intraLATA traffic that is carried over an LEC's network travels directly between LEC end offices rather than make an excursion through an IXC's POP and switch.

It is important to emphasize, however, that IXCs' current network configurations are the product of state regulatory environments that largely ban IXCs from carrying intraLATA traffic. If IXCs were generally allowed to carry intraLATA traffic, it seems reasonable to expect that their network configurations would change over time. Since carriers such as US Sprint and MCI built much of their national networks over a period of only four or five years, it seems reasonable to assume that IXCs could add intraLATA components to their network configurations very quickly. Thus, the notion that IXC networks are less efficient than LEC networks in carrying intraLATA traffic assumes that a ban on 1+ (and even

10XXX) intraLATA competition continues, and IXCs will not configure their networks to carry intraLATA traffic.

IntraLATA Competition. Broadly speaking, there are two intraLATA competition alternatives—presubscription and no presubscription. In a presubscription environment, LECs would not retain their rights to carry all 1+ intraLATA traffic. Customers would select their primary intraLATA carrier just as they select their primary interLATA carrier. Only four states have ordered intraLATA presubscription: Iowa, Minnesota,[16] South Dakota,[17] and Kentucky.[18] Typically, presubscription is not favored by regulators because of customer confusion—it requires customers to select an intraLATA carrier and an interLATA long distance carrier when many customers do not know what a LATA is. For example, a recent Southern Bell survey of Florida customers found that only 16.6 percent of residential customers and 44 percent of business customers surveyed indicated that they had even heard of the term "LATA".[19] Similarly, a South Central Bell survey of Kentucky customers reported that only 8.1 percent of residential customers and 25.8 percent of business customers surveyed indicated that they had heard of LATAs.[20] Also, it is often argued that presubscription unfairly disadvantages BOCs since customers are unlikely to select a primary long distance carrier that cannot carry both inter and intraLATA traffic.

In most states that permit intraLATA competition, the LEC carries the switched 1+ intraLATA traffic and customers may access other long distance carriers by dialing a 10XXX access code, just as they may do in equal access offices with their interLATA traffic. Since it is impossible, as a practical matter, to prefix intraLATA calls that employ dedicated access with a 10XXX code, such intraLATA traffic is typically carried by the IXC without a 10XXX code.

A number of states distinguish between facilities based intraLATA competition and resale competition. Facilities based intraLATA competition usually refers to an IXC's use of its own transmission facilities to carry intraLATA traffic. Resale competition refers to an IXC's resale of an LEC's intraLATA services. For example, a reseller might purchase bulk-billed intraLATA WATS[21] services from an LEC and resell those services to its customers as intraLATA MTS[22] services.

Florida and Illinois employ unusual mechanisms to regulate intraLATA competition. Florida generally allows facilities based intraLATA competition, but has subdivided the state into the geographic regions served by its LECs' toll centers, called Equal Access Exchange Areas (EAEAs).[23] Florida's LECs possess a transmission monopoly for all intraEAEA traffic, but must compete with IXCs for interEAEA traffic. IXCs that have the ability to block intraEAEA calls may compete with LECs only by reselling LEC WATS and MTS services. IXCs that do not have the ability to block intraEAEA calling are required to pay compensation to the LEC. An IXC that can demonstrate that it can provide intraEAEA services over its facilites in a more economical manner than the LEC is exempt from the general facilities-based intraEAEA ban.

The rationale for the Florida plan is that traffic that is carried between LEC toll centers is comparable to traffic that travels between an IXC's POPs. LEC transport of intraEAEA traffic is theoretically more economical and efficient than IXC transport since the leg between the toll center and the POP is eliminated.[24] While the Florida Commission ordered that LECs be granted transmission monopolies for intraEAEA traffic, it ordered such monopolies on an iterim basis "in order to provide a transitional period during which LECs can adjust to competitive circumstances."[25] The Florida Commission recently opened a docket to reconsider its intraEAEA policy, and decided to substantially eliminate its compensation requirements and relax its ban on facilities based intraEAEA competition.[26]

Illinois adopted a similar plan, but subdivided the state into Market Service Areas (MSAs).[27] Historically, IXCs were prohibited from providing facilities based intraMSA services, but by statute, the intraMSA prohibition was lifted in 1986.[28] Generally, IXCs may not carry 1+ intraMSA services, except for 800 services and services that employ a dedicated access arrangement; only LECs are permitted to provide 1+ switched intraMSA toll services.[29]

Table 1 lists the general status of intraLATA competition by state. It is important to note, however, that even though a state may authorize intraLATA competition, it may also impose compensation or blocking requirements for certain intraLATA services. In other words, a state that permits intraLATA facilities based competition may impose a blocking or compensation requirement for some services.[30]

When intraLATA competition is ordered, regulators must wrestle with how to prevent LECs from using their control over access charges and facilities to disadvantage their intraLATA competitors. For example, IXCs cannot compete with LECs that might set the price of their toll services without regard for access charges, which comprise a major component of IXCs' costs. A recently released study of the viability of intraLATA competition in Michigan found that the average incremental cost facing IXCs for providing an additional unit intraLATA traffic was about 18 cents per minute, and that 95 percent of those incremental costs were access charges. In contrast, the study also found that since an LEC does not pay access charges, its average incremental cost for an additional unit of intraLATA traffic was .4 cents per minute, or about 3 percent of the costs facing an IXC intraLATA market entrant.

In order to prevent abuse of control over essential facilities in intraLATA markets, regulators can require that LECs face similar costs as do IXCs in providing intraLATA services—i.e., regulators can require that LECs impute their own access charges in setting the price of their intraLATA toll services.[31] Imputation of access charges has been ordered by state public utility commissions in Minnesota,[32] Missouri,[33] Oregon,[34] Washington,[35] Vermont,[36] and West Virginia.[37] Imputation of access charges is required by statute in Minnesota[38] and, arguably, Colorado.[39] In 1985 the FCC ordered the imputation of access charges for interstate, intraLATA services, and corridor services.[40]

It is important to note that while there are few states that require imputation, this does not mean that imputation has been rejected by most state regulators. In the states that do not allow intraLATA competition, or in the states that allow

Table 1. Status of IntraLATA Competition by State—1990[1]

State	Does the state permit Facilities Based IntraLATA Competition	Does the state permit Resale of LEC IntraLATA Services	State	Does the state permit Facilities Based IntraLATA Competition	Does the state permit Resale of LEC IntraLATA Services
Alabama	No	Yes	Montana	Yes	Yes
Alaska	Pending	Pending	Nebraska	Yes	Yes
Arizona	No	No	Nevada	No	No
Arkansas	Partial[2]	Yes	New Hampshire	Pending	Pending
California	Partial[3]	No	New Jersey	No	Yes
Colorado	Yes	Yes	New Mexico	Yes[10]	Yes
Connecticut	Partial[4]	Yes	New York	Yes	Yes
Delaware	Pending	Pending	North Carolina	No	Yes
Florida	Partial[5]	Yes	North Dakota	No	Yes
Georgia	No[6]	Yes	Ohio	Yes	Yes
Hawaii	Partial[7]	No	Oklahoma	Partial[11]	Yes
Idaho	Yes	Yes	Oregon	Yes	Yes
Illinois	Yes	Yes	Pennsylvania	Yes	Yes
Indiana	No	Yes	Rhode Island	No Action	No Action
Iowa	Yes	Yes	South Carolina	Partial[12]	Yes
Kansas	No	No	South Dakota	Yes	Yes
Kentucky	Yes	Yes	Tennessee	Partial[13]	Yes
Louisiana	Partial[8]	Yes	Texas	Yes	Yes
Maine	Yes	Yes	Utah	Yes	Yes
Maryland	Yes	Yes	Vermont	Yes	Yes
Massachusetts	Yes	Yes	Virginia	No	Yes
Michigan	Yes[9]	Yes	Washington	Yes	Yes
Minnesota	Yes	Yes	West Virginia	Yes	Yes
Mississippi	No	Yes	Wisconsin	Pending	Yes
Missouri	Yes	Yes	Wyoming	No	Yes

Notes:
1. Surveys of IntraLATA competition can be found in *Eastern States Move Slowly on Intra-LATA Toll Competition Issues*, 7 State Telephone Regulation Report 1 (April 20, 1989) and *Intra-LATA Toll Competition Allowed in Most Western States*, 7 State Telephone Regulation Report 1 (May 4, 1989).
2. Limited to the intraLATA traffic associated with high volume, dedicated access products, such as MEGACOM.
3. IntraLATA competition limited to T-1 data services. A docket is pending to consider general intraLATA competition and compensation.
4. Facilities based intraLATA competition in Connecticut is limited to non-switched private line services and specialized services that are ancillary to the same specialized services offered on an interstate basis. IntraLATA MTS and WATS services may only be provided as resold MTS and WATS.
5. Florida generally permits intraLATA competition, but restricts intraEAEA competition.
6. Georgia recently held hearings to consider intraLATA compensation, and whether IXC should be allowed to provide intraLATA services was raised by several parties. The Georgia Commission is not expected to allow facilities based intraLATA competition as a result of that docket, although its final decision is pending.
7. Hawaii permits intraLATA competition for services that employ private lines.
8. Louisiana LECs may compete in intraLATA markets, but IXCs may not.
9. Michigan is currently considering how to structure access charges and implement intraLATA competition.
10. New Mexico is currently conducting an inquiry into intrastate competition.
11. Limited to intraLATA traffic from high-volume, dedicated access services, such as MEGACOM.
12. Only one IXC has intraLATA authority in South Carolina.
13. Limited to the intraLATA traffic associated with high-volume, dedicated access products, such as MEGACOM.

intraLATA competition only by resellers, imputation of access charges to LEC intraLATA toll rates is not an issue. Among the states that allow facilities based intraLATA competition, only two states, Pennsylvania[41] and Texas, have explicitly rejected imputation of access charges.

IntraLATA Compensation. IntraLATA Compensation plans require IXCs to pay compensation to LECs for any "unauthorized" intraLATA traffic. The method of calculating compensation that is adopted depends on the economic objective that regulators wish to achieve through a compensation mechanism. Conceptually, there are at least four categories of compensation plans:

1. *Lost Revenues.* Compensation should be equal to the revenues the LECs would have realized but for the unauthorized intraLATA traffic. Such compensation plans calculate compensation as

$$\text{Compensation} = P_L Q_I - A_I$$

 where P_L is the LEC's average toll revenues per minute; Q_I is the IXC's unauthorized intraLATA minutes; and, A_I are the access charges that the IXC paid on its unauthorized intraLATA traffic.

2. *Lost Net Revenues.* These are similar to *Lost Revenues* compensation plans, but adjust the compensation obligation with any cost savings realized by the LEC as a result of not actually carrying the unauthorized intraLATA traffic. Such compensation plans calculate compensation as

$$\text{Compensation} = P_L Q_I - A_I - V_I$$

 where V_I represents any avoided (i.e., variable) costs associated with the unauthorized intraLATA traffic. Typical avoided costs range between 20 and 35 percent of toll revenues, the remainder of costs being common costs that are not subtracted from the compensation obligation.

3. *Net Contribution.* These compensation plans seek to replace any lost local service contribution. The prices of LEC provided intraLATA toll services and access services are generally greater than the costs of providing such services. The difference, i.e., profits, is considered the contribution, or subsidy, that the services provide toward local service rates. Such compensation plans calculate compensation as

$$\text{Compensation} = \text{TollContribution} - \text{AccessContribution}$$

 where *Toll Contribution* is the contribution provided to local services by the LEC's intraLATA toll offerings that is lost to unauthorized intraLATA traffic; and, *Access Contribution* is the contribution to local services that the LEC gains from the access charges paid by the LEC for its unauthorized intraLATA traffic.

4. *Access Charges.* Conceptually, access charges are payments for the economic resources used by the LEC to provide access services, plus an

appropriate contribution toward local service rates. Thus, access charges provide the only appropriate compensation that is due to the LECs.

Table 2 uses data presented in a recent Georgia intraLATA compensation proceeding to illustrate how each of the above four compensation plans might be applied.

Table 2. Calculating Compensation			
	Revenues per Minute[1] (Cents per minute)	Contribution to Local Service[2] (Percent)	Contribution per Minute[3] (Cents per minute)
Toll Loss	22.6	41%	9.27
Less Access Gain	11.67	57%	6.65
= Lost Revenues	10.93	= Net Contribution	2.62
Less Avoided Costs[4]	- 6.78		
= Lost Net Revenue	4.15		
Notes:			
1. These are the average toll and access revenues per minute reported by Southern Bell for its Georgia intraLATA MTS toll services and its intrastate switched access services.			
2. These are the percentage contributions made by Southern Bell's Georgia toll and intrastate access services. An access charge contribution of 57% means that for every dollar of intrastate access charges collected by Southern Bell, 43 cents are used to cover the costs of providing access services and 57 cents are available for contribution. The reported percentage figures were derived from Southern Bell's 1987 Embedded Direct Analysis for Georgia.			
3. This is simply the average rate per minute multiplied by the percentage contribution.			
4. Avoided costs were calculated as 30 percent of revenues. The 30 percent figure is assumed.			

The distinctions between each of the above compensation plans are the public policy purposes for imposing compensation and the assumptions that form the basis for requiring compensation. The *Lost Revenues* and *Lost Net Revenues* plans assume that the presence of unauthorized intraLATA traffic harms the LEC in some manner, and represent two mechanisms to recompense the LEC for its harm. Both assume that the LEC is entitled to all revenues or profits associated with intraLATA traffic. The *Lost Revenues* approach uses the simple difference between the toll revenues lost and the access revenues gained as a result of the unauthorized intraLATA traffic. A *Lost Net Revenues* plan attempts to use lost profits as the metric for measuring the harm associated with unauthorized intraLATA traffic. *Lost Net Revenues* plans are based on the notion that when toll revenues are lost to unauthorized traffic, so are a portion of the LEC's toll costs, and IXCs should not be liable to provide compensation for such a reduction in costs.

A *Net Contribution* plan assumes that LEC intraLATA toll revenues are used to subsidize local service rates, and that unauthorized intraLATA traffic threatens that subsidy flow. A *Net Contribution* plan seeks to provide compensation to maintain the toll-to-local subsidy lost as a result of unauthorized intraLATA traffic.[42]

Generally speaking, $1 of access revenues provides more contribution than does $1 of LEC toll revenues since intrastate access charges often consist of rate elements that are "pure" local service subsidy.[43] Also, generally speaking, when an LEC loses a minute of intraLATA toll traffic to a competing IXC, it gains a minute of access traffic for which it collects access charges. Thus, depending on the relative prices of toll and access services, there may be no net reduction in contribution levels even though an LEC may experience a loss of toll traffic and realize a net reduction in total revenues.

An *Access Charge* plan assumes that LECs do not suffer any harm to their revenue streams as a result of unauthorized intraLATA traffic and seeks to provide compensation for the LEC's costs associated with providing access services.

Since compensation is typically stated in terms of a per minute payment, a critical step in any compensation calculation is deciding which intraLATA minutes should be used in compensation calculations. In other words, which intraLATA minutes are unauthorized? For example, many states permit the resale of LEC intraLATA MTS and WATS services, so resold intraLATA minutes would not be included in these states' compensation plans.

A more complex segregation of minutes is required than simply classifying minutes as resold and facilities based. Compensation plans generally seek to replace revenues, net revenues or contribution that is lost due to the unauthorized intraLATA traffic. Thus, the threshhold issue for compensation calculations is a showing that the LEC was somehow harmed by the unauthorized traffic. As discussed in Section 2, below, evidence is, at best, mixed regarding whether LECs are harmed by intraLATA competition.

If an IXC offers intraLATA services that an LEC does not offer, or customers would not otherwise purchase similar services from an LEC, then an LEC cannot have been harmed by the unauthorized traffic. Indeed, to the extent that an LEC collects access charges on these non-comparable services, an LEC benefits from unauthorized intraLATA traffic. Such noncomparable traffic should be excluded from compensation calculations. For example, US Sprint offers FONCARD service which allows its customers to place long distance telephone calls over US Sprint's network anywhere in the country by dialing an 800 number and entering an authorization code. FONCARD service is especially valuable to persons who travel and make long distance calls from phones throughout the country that they wish to have billed to their residence or business. A traveler that places an intraLATA call with a FONCARD arguably does not displace LEC toll services since comparable services may not be available. Even if an LEC offers a similar calling card service, such services may not be readily available to persons who live outside of the LEC's service areas but travel to cities within the LEC's service areas.

Even when comparable services are involved, correct compensation calculations should exclude stimulated traffic. For example, if the price of an IXC's services are generally lower than the LEC's prices, then ceterus paribus, the IXC will carry more intraLATA traffic than the LEC.[44] The LEC's intraLATA traffic

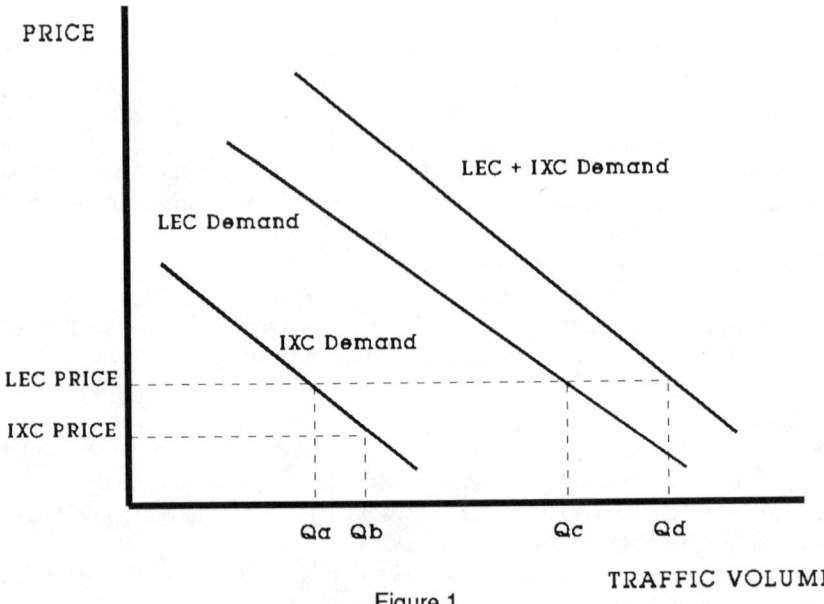

Figure 1.

loss, if any, is the traffic it would have carried if the IXC's intraLATA customers faced the LEC's higher prices. Also, an adjustment should be made to account for the differences in demand between IXC and LEC intraLATA customers. For example, if an IXC's intraLATA customers must dial a 10XXX access code whereas an LEC's intraLATA customers need only dial 1+ to make intraLATA calls, then arguably the demand characteristics of IXC intraLATA customers are different than LEC customers. Intuitively, the toll demand of such IXC intraLATA customers are probably more price elastic than the toll demand of LEC intraLATA customers, since the IXC's customers are willing to go to greater lengths than other customers to make intraLATA calls using a lower priced carrier.

In short, to calculate compensation correctly, a demand study should be performed to estimate the demand that the LEC would have faced but for the unauthorized intraLATA traffic. Figure 1 illustrates the concepts and critical volumes that should be involved in such a demand study.[45]

In addition to demand studies to estimate the appropriate quantities for use in compensation calculations, it is also important to note that access minutes of use are different than conversation minutes by as much as a factor of 20 percent.[46] Thus, an IXC's intraLATA access minutes cannot be used to calculate the intraLATA revenues that the LEC would have earned (i.e., Q_I in the above formulas) without first applying a factor to convert those access minutes into conversation minutes.

Even when accurate intraLATA traffic volumes are available, compensation calculations are often complicated by other factors. For example, when the North Carolina Utilities Commission adopted its compensation plan,[47] basically a *Lost*

Net Revenues plan, it struggled with the appropriate service to use for calculating the average intraLATA price. Since unauthorized intraLATA traffic can be MTS, WATS or private line services, the North Carolina Commission questioned whether it was proper to use average MTS revenues as the appropriate intraLATA price for calculating intraLATA compensation.

Finally, it is worth noting that compensation plans can be designed as methods of punishing IXCs for carrying intraLATA traffic on the theory that such financial punishments will deter unauthorized intraLATA traffic. At least one state imposed compensation plans that penalize IXCs for carrying intraLATA traffic. Alabama adopted a *Lost Revenues* plan but ordered an additional 1.5 cents per minute above ordinary compensation.[48] Unfortunately, such plans are fatally flawed since compensation is not passed onto customers, but simply paid by IXCs for their intraLATA traffic. If state law prohibits an IXC from providing intraLATA services, an IXC cannot tariff a set of intraLATA services and prices, since it is not authorized to provide those services in the first place. Thus, the notion that intraLATA compensation will deter unauthorized intraLATA traffic is incorrect since IXCs' customers, who make the decision to place intraLATA calls, do not face a penalty (i.e., pay compensation) for their intraLATA calling decisions.

IntraLATA Blocking. Blocking unauthorized intraLATA traffic is an alternative to allowing IXCs to carry intraLATA traffic, or requiring IXCs to pay compensation for unauthorized intraLATA traffic. As an option, blocking faces several technological and marketing constraints that make it the least desirable of all three options.

A major difficulty associated with blocking is deciding who is responsible for blocking unauthorized intraLATA traffic. As noted above, in equal access end-offices, LECs have the ability to automatically carry 1+, switched intraLATA traffic, and can block attempts to use 10XXX access codes to place intraLATA calls over alternative carriers. When 10XXX intraLATA call attempts are blocked by an LEC, however, customers may not realize that the IXC they are trying to access does not have intraLATA authority and assume that their call was blocked because of a problem with the IXC's network.

Since LECs cannot block calls that are originated with FGA and FGB access arrangements, responsibility for blocking must be borne by IXCs. However, since calls that originate with FGA and FGB access employ a local access number and an authorization code, IXCs may not be able to correctly identify whether a call is inter- or intraLATA. For example, if a customer calls the local access number from a location other than his/her billing address, the IXC may not be able to determine whether the calling location and the called number's location are located in the same LATA.

As with FGA and FGB, LECs cannot block calls that are originated over dedicated access facilities; only the IXC can potentially block such traffic. Requiring IXCs to block unauthorized intraLATA traffic that originates over dedicated access facilities requires that they install and maintain potentially large "look-up" tables in their network switches that list all the NPA-Nxx combinations[49] in every LATA. For LATAs that encompass several area codes and/or local exchanges, the "look-up" table required to screen all calls for potential unauthorized intraLATA traffic could be quite large and complex. The addition of such screening tables could consume a significant portion of an IXC's switches and limit its ability to add customers or services to its network.

Dedicated access arrangements are typically employed by customers that have large volumes of traffic and sophisticated telecommunications needs. For example, a customer that owns and operates its own private telephone network may employ some form of dedicated access to link its private network with an IXC's network in order to establish communications with the customer's remote network locations. In such circumstances, an IXC may be unable to identify inter- and intraLATA traffic. If a customer's private network extends over LATA boundaries (or even state boundaries), an IXC whose only point of contact with the customer is a dedicated access link at one location cannot know whether the originating call crossed state or LATA boundaries before it was passed to the IXC's dedicated access link.

In addition to the technical considerations of blocking, there are some significant *moral harzards*. An IXC that carries all traffic, both inter- and intraLATA, can more easily market its products in a state than an IXC that tells its customers that it can only carry interLATA traffic. A loosely enforced blocking requirement creates an incentive for IXCs to "cheat", and not block significant portions of intraLATA traffic. This may be especially true for smaller carriers who may not have the resources to install and maintain switches capable of screening and blocking unauthorized intraLATA traffic or who are anxious to enter or remain in hotly contested markets.

A pure blocking requirement that is rigorously enforced is rare in the United States, probably owing to regulators' recognition of the difficulties associated with blocking. Most blocking orders require that IXCs either block unauthorized intraLATA traffic, divert intraLATA traffic to the LEC, or pay compensation for unauthorized intraLATA traffic.

2. IntraLATA Competition

Should intraLATA competition be allowed in a state? There are a number of studies that show that there are significant societal benefits to be realized from the introduction of intraLATA competition. On the other hand, LECs often argue that the introduction of intraLATA competition will reduce their toll revenues and threaten contributions that are applied to minimize local service rates.

IntraLATA competition is a difficult issue for state regulators, and since divestiture a number of surveys and analyses have been performed by or for state regulators. (e.g., Virginia State Corporation Commission 1985, Rogers and Morelli 1985, NRRI 1989, 128-139) Some state regulators do not allow intraLATA competition simply because of uncertainty about the benefits and costs. For example, when the Public Utilities Commission of California examined whether to allow general intraLATA competition,[50] it observed that a decision to allow intraLATA competition is irreversable—once IXCs are allowed to enter intraLATA markets, the Commission will not be able to restrict subsequent intraLATA entry. Because the California Commission was concerned about the possible loss of LEC toll revenues and the potential relationship between toll revenues and local service rates, it declined to allow general intraLATA competition.[51]

Other states have allowed intraLATA competition, usually noting that competition yields substantial benefits for telephone consumers. For example, in its order permitting intraLATA market entry, the Missouri Public Service Commission found that authorizing intraLATA toll competition will result in new and improved services, lower prices and faster responses to customers' needs which will benefit the public. Not only will the ratepayers be benefitted, the telecommunications industry in Missouri should be stimulated by the opening of this new market and encouraged to develop new technology and efficiencies in the industry.[52]

Pragmatically, state regulators may not be able to prevent intraLATA market entry. So long as firms have an economic incentive to seek out or provide alternative intraLATA services, they will enter intraLATA markets and seek methods of avoiding intraLATA regulation. For example, a private network that links several large users may carry intraLATA traffic and, thus, compete with the LECs' exclusive rights to carry intraLATA traffic and may be exempt from state regulation.[53] Perhaps because they cannot limit intraLATA entry in some areas, some state regulators break intraLATA markets into several "submarkets" and allow entry in some and forbid intraLATA entry in others.[54]

2.1. Benefits of IntraLATA Competition

Two studies have been recently released which empirically estimated the benefits associated with intraLATA competition. In June 1988, an economist at the Federal Communications Commission (FCC) released an econometric study that showed that toll rates were lower in states that allowed IXCs to provide facilities based intraLATA services. (Frentrup 1988) The study found that the toll rates charged by Bell Operating Companies were three to four percent lower in states that allowed intraLATA competition than in states that forbid intraLATA competition.

In November 1988, economists at the Federal Trade Commission (FTC) released an econometric study that showed toll rates were lower in states that allowed intraLATA competition and significantly higher in states that imposed punitive measures, such as requiring compensation, to enforce a ban on unauthorized intraLATA traffic. (Mathios and Rogers 1988) Specifically, the study reported that states that restrict all entry into intraLATA markets have toll rates that are about 7.5 percent higher than other states. The study also found that states that adopt regulations to enforce a ban on unauthorized intraLATA traffic, including intraLATA compensation, blocking, and fines, had toll rates that are about 10.3

percent higher than other states. The study estimated that telephone consumers would save at least $200 million annually if the states that restrict intraLATA competition eliminated their restrictions.

The results of the FTC study were derived from a regression model that regressed the 1986 price of intraLATA toll services against a variety of explanatory variables. The explanatory equation included three dummy variables for state regulation: (1) whether the state prohibited provision of intraLATA toll services by facilities based carriers (*FBENTRY*); (2) whether the state banned all entry into intraLATA markets (*NOENTRY*); (3) whether the state imposed sanctions against those carried unauthorized intraLATA traffic (*BLOCK*); and, (4) a composite variable defined as the product of *BLOCK* and *NOENTRY*. The study found that the coefficients on the *FBENTRY* and the composite variable were statistically insignificant.[55]

The empirical evidence provided by these studies illustrates a basic economic principle—in the absence of competition, firms have an incentive and the ability to raise their prices above the level that would otherwise prevail in a competitive environment. While regulators can exert some influence over the exercise of this economic incentive, these studies show that regulators' abilities to constrain intraLATA prices to competitive levels are limited. Indeed, as the FTC study shows, regulatory attempts to limit intraLATA competition and enforce that limit with sanctions (e.g., blocking and compensation) resulted in even higher intraLATA prices.

There are several other economic benefits associated with intraLATA competition in addition to the price benefits estimated by these two empirical studies. First, as a matter of basic economics, a reduction in intraLATA toll prices will be associated with an increase in toll volumes. One of the most comprehensive surveys of telephone demand studies concluded that the price elasticity[56] of intrastate MTS calls is .65 ($\pm$ .15), (Taylor 1980, 170) which means that a one percent decrease in the price of intrastate MTS services would result in a .65 percent increase in the volume of intrastate MTS traffic. Thus, based on this elasticity estimate and the price differentials cited above, the volume of intraLATA toll calls in a state that allows intraLATA competition could be expected to increase between two and five percent higher than states that prohibit intraLATA competition, everything else held equal.[57]

Second, with the introduction of intraLATA competition, telephone consumers will have a wider variety of suppliers and services to choose from when placing long distance intraLATA calls. For example, if a consumer is dissatisfied with the long distance services he receives from its LEC, and if intraLATA competition is allowed, he could select another carrier that he believes will better serve his needs. The potential loss of customers to competing intraLATA carriers could increase LECs' sensitivity and responsiveness to telephone customer demands, and thus, would provide an economic incentive to increase the quality of intraLATA toll services.

Third, permitting intraLATA competition is probably administratively simpler than the alternatives—intraLATA compensation or blocking. If intraLATA competition is allowed, a state regulator need only administer the enforcement of intraLATA access charges, just as interLATA access charges are administered, rather than become mired in the minutia of calculating unauthorized minutes, compensation rates, and the technical aspects of blocking. States that implement compensation plans must devote resources to a continual administration of LEC-IXC disputes. Which minutes do the compensation charges apply to? Who is responsible for tracking those minutes (LECs or IXC), and how will accuracy be guaranteed? How often will the plan be reviewed to determine whether the parameters continue to be valid, or whether the objectives of the compensation plan are being met? How will non-payment or over-charging disputes be resolved?

The relative administrative costs of various methods of regulating intraLATA traffic are important for two reasons. First, to the extent that regulatory compliance costs are included in LECs' operating costs and the assets used to comply with regulation (such as lawyers' office space, word processing equipment, etc.) are considered rate base assets, LEC customers pay for the administrative costs of regulation in their telephone rates. Second, administrative burdens may have significant associated opportunity costs. Most state regulatory commissions have small staffs that must deal with a broad range of regulatory issues in the telephone industry and in other utility industries. The staff and resources devoted to the administration of a compensation or blocking plan will not be available for other regulatory matters that could be of greater importance to a state's utility consumers.

2.2. Costs of IntraLATA Competition

A common allegation in regulatory proceedings where intraLATA authority is an issue is that if IXCs are allowed to carry intraLATA traffic, LECs' toll revenues will fall and contribution to local service will be threatened. For a number of reasons, however, empirical evidence and analyses indicate that the threat to local service prices is illusory.

First, empirical studies report that the demand for WATS is price elastic or close to unit elasticity. (Taylor 1980, 130-144) Thus, even if competition forces intraLATA prices down by 3 to 10 percent, as indicated by the studies discussed above, there may be some intraLATA services for which price decreases are not associated with revenue losses.

Second, the introduction of competition in interLATA markets resulted in substantial increases in the total volume of long distance traffic. Since divestiture in 1984, national traffic volumes have grown by about 22 percent in interstate, interLATA markets. Part of this traffic stimulation is due to price reductions in interLATA markets and part is due to the marketing efforts of alternative carriers. A similar growth of total market volume in intraLATA markets could result in an increase in the LECs' toll revenues even though their share of the total intraLATA market decreases.

Third, LEC shares in intraLATA traffic do not decline significantly when intraLATA competition is introduced. Most states that permit intraLATA competition grant LECs the exclusive right to carry all 1+ switched access traffic and allow IXCs to "compete" by permitting them to carry 10XXX intraLATA switched traffic and dedicated access traffic. As a practical matter, few telephone consumers will take the time to dial a 10XXX access code to reach an alternative IXC. The Washington Utilities and Transportation Commission recently surveyed its experiences with intraLATA competition and found that in 1986, LECs carried 93.93 percent of intraLATA traffic. By 1988, that market share had fallen to 93.71 percent, a change of only .22 percentage points. (Washington Utilities and Transportation Commission 1989, 65)

This lack of market share erosion reflects both customers' unwillingness to dial a 10XXX access code as well as customers' general lack of knowledge of LATAs and LATA boundaries. For example, in a Southern Bell survey of Florida customers, after defining LATAs, surveyors asked customers whether they would be willing to select a carrier other than Southern Bell to carry their intraLATA traffic. 69.4 percent of the residential customers and 71.7 percent of the business surveyed answered "no."[58] When South Central Bell asked the same question of Kentucky customers, 63 percent of the residential customers and 62.2 percent of the business customers surveyed indicated that they were not willing to change carriers.[59]

Fourth, the introduction of competition in intraLATA markets will result in an increase in LECs' intraLATA access charge revenues. As noted above, when an LEC loses a minute of toll traffic to a competitor, generally speaking, it gains a minute of access charge revenue. The net result of these four factors could be a net increase in revenues for LECs.

Table 3 uses data from a recent Georgia intraLATA compensation case to show how an LEC's revenues might be impacted by IXC carried intraLATA traffic. Table 3 shows that even though there was a 1200 percent increase in "unauthorized" intraLATA traffic between 1984 and 1988, the LECs realized a total revenue

Table 3. Revenue Impact of IntraLATA Competition			
Before IXC IntraLATA Market Entry			
Service	Average Price (per minute)	Quantity (minutes)	Total Revenue
Toll Services	$0.2260	672,810,624	$152,055,201
Access Services	$0.1167	3,928,300	$458,433
After IXC IntraLATA Market Entry			
Service	Average Price (per minute)	Quantity (minutes),	Total Revenue
Toll Services	$0.2260	820,726,250	$185,484,133
Access Services	$0.1167	50,924,724	$5,942,915
		Revenue Gain	$38,913,414
		Percentage Gain	25.5%
Sources: Average prices and quantity data were reported by Southern Bell in *In Re: IntraLATA Toll Compensation*, Docket 3821-U (Georgia 1989). Because Southern Bell's average toll revenues increased by 1.25 percent over this period, no price decrease was assumed to accompany the unauthorized intraLATA traffic.			

increase of about 25 percent. Both its toll revenues and its access service revenues increased over this time period.

Some state regulators have also questioned whether intraLATA competition necessarily harms local service rates. For example, in its decision to permit intraLATA competition, the Vermont Public Service Board questioned whether local service prices would necessarily increase as a result of the introduction of intraLATA competition.[60] Indeed, even though a number of states have introduced intraLATA competition in some form or another, local rates have been decreasing in recent years and a number of LECs have been cited by state regulators for over-earnings.

Time series data has begun to be gathered on telephone rates, and these data do not indicate that local service rates are negatively impacted by long distance competition. In their survey of telephone price indexes, FCC economists concluded that prior to divestiture, local and long distance rates tended to follow the same patterns. (Lande and Wynne, 1987) However, after 1984, long distance prices began to fall, while local service prices continued to increase, but at a lower rate than before divestiture. If long distance revenues are necessary to maintain low local service rates, then why have the increases in local service rates been smaller after divestiture than before.

Other telephone price index data show that average local service rates are not higher in states that allow intraLATA competition than in states that forbid intraLATA competition. In fact, average local service rates are generally lower in states that allow intraLATA competition.[61] Admittedly, a simple average monthly rate is an imprecise measure of the impact of intraLATA competition, but if intraLATA competition necessarily implied higher local service rates, then one would have expected the opposite results.

LECs that oppose intraLATA competition often make an equity argument—it's not fair to allow intraLATA market entry when LECs are forbidden by the MFJ from entering interLATA markets. Such an argument casts the MFJ's intraLATA restrictions as a *quid pro quo*—LECs should be given an intraLATA monopoly to compensate them for their lack of interLATA authority. As noted above, however, the purpose of the MFJ's interLATA restriction was to prevent BOCs from using their control over local facilities to retard long distance competition. No *quid pro quo* was intended by the inter-and intraLATA provisions of the MFJ.

Also, it is important to emphasize that the MFJ was a consent decree that applies only to the BOCs and GTE—other LECs are not bound by the MFJ's interLATA restriction. The BOCs and GTE agreed to the terms of the MFJ in exchange for settlement of their antitrust case. Thus, it is disingenous to argue that other carriers should not be allowed into intraLATA markets because the BOCs and GTE voluntarily agreed to be bound by the MFJ's interLATA restriction.

3. Recommendations

As the above discussion implies, this author believes that the benefits of intraLATA competition far outweigh the potential costs. The alternatives to intraLATA competition (intraLATA compensation and intraLATA blocking) are, for the reasons discussed above, impractical or unworkable. If intraLATA competition is allowed, then how should the market be structured?

As long as LECs are forbidden from entering interLATA markets, they should retain the right to carry 1+ intraLATA switched traffic, and IXCs should be allowed to carry switched intraLATA traffic when that traffic is prefixed with a 10XXX access code or carried over dedicated access facilities. Such an arrangement is very close to what exists in today's market in many states. Presubscription for intraLATA markets, with the possibility of different inter- and intraLATA carriers, would likely be extremely confusing for many telephone consumers. Also, when given a choice, few consumers could be expected to select a long distance carrier that could not carry both their intra and interLATA traffic.

LECs should not be given the exclusive right to carry 1+ intraLATA traffic that employs dedicated access lines or 800 traffic. As noted above, it would be impossible for customers to know when to prefix 800 calls with a 10XXX access code and impossible to prefix 800 calls with a 10XXX code. Also, since the called party pays the charges on 800 calls, the calling party has no incentive to prefix the 800 call with the called party's desired 10XXX code.

For several reasons, IXCs should be allowed to carry intraLATA traffic that employs dedicated access arrangements[62] without requiring a 10XXX prefix. First, routing such traffic from the IXC to the LEC will add to the cost of such arrangements. The IXC would have to identify intraLATA traffic and make arrangements to route that traffic back to the LEC for transmission over the LEC's facilities. Second, routing dedicated access traffic to the LEC may result in a degradation of service especially if the LEC's network is inferior to the IXC's[63] or if the IXC's screening adds to its call set up times.[64] Third, because dedicated access lines are typically purchased from the LEC's interstate tariffs and the costs of such lines are fully allocated to the LEC's interstate jurisdiction, routing 1+ dedicated access traffic to the LEC will result in a double recovery of costs—it will recover its access costs through its federal tariff and will realize intrastate revenues from rerouted 1+ traffic.

The benefits of intraLATA competition will be realized only to the extent that competition exists. As noted above, IXCs will be reluctant to enter intraLATA markets if their major competitor, the LEC, does not face similar costs, or if their major competitor control their access costs. Imputation of comparable access charges on LEC intraLATA services is the simplest means of remedying these problems. It eliminates the need for extensive, burdensome cost studies to determine the local loop and local switching costs of providing a service. It also mitigates LECs' incentives to manipulate the level of access charges to discourage intraLATA competition.

Notes

The materials in this paper represent the opinions and analyses of the author, and not necessarily those of United Telecommunications, Inc., US Sprint or any of their affiliates.

1. The MFJ was approved by the Court in and can be found at *United States v. Western Electric Company, Inc.*, 552 F. Supp. 131 (D. D.C. 1982).
2. The GTE local operating companies operate under a similar antitrust consent degree that limits their provision of interLATA services in a similar manner. The GTE consent decree can be found at *United States v. GTE Corp.*, 603 F. Supp. 730 (D. D.C. 1984).
3. *United States v. Western Electric Company, Inc.*, 569 F. Supp. 990, 993-995 (D. D.C. 1983).
4. *United States v. Western Electric Company, Inc.*, 673 F. Supp. 525 (D. D.C. 1987), *reversed on other grounds, United States v. Western Electric Company, Inc. et al.*, Nos. 87-5388 & 87-5389 (D.C. C.A. slip op. April 3, 1990).
5. See the Court's discussion in *United States v. Western Electric Company, Inc.*, 569 F. Supp. 990, 995-1003 (D. D.C. 1983).
6. The Court also observed that if LATAs were too small, competing IXCs, such as MCI and US Sprint, would not extend service to remote rural areas, and that since AT&T was the default long distance carrier, it would retain its long distance monopoly in those areas.
7. *United States v. Western Electric Company, Inc.*, 569 F. Supp. 1057, 1108 (D. D.C. 1983).
8. *United States v. Western Electric Company, Inc.*, 569 F. Supp. 1057, 1105 (D. D.C. 1983).
9. Id., 569 F. Supp. at 1109.
10. *United States v. Western Electric Company, Inc.*, 569 F. Supp. 990, 1005 (D. D.C. 1983).
11. Id., 569 F. Supp. at 1005-1006; and, *United States v. Western Electric Company, Inc.*, 569 F. Supp. 1057, 1105-1107 (D. D.C. 1983).
12. A review of access service arrangements is in Wnorowski (1985, 75-79).
13. For example, to use US Sprint's network to place a long distance, interLATA call in equal access offices, customers dial 10333 and then the ten digit long distance number that they wish to call. Billing for the US Sprint call is then handled by the LEC.
14. Because FGA and FGB access arrangements are often priced lower than FGD, long distance resellers and smaller IXCs sometimes use FGA and FGB to originate calls and supply their customers with automatic dialers to overcome the dialing disadvantage. Also, some IXCs terminate calls over FGB access arrangements.
15. A Point of Presence (POP) is the point where a long distance carrier's network connects with LECs' local networks. In theory, a POP could be located on the border of two LATAs, and thus, an IXC could operate with fewer POPs than LATAs.
16. *Minnesota Committee Requests Information from Switch Vendors in Effort to Nail Down Price, Timetable for IntraLATA '1+' Presubscription; IXCs Press Issue in Other States*, Telecommunications Reports 16 (Aug. 29, 1988). Hawaii allows its residents to select different interstate and intrastate carriers, but not different inter and intraLATA carriers.
17. *South Dakota PUC Orders Intra-LATA '1+'*, State Telephone Regulation Report, 12 (Mar. 23, 1989).
18. *An Inquiry into IntraLATA Toll Competition and Appropriate Compensation Scheme for Completion of IntraLATA Calls by Interexchange Carriers and WATS Jurisdictionality*, Interim Order, Admin. Case No. 323, Phase I (Mar. 29, 1990).
19. Survey presented in *In re: Investigation into Equal Access Exchange Areas, 1+ Restrictions to the local exchange companies and elimination of the access discount*, Docket 880812-TP, Testimony of Alphonse Varner (Oct. 1989).
20. Survey presented in *In the matter of An Inquiry into IntraLATA Toll Competition, An Appropriate Compensation Scheme for Completion of IntraLATA Calls by Interexchange Carriers, and WATS Jurisdictionality*, Administrative case No. 323 (1989).
21. WATS stands for Wide Area Telecommunications Services. It is a service that allows customers to make (Out-WATS) or receive (In-WATS or 800 service) long distance calls and have those calls billed on a bulk basis rather than individually.
22. MTS stands for Message Telecommunications Service. It is generic long distance services that pass through the LEC's switch.

23. Florida's plan is described in *In Re: Intrastate Telephone Access Charges for Toll Use of Local Exchange Services: Order,* Docket No. 820537-TP, Order No. 13750 (Oct. 5, 1984).

24. This relative efficiency may not hold if one leg of the transmission path is a dedicated access link between the customer and the IXC's POP.

25. Id. at p. 11.

26. The Florida Commission decided to allow IXCs to carry intraEAEA traffic without paying compensation or reselling LEC MTS or WATS if the intraEAEA traffic carried by the IXC is not carried over the IXC's facilities. Thus, an IXC with only one POP in an EAEA would not pay compensation or be required to block intraEAEA call attempts over its network. Also, if the EAEA has more than one access tandem, an IXC may carry intraEAEA traffic over its own facilities between POPs without paying compensation so long as the call originated at one access tandem and terminated at another.

27. MSAs were established in *Investigation into the Determination of Telephone Exchange Boundaries in Illinois: Order,* Docket 82-0268 (Feb. 9, 1983).

28. ILL. REV. STAT. ch. 111 2/3, Sec. 13-403.

29. Exemptions for dedicated access and 800 services were added to Illinois statutes in 1988. See 1988 Ill. Laws, Pub. Act 85-1161.

30. On the other hand, states that ban intraLATA competition generally enforce that ban with a compensation or blocking requirement.

31. For a discussion of imputation issues, see Dingwall (1988).

32. *In the Matter of a Summary Investigation Into IntraLATA Toll Access Compensation for Local Exchange Carriers Providing Telephone Service Within the State of Minnesota: Findings of Fact, Conclusions of Law and Order Initiating Summary Investigations,* Docket P-999/CI-85-582 at 38-41 (Nov. 2, 1987) [Ordered that average toll rates should cover average access charges imposed by LECs on other toll carriers.]

33. *In the matter of the investigation into WATS resale by hotels/motels: Order of Clarification and Denying Rehearing,* Docket TO-84-222, et al. (Dec. 11, 1987).

34. *In the Matter of the Investigation into Exchange Carrier Toll Rates: Order,* Docket UT 47, Order No. 88-665 (June 30, 1988).

35. *Washington Utilities and Transportation Commission v. Pacific Northwest Bell Telephone Company: Eighteenth Supplemental Order,* Cause No. U-85-23 et al. (Dec. 30, 1986); and, *Washington Utilities and Transportation Commission v. Pacific Northwest Bell Telephone Company: Fifth Supplemental Order,* Docket No. U-87-1083-T (May 26, 1988).

36. *Investigation of Proposed "Vermont Telecommunications Agreement": Order,* Docket No. 5252, pp. 56-61 (July 12, 1988) [approving an imputation of access charges based on a comparison of the weighted average rate per minute for DDD toll with the total weighted premium switched access rate per minute].

37. *In Re MCI Telecommunications: Order Lifting Moratorium on IntraLATA Competition Effective January 1, 1989 and Approving Stipulation,* Case Nos. 83-259-T-SC, et al., 92 PUR4th 39 (April 27, 1988) [approving stipulation that required imputation].

38. 16 MINN. STAT. ANN. Sec. 237.60, Subd. 4 (Supp. 1988). "Prices of rates charged for competitive services must cover the incremental costs of providing the service. If a telephone company provides both local service and long-distance services, that company shall, in determining the cost of the long distance service, include at least the same level of contribution to common and joint costs as is contained in the access charges to other telephone companies. The company may do so on an aggregated basis, instead of on a time or mileage band basis."

39. COLO. REV. STAT. Sec. 40-15-1501(1) (Supp. 1988). "No local exchange provider shall, as to its pricing and provision of access, make or grant any preference or advantage to any person providing telecommunications service between exchanges nor subject any person to, nor itself take advantage of, any prejudice or competitive disadvantage for providing access to the local exchange network. Access charges shall be cost-based, as determined by the commission, but shall not exceed its average price by rate element and by type of access in effect in the state of Colorado on July 1, 1987."

40. *In the Matter of Application of Access Charges to the Origination and Termination of Interstate, IntraLATA Services and Corridor Services: Memorandum Opinion and Order,* FCC 85-172 at pars. 9-11 (April 12, 1985).

41. *Pennsylvania Public Utility Commission v. Bell Telephone Co. of Pennsylvania,* 60 Pa. PUC 435, Docket R-842779 (Oct. 24, 1985).

42. Some state regulators have questioned whether intraLATA toll services provide any subsidy to local services. See, for example, the discussions in *Re Investigation into Non-Traffic Sensitive Cost Recovery: Order*, Docket 860984-TP, Order 18598, 89 PUR 4th 259, 263-266 (Florida PSC, Dec. 24, 1987), aff'd., 94 PUR 4th 145 (April 7, 1988); and, *Re Revenue Transfer from Long-Distance Carriers to Local Exchange Customers*, Docket UT 42, Order No. 87-405 (Oregon PUC, Mar. 31, 1987). The Florida Commission order used incremental and stand-alone cost standard and found no evidence of a cross-subsidy. The Oregon Commissioner order argued that the existence of a subsidy critically depends on how one allocates common costs, and since there is no single correct method of allocating common costs, there is no reliable evidence of a toll-to-local subsidy.

43. For example, Carrier Common Line (CCL) charges are per minute charges paid by IXC that are used to recover fixed non-traffic sensitive (NTS) costs that do not vary with minutes of use. Thus, the more long distance traffic that is carried over an LEC's network the greater will be its CCL revenues even though its NTS costs are the same regardless of traffic volume.

44. The Texas Public Utilities Commission recently reported that LEC intraLATA rates may be anywhere from 40 to 100 percent higher than comparable IXC rates. (Texas Public Utilities Commission 1989, 49)

45. The Tennessee Public Service Commission adopted a compensation plan that consisted of simply switched access charges when it noted that per minute switched access charges were approximately the same as a *Net Revenue* plan proposed by an LEC, but considerably simpler to calculate than net revenues. *Re AT&T Communications of the South Central States, Inc.*, Docket U-87-7492, 91 PUR 4th 1 at 5-8 (Tenn. PSC, Mar. 17, 1988). The Tennessee Commission also required that IXCs bill their customers the same rates as charged by the LEC for intraLATA traffic.

46. For example, see the Commission's discussion in *Re Compensation to telephone Companies by Interstate Common Carriers for Unauthorized Intrastate Calls*, Docket No. 85-05-23, 69 PUR 4th 645, 658 (Conn. DPU, Aug. 21, 1985). The reason for this divergence is that IXCs pay access charges from the time that a customer establishes local dial tone until the customer disconnects the call. Thus, access minutes include the time spent in call attempts and waiting for the called party to answer. In contrast, customers are billed on the basis of conversation minutes, which run from the time the called party answers until the call is disconnected.

47. *Re Competitive Intrastate Offerings of Long Distance Telephone Services*, Docket No. P-100, Sub 72, 69 PUR 4th 629 (N. Car. Sept. 30, 1985).

48. *Re Telephone Companies Operating in Alabama*, Docket 19536, Phase II, 97 PUR 4th 233 (Ala., Nov. 10, 1988).

49. NPA-Nxx is the North American Numbering Plan for telephone numbers. NPA is the area code and Nxx is the local exchange. There are many local exchanges within the region encompassed by an area code, and a LATA may contain several area codes. Also, some area codes extend into different LATAs.

50. *Order Instituting Investigation to Determine Whether Competition Should be Allowed in the Provision of Telecommunications Transmission Services Within the State: Opinion*, OII 83-06-01, et al. (June 13, 1986).

51. The California Commission is currently reexamining its intraLATA market structure.

52. *In the matter of the investigation into WATS resale by hotels/motels, et al.*, Case No. TO-84-222, p. 11 (June 24, 1986).

53. Generally speaking, state utility regulation is limited to common carriers — firms that provide service to the public at large. If a firm builds a private network that links several large users together and then transports those users traffic to a remote location (e.g., another city), that traffic may be intraLATA traffic, but the carrier may not be a common carrier since it does not market its services to the public at large.

54. For example, see the decision of the Connecticut Department of Public Utility Control in *DPUC Investigation into Authorization of Competition for Intrastate Interexchange Telecommunication Services Pursuant to Public Act 87-415, Phase I and II: Decision*, Docket 87-08-24 (March 15, 1989). The DPUC found that general, facilities based intraLATA competition was not in the public interest, but allowed intraLATA competition when the services were provided as resold LEC services, private line services, and ancillary and specialized services.

55. The lack of statistical significance may not mean that there are no price effects when a state prohibits facilities based intraLATA competition. The four policy variables included in the FTC's

model were likely highly correlated, and the resulting multicollinearity could have resulted in a distortion of the variables' t-statistics. Also, this author knows of no states that prohibit facilities based intraLATA market entry and do not impose some form of blocking or compensation requirement. Thus, the effects of the *FBENTRY* variable were likely captured entirely by the *BLOCK* and *NOENTRY* variables.

56. Price elasticity is defined as the percentage change in the quantity demanded for a one percent change in price. Thus, a price elasticity of 2 means that if the price of a product increased by one percent, the quantity demanded would decrease by two percent.

57. It is important to note, however, that this price elasticity estimate is based on a survey of demand studies done prior to 1980, before there was substantial competition in the telecommunications industry. Thus, the estimate is extremely conservative. In today's telecommunications environment where consumers have a number of alternatives, the price elasticity of intrastate toll services is likely much larger than .65. It is also important to emphasize that this volume increase is the volume increase associated with a price decrease; it does not include the increase in volumes associated with the general growth of toll markets, nor does it include the stimulation associated with the introduction of new intraLATA carriers and their marketing efforts.

58. Survey presented in *In Re: Investigation into Equal Access Exchange Areas, Toll Monopoly Areas, 1+ Restrictions to the local exchange companies and elimination of the access discount*, Docket 880812-TP, Testimony of Alphonse Varner (Oct. 1989). Note, however, that 14 percent of residential customers and 9 percent of business customers responded that they "did not know" whether they would select another carrier. Thus, if the LEC remains the default 1+ carrier, it seems reasonable to assume that the customers who responded "I don't know" would continue to consume the LEC's intraLATA services.

59. Survey presented in *In the Matter of An Inquiry into IntraLATA Toll Competition, An Appropriate Compensation Scheme for Completion of IntraLATA Calls by Interexchange Carriers and WATS Jurisdictionality*, Admin. Case No. 323 (1989). Among those surveyed in Kentucky, 25.5 percent of the residential customers and 20.6 percent of the business customers said they did not know whether they would be willing to switch intraLATA carriers.

60. *Re IntraLATA Access Charges*, Docket Nos. 5092 et al., 86 PUR 4th 319, 330 (Vt. Public Service Board, Sept. 4, 1987).

61. The average monthly rate for local service in states that allow intraLATA competition is $12.81. The average local monthly service rate in states that forbid intraLATA competition is $13.44. Based on data from Lande and Wynne (1989).

62. A dedicated access arrangement refers to a situation where the customer has a direct line between his premises and his IXC. The direct line can either be rented from the LEC (special access), owned and operated by the customer, or owned and operated by the IXC.

63. An LEC's network may be physically inferior to an IXC's network, or an LEC may not offer the same services that an IXC offers in conjunction with the dedicated access arrangement.

64. If an IXC must screen its traffic for intraLATA calls (assuming that technology is available for such screening), the screening could add to the IXC's call set up time and degrade the quality of *all* calls placed through the IXC's network.

References

Dingwall, Craig. 1988. "Imputation of Access Charges — A Prerequisite for Effective IntraLATA Toll Competition." *Administrative Law Review* 40:433-450.

Federal Communications Commission. 1990. *Trends in Telephone Service*.

Frentrup, Chris. 1988. "The Effect of Competition and Regulation on AT&T's Intrastate Toll Prices, and of Competition on Bell Operating Company IntraLATA Toll Prices." Federal Communications Commission report.

Horning, John S. et al. 1989. "Evaluating Competitiveness of Telecommunications Markets: A Guide for Regulators." National Regulatory Research Institute report.

Lande, James L. and Peyton L. Wynne. 1987. "Primer and Sourcebook on Telephone Price

Indexes and Rate Levels" Federal Communications Commission publication.
Mathios, Alan D. and Robert P. Rogers. 1988. "The Impact of State Price and Entry Regulation on Intrastate Long Distance Telephone Rates." Federal Trade Commission report.
Rogers, Paul and G. Morelli. 1985. "Intrastate Telecommunications Competition." National Association of Regulatory Utility Commissioners report.
Taylor, Lester. 1980. *Telecommunications Demand: A Survey and Critique.* Cambridge, Mass: Ballinger.
Texas Public Utilities Commission. 1989. *Status of Competition in Long Distance and Local Telecommunications Markets in Texas.*
Virginia State Corporation Commission. 1985. *Competition in the IntraLATA Market.*
Washington Utilities and Transportation Commission. 1988. *The Status of the Washington Telecommunications Industry.*
Wnorowski, Adalbert K. 1985 "Will Equal Access Truly Equal Competition?." in *The New Telecommunications Era After the AT&T Divestiture: The Transition to Full Competition.* edited by Herbert E. Forrest and Richard E. Wiley. Washington, D.C.:Practicing Law Institute.

3

DIVERSIFICATION AND REGULATED MONOPOLY

Michael A. Crew
Keith J. Crocker

Although the merits of diversification by regulated utilities into competitive markets have been widely debated by economists, regulators, and public interest advocates, the efficiency consequences of relaxing line-of-business restrictions remains unclear.[1] One argument, most recently advanced by Baumol and Willig [1985] and McAvoy and Robinson [1985], contends that diversification restrictions are both unnecessary and result in significant inefficiencies through the loss of economies of scope.[2] The alternative position, which was enunciated most cogently by Posner [1968], is that "... regulation ... creates an incentive ... to diversify, regardless of efficiency considerations ... for diversification may enable the [regulated firm] to evade the constraint of regulation" (p. 605). This paper reconciles these two conflicting positions by examining the incentives facing the regulated firm to diversify into competitive markets. We conclude that, under rate of return regulation, the existence of economies of scope is a necessary, but not a sufficient, condition for efficiency because any benefits are sensitive to the precise regulatory form and cost attribution rules adopted by regulators.

The debate on the merits of diversification reflects differing opinions regarding the incentive facing regulated firms to enter competitive markets. The traditional concerns have been that diversification might allow (i) cross-subsidization between the regulated and competitive sectors of the firm, providing revenues to the unregulated subsidiary to allow predatory behavior against competitors, or (ii) the diversion of revenues to the competitive subsidiary (through internal equipment sales at an upcharge or strategic assignment of common costs), thereby circumventing regulatory constraints on allowable profit.[3] More recently, it has become apparent that to disallow diversification may result in forgone economies of scope, whose benefits may at least in part accrue to the customers of the regulated subsidiary.[4] As it turns out, there is more than a grain of truth in both of these arguments.

That economies of scope are necessary for diversification by traditionally regulated monopolies into competitive markets to be efficient is straightforward. Consider, for the moment, a case where a firm produces products x and y that are sold in rate-of-return-regulated and competitive markets, respectively, and are produced by means of distinct (separable) production technologies (implying no economies of scope) to which the labor and capital inputs can be precisely attributed. The only potential benefit to ratepayers would be if profit from the competitive market were used to subsidize production of the regulated product. But if the market for y is truly competitive, and the regulated firm has no technological advantage over its competitors, then that market cannot be a long run source of profit.[5] And the consumers of y are indifferent about whether the diversified firm enters their market or not, since, presumably, there exists a perfectly elastic supply of alternative producers possessing the identical production technology poised as potential entrants. Consequently, diversification by the regulated firm having no technological advantage cannot be efficiency improving.[6] On the other hand, if the regulator can attribute inputs to the production processes only imperfectly or at positive (monitoring) cost, then significant inefficiency can result since diversification would provide yet another opportunity to inflate the regulated rate base. The addition of capital used in the production of y is effectively costless (since zero profit is guaranteed in the competitive market) and would relax the rate of return constant, allowing a restriction of output and higher profit in the regulated market.[7] Diversification without economics of scope, therefore, cannot improve efficiency and may allow circumvention of the rate-of-return constraint, with deleterious effect.

Although economies of scope imply the existence of potential Pareto improvements from diversification, whether such benefits obtain will depend on the incentives generated by the regulatory structure. We first consider a situation where the regulated monopoly and competitive subsidiary operate under an "umbrella" rate of return constraint and demonstrate that, if the nature of the production technology is exogenously specified, then diversification is efficient. Alternatively, if the firm is able to select among distinct production technologies with different x- and y- output proportions, then diversification may be inefficient even with the presence of economies of scope. The second section examines the "partially regulated" firm where a constant proportion of common costs are attributed to the regulated monopoly, which operates under the resulting rate-of-return constraint, and the residual attributed to the competitive subsidiary operating with no profit restrictions. Although ". . . allocation of joint or common costs among services is not merely difficult; it is inherently arbitrary," (Posner, p. 605) may seem to be a virtual tautology, we show that, from the perspective of obtaining Pareto improvements from diversification, the nature of the allocation rules is critical. Indeed, we find that the only constant allocation rule which *guarantees* diversification to be efficient is the one which attributes *all* of the common cost to the regulated subsidiary; other constant allocators have ambiguous consequences. In particular, equity-based cost allocation rules designed to have the competitive subsidiary shoulder a "fair" proportion of common costs could disadvantage ratepayers even when diversification generates economies of scope.

The paper proceeds as follows. The next section presents the environment and examines the firm which diversifies while operating under an umbrella rate of return. The third section examines the partially regulated firm, and concluding remarks are contained in the final section. Proofs of the principal results are given in the Appendix.

1. The Environment and Total Regulation

In general, production technologies which allow joint production and the realization of economies of scope are not unique. In the case of cogeneration, for example, there exists a wide range of technologies which produce different proportions of heat and electricity for a given level of input usage. Similarly, with local telephone services, the technology chosen determines the mixture of basic local service and enhanced services available for a given investment. Consequently, the diversification decision not only entails the selection of factor inputs, but also the choice of the basic technology which determines the relative output proportions.

To illustrate these concerns, consider a firm possessing a technology which produces the outputs x and y from common capital and labor inputs according to

$$\begin{bmatrix} x \\ y \end{bmatrix} = \begin{bmatrix} t \cdot f(K, L) \\ (1-t) f(K, L) \end{bmatrix}$$

where f is strictly quasi-concave and $t \in [0, 1]$ is a technology parameter. We also assume that neither input is inferior.[8] This technology exhibits fixed-proportions output for a given t and variable-production when t is a choice variable. Moreover, this joint production function generates economies of scope.

Let the firm sell x as a rate-of-return regulated monopolist who faces the strictly concave (as a function of x) revenue function $R^x \equiv xP(x)$ where $P(x)$ is the inverse demand and assume that y is sold in a perfectly competitive market at a price m.[9] We are assuming that there exists a perfectly elastic supply of potential producers in the competitive market and that the regulated firm is small relative to the market so that m is constant and independent of the regulated firm's diversification decision.

For the remainder of this section, we consider the effects of diversification when the firm operates under an "umbrella" rate of return constraint where all revenues are considered in the revenue requirements decision. Currently, this is the regulatory regime which obtains whenever a traditionally regulated firm sells a product in a competitive market, unless regulators explicitly act to exclude those revenues from the rate of return calculations. Letting $R^y \equiv my$ represent the total revenues obtained by the firm from the competitive market, the rate of return constraint may be written as

$$R^x + R^y - wL - rK \leq (s-r)K$$

where s is the allowed rate of return on the capital base K.[10] Before proceeding, we present an assumption necessary for our results and discuss its implications.

Assumption 1: $f_{LL} < 0$.

This assumption implies diminishing returns to labor but, since we may have $f_{KK} > 0$, does not preclude increasing returns to scale of production. The import of this assumption is that it implies diminishing *revenue* returns to labor ($R_{LL} < 0$), which is required in order that the first order conditions examined below be sufficient for a maximum (see Baumol and Klevorick (1970), Klevorick (1973), and Bailey (1973)). Our first result examines the effect of diversification on the output of the regulated product when the firm has (for the moment) no discretion in selecting the technology choice parameter t.

Theorem 1: If $f_{LL} < 0$ and t (>0) is exogenously specified, then $\dfrac{dx}{dm} > 0$.

The implication of this result is that, when the technology t is not a choice variable, the output of the regulated product x is higher when the firm is allowed to diversify ($m > 0$) than when diversification is disallowed ($m = 0$). This implies that diversification is Pareto improving since (i) the consumers in the competitive market are indifferent; (ii) the expansion of output reduces the price of the regulated product so ratepayers benefit; and (iii) the firm has higher profit since K increases and the allowed profit equals $(s-r)K$. The incentives generated by this regulatory structure ensure that the consumers of the regulated product enjoy part of the benefits generated by the economies of scope produced by diversification. However, if the firm is able to alter the output proportions of production through the choice of the technology t, then the implications for the efficiency of diversification are less clear. Let $\hat{x}$ denote the profit maximizing output of the undiversified regulated monopoly and $MR(\hat{x})$ be the associated marginal revenue.[11]

Corollary: When the regulated firm selects t, the output of the regulated product increases (decreases) after diversification if $MR(\hat{x}) > (<) m$.

The intuition behind this result is that the profit maximizing firm selects the technology which equates the marginal addition to profit in both markets. And, for a given input cost, this entails equating the marginal revenue obtained in the regulated market and the price of the competitive output. This will imply a contraction in the production of the regulated market if the profit maximizing level of marginal revenue for the undiversified firm were less than the competitive price m.[12] Such a reduction in the output of the regulated product would imply that a movement from the nondiversified to the diversified regime could not constitute a Pareto improvement, since the customers of the regulated product are disadvantaged as a result of the higher price for x. On the other hand, such a movement could allow a *potential* Pareto improvement if the "winners" from a reduction in x

(firms) were able, in principle, to compensate the losers (consumers). Whether such compensation is possible would depend, inter alia, on the elasticity of demand for the regulated product and the price of the competitive good. If the demand were fairly elastic, then reductions in x would result in a modest reduction in consumer surplus, whereas a large value of m would imply substantial profit to the firm which diversifies. Alternatively, a very inelastic demand for the regulated product coupled with a relatively low competitive price m would, ceteris paribis, indicate a large cost to consumers while promising modest gains to the diversified firm.

From a policy perspective, however, the corollary does provide some practical guidance. One suspects that regulators, when contemplating a movement from a nondiversified status quo, would be particularly concerned about permitting diversification which, while perhaps allowing a potential Pareto improvement, explicitly disadvantaged the consumers of the traditionally regulated product. Since the nondiversified regime is the status quo, $MR(\hat{x})$ is potentially observable prior to diversification, as is the price m in the (extant) competitive market.[13] Thus, whether diversification would result in an actual Pareto improvement relative to the nondiversified regime can, in principle, be ascertained ex ante.[14] Perhaps paradoxically, the more attractive the competitive market (higher m), the more likely ratepayers are to suffer from an adverse technology choice after diversification.

2. Diversification with Partial Regulation

An alternative to the approach of total regulation considered in the previous section is to partition the diversified firm into independent rate-of-return-regulated and competitive divisions where the rate of return constraint applies only to the regulated portion. This requires that common costs be divided between the regulated and competitive divisions in order to provide a well defined capital base for rate-of-return calculations in the regulated market. We assume that the regulator assigns the constant proportion θ of the total costs to the regulated product.[15] We adopt the environment from the previous section, but assume that the technology is fixed exogenously at $\bar{t} \in (0, 1)$ in order to concentrate on the incentive effects of differing (constant) cost allocation rules.

Given the value of θ set by the regulator, the relevant maximization problem for the diversified firm is represented by the Lagrangean expression

$$H = \pi + \lambda[\theta(wL + sK) - R^x]$$

where $R^x \equiv xP(x)$; $R^y \equiv my$;

$$\pi = R^x + R^y - rK - wL;$$

and the rate-of-return constraint is written as[16]

$$R^x \leq \theta(wL + sK). \tag{1}$$

Before proceeding, we introduce the following assumption which we will use to obtain the results below.

Assumption 2: $R^x(K, L)$ is a strictly concave function.

This is a common assumption in the rate of return literature dating back to Averch and Johnson, Klevorick, Baumol and Klevorick, and Bailey. While concavity of revenue does not preclude increasing returns to scale of production, since R^x may be strictly concave even when $f(K, L)$ is not, it does place limitations on the extent of increasing returns for a given demand function.[17]

Letting $\frac{dK}{dL}|_R$ denote the slope of the rate of return frontier $R^x - wL - sk = 0$, assumption 2 allows the following technical, but important, conclusion.

Lemma: When R^x is strictly concave, $\frac{dK}{dL}|_R < 0$ implies that $\frac{d}{dL}\left\{\frac{dK}{dL}|_R\right\} < 0$.

This result implies that the rate of return frontier is strictly concave when it has a negative slope (see figure 2).

For the partially regulated firm, the first order conditions for an interior maximium (in K and L) are

$$\frac{\partial H}{\partial L} = \pi_L + \lambda[\theta w - R^x_L] = 0; \text{ and} \quad (2)$$

$$\frac{\partial H}{\partial K} = \pi_K + \lambda[\theta s - R^x_K] = 0. \quad (3)$$

There are two classes of solutions to this problem, depending on whether or not the rate of return constraint binds after diversification. First, if $\lambda = 0$, the first order conditions reduce to $\pi_L = \pi_K = 0$ which implies unconstrained profit maximization and $R^x < \theta(wL + sK)$, so that the firm is not making the allowed rate-of-return in the regulated market. The alternative solution occurs when $\lambda > 0$. In this case, dividing (2) by (3) yields

$$-\frac{\pi_L}{\pi_K} = -\frac{R^x_L - w\theta}{R^x_K - s\theta} \quad (4)$$

where the left hand side is the slope of an isoprofit contour and the right hand side is the slope of the (binding) constraint frontier. Since the rate-of-return constraint holds with equality, it may be rewritten as $\pi = (\theta - 1)wL + (\theta s - r)K + R^y$, so that (4) yields the expansion path

$$-\frac{R^y_L + w(\theta - 1)}{R^y_K + s\theta - r} = -\frac{R^x_L - w\theta}{R^x_K - s\theta}. \quad (5)$$

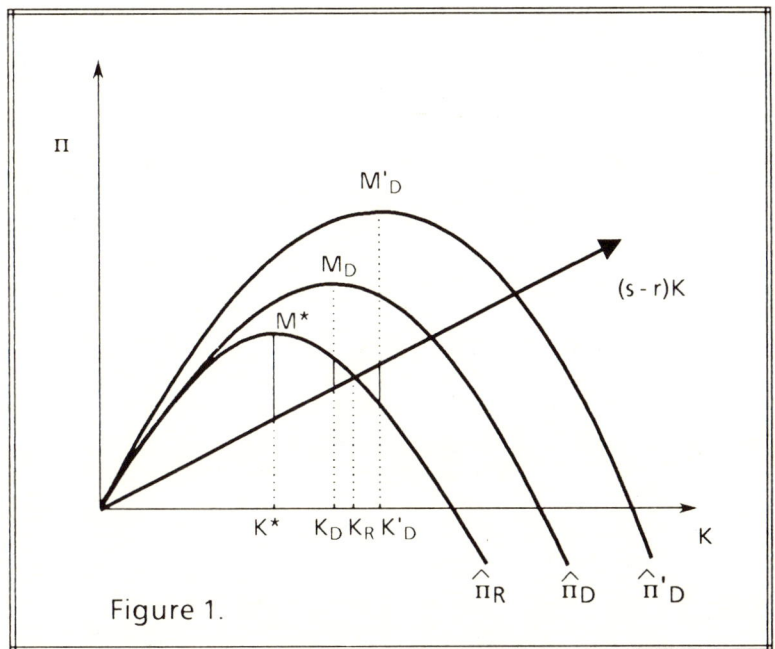

Figure 1.

The relationship between these cases can be illustrated with reference to figure 1.[18] Let $\hat{\pi}(K) \equiv \pi(K, L^*)$ where L^* solves $\pi_L = 0$, so that $\hat{\pi}$ represents the maximum obtainable profit for every K (where L is picked optimally). Then $\hat{\pi}_R$ denotes the profit function of the undiversified firm, and K_R is the capital choice which maximizes profit subject to the rate-of-return constraint $\pi_R \leq (s-r)K$. Diversification results in a shift in the profit function to either $\hat{\pi}_D$ or $\hat{\pi}'_D$. In the former case, the unconstrained profit (M_D) is not allowed since, at K_D, $\hat{\pi}_R(K_D) > (s-r)K_D$. Then the rate-of-return constraint binds, and $\lambda > 0$. Alternatively, if the shift in the profit function is sufficiently large ($\hat{\pi}'_D$), then $\lambda = 0$ and the unconstrained profit maximum (M'_D) can be obtained since, at K'_D, we have $\hat{\pi}_R(K'_D) < (s-r)K'_D$.

Whether diversification results in a relaxation of the rate-of-return constraint depends on the nature of the production technology as well as the price of the competitive output. To see this, note that an application of the envelope theorem to post-diversification profit yields

$$\frac{d\hat{\pi}_D}{dK} = R_K^x + R_K^y - r$$

where $R_K^y = m(1-\bar{t})f_K$. Thus, the relationship between the pre- and post-diversification unconstrained profit maximization solutions depends on the marginal revenue product (R_K^y) of the competitive product. This occurs when the competitive

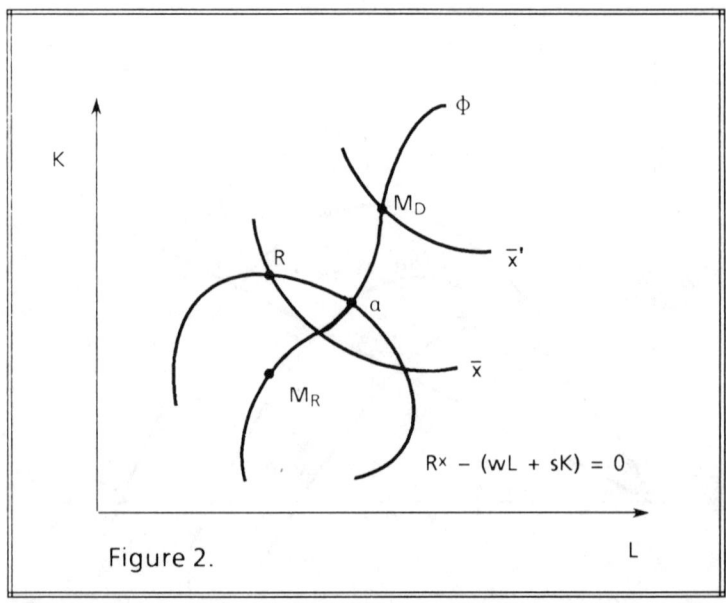

Figure 2.

venture is so profitable that the firm is willing to accept less than the allowed rate of return in the regulated sector in order to sell more of the competitive product (when R_K^y is large so that $d\hat{\pi}'_D/dK$ is still positive when the rate-of-return constraint in the regulated market is met with equality at K_R). Whether this case would apply in practice depends on the extent to which rate of return regulation constrains the undiversified firm, as well as on the profitability of the competitive venture. But, were this situation to obtain, the ratepayers would benefit from diversification.

Theorem 2: The production of the regulated output increases if the rate-of-return constraint does not bind after diversification.

The intuition behind this result, which is proved in the appendix, may be explained with reference to figure 2. The locus of input combinations which satisfies the binding rate of return constraint for the undiversified firm is given by $R^x - wL - sK = 0$.[19] Prior to diversification, $\lambda > 0$ and the firm operates at point R which maximizes profit along the rate of return frontier (recall that $\pi = (s - r)K$ when the rate of return constraint is met with equality). After diversification, the rate of return constraint is $R^x - \theta(wL + sK) \le 0$. When $\lambda = 0$ after diversification, this constraint is satisfied with a strict inequality, which implies (since $\theta < 1$) that $R^x - wL - sK < 0$ as well. Then the firm attains the unconstrained profit maximum M_D on the efficient expansion path (denoted ϕ). A movement from R to M_D results in production on a higher isoquant, so that output increases from $\bar{x}$ to $\bar{x}'$.

When diversification does not permit a relaxation of the rate of return constraint,

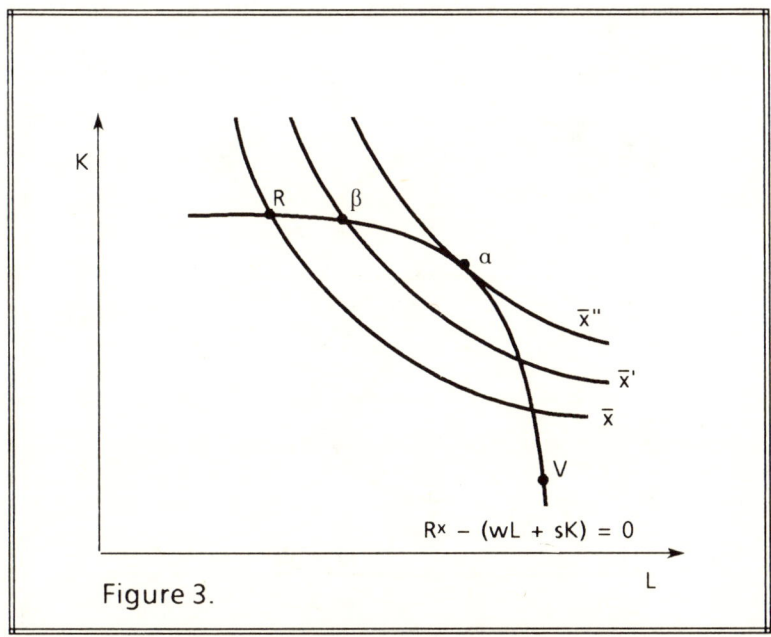

Figure 3.

the efficiency consequences of diversification are more mixed. First, consider the case where the rate of return constraint binds post-diversification and suppose that $\theta = 1$. Then (5) reduces to

$$-\frac{R^y_L}{R^y_K+s-r} = -\frac{R^x_L-w}{R^x_K-s} \tag{6}$$

where the right hand side is the slope of the rate of return frontier $\frac{dK}{dL}|_R$. As a benchmark for comparison, consider the case where the firm does not sell the competitive product. Then $m = 0$ and the firm operates at a point on the rate of return constraint with zero slope, depicted as R in figure 3. If $m > 0$, we obtain from (6)

$$-\frac{my_L}{my_K+s-r} = -\frac{R^x_L-w}{R^x_K-s} \tag{7}$$

which implies that the firm operates on a negatively sloped portion of the rate of return frontier such as β. Since the isoquants are strictly convex as a result of the strict quasiconcavity of f and the rate of return frontier is strictly concave in the negatively sloped region, this movement from R to β entails an increase in production from $\bar{x}$ to $\bar{x}'$. Moreover, as m increases, the left hand side of (7) approaches $-f_L/f_K$ and production moves toward point γ. This proves the following result.

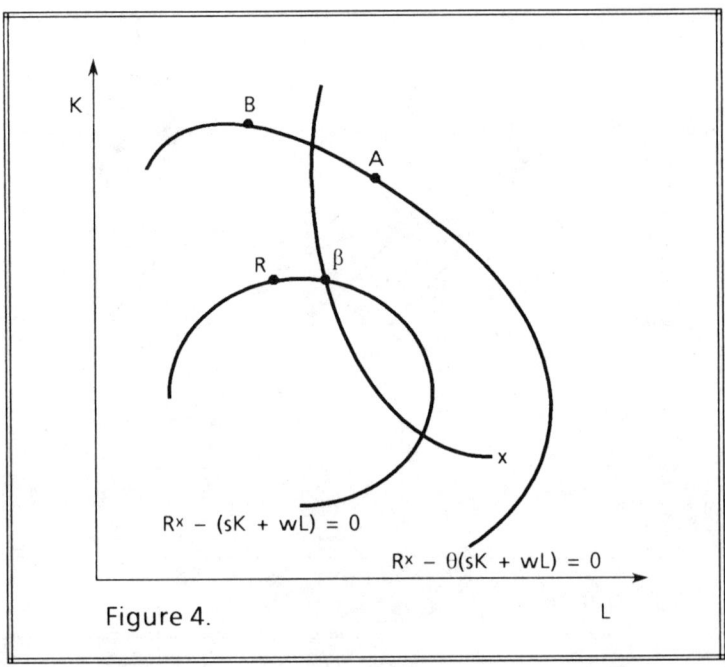

Figure 4.

Theorem 3: If the regulator attributes all of the common costs to the regulated subsidiary ($\theta = 1$) and the rate of return constraint binds after diversification, then diversification increases the output of the regulated product.

When all common costs are attributed to the regulated output (so that the competitive output is sold, essentially, as a "free" good), the consumers of the regulated product unambiguously benefit from diversification. Diversification partially mitigates the capital bias under which the undiversified firm operates and increases the output of the regulated commodity.

Unfortunately, the efficiency consequences of diversification under other cost attribution rules are ambiguous unless additional restrictions are placed on either production technologies or demand. The effect of an increase in θ is to shift the rate of return frontier outward as in figure 4. Any point on the rate of return frontier for $\theta = 1$ violates the rate of return constraint for $\theta < 1$ since $R^x = sK + wL > \theta(sK + wL)$. Therefore, the rate of return frontier for $\theta = 1$ lies entirely inside of the frontier for $\theta < 1$. But the output effects of a reduction in θ relative to $\theta = 1$ (point B) are ambiguous, as either A or B may satisfy the tangency condition and result in production on the negatively sloped portion of the rate of return frontier but have differing output consequences. Without additional assumptions regarding the behavior of the rate of return frontier and, therefore, restrictions on production technologies and demand, no definitive conclusions can be derived regarding the output effects of other constant cost allocation rules.

3. Conclusions

Recent public policy debate has focused attention on the desirability of permitting diversification by regulated monopolies into competitive markets. While many proposals for diversification allow economies of scope and, hence, the potential for increased efficiency, our analysis indicates that the existence of such economies is not sufficient for actual benefits to obtain. Where both the monopoly and competitive subsidiaries operate under an umbrella rate-of-return constraint (which, as we argue above, is equivalent to revenue-based fully distributed cost allocation), circumvention of restrictions on allowable profit may be achieved by the strategic selection of output intensities through technology choice. In the alternative regime where only the monopoly is subject to rate-of-return regulation and the competitive subsidiary pays a portion of common costs, the efficiency consequences of diversification are highly sensitive both to the relative size of the competitive venture and to the particular joint cost attribution rules adopted by the regulator. While equity norms might suggest some type of cost sharing to be appropriate, we found, perhaps paradoxically, that the only percentage cost allocator guaranteeing beneficient efficiency effects from diversification allocated all of the common costs to the regulated subsidiary. Without further restrictions on production or the structure of demand, other percentage cost attribution formulae have ambiguous efficiency consequences.

This analysis suggests that the efficiency effects of diversification under non-revenue based fully distributed cost rules, such as those based on directly attributable costs or relative output levels, is still an open question.[20] Clearly, regulators cannot proceed as if economies of scope guaranteed beneficent results from diversification. Whether diversification by the regulated monopolist is desirable depends not only on the existence of economies of scope, but also upon the precise regulatory and cost allocation structures adopted in regulation. Both of the regulatory regimes seem likely to provide another manifestation of McKie's (1970) "tar baby" effect: extending the scope of the regulated firm requires the expansion of regulatory control, in this case to the fundamental choice of production technology and to the nature of internal cost attribution rules.

Appendix

This appendix provides the proofs of the Theorems. The general approach is similar to that of Bailey (1973).

Proof of Theorem 1.

The relevant Lagrangean expression is

$$G = \pi + \lambda[(s-r)K - \pi] \tag{A1}$$

where $\pi \equiv R^x + R^y - rK - wL$. The first order conditions for an interior solution in

(K, L) are

$$G_K = (1 - \lambda)(R_K^x + R_K^y - s) + s - r = 0; \text{ and} \quad (A2)$$

$$G_L = (1 - \lambda)(R_L^x + R_L^y - w) = 0 \quad (A3)$$

where R_j^i denotes the partial derivative of R^i with respect to input j. Totally differentiating the (binding) rate of return constraint yields[21]

$$dK(R_K^x + R_K^y - s) + dL(R_L^x + R_L^y - w) + y\, dm = 0$$

which, from (A3), gives

$$\frac{dK}{dm} = -\frac{y}{R_K^x + R_K^y - s} \quad (A4)$$

Since $s > r$ and $0 < \lambda < 1$,[22] equation (A2) implies that the denominator is negative, so that $dK/dm > 0$.

Now, totally differentiate (A3) to obtain

$$dK(R_{LK}^x + R_{LK}^y) + dL(R_{LL}^x + R_{LL}^y) + y_L dm = 0$$

which implies

$$\frac{dL}{dm} = \frac{-\frac{dK}{dm}(R_{LK}^x + R_{LK}^y) - y_L}{R_{LL}^x + R_{LL}^y}. \quad (A5)$$

Noting that $\frac{dx}{dm} = x_L \cdot \frac{dL}{dm} + x_K \cdot \frac{dK}{dm}$, substitution of (A5) and rearranging terms yields

$$\frac{dx}{dm} = \frac{1}{R_{LL}^x + R_{LL}^y} \left\{ \frac{dK}{dm}[-x_L(R_{LK}^x + R_{LK}^y) + x_K(R_{LL}^x + R_{LL}^y)] - x_L y_L \right\}. \quad (A6)$$

We now sign the terms in this expression. Expanding the denominator yields

$$R_{LL}^x + R_{LL}^y = x_{LL}\left[MR + m\left(\frac{1-t}{t}\right)\right] + MR'(x_L)^2$$

where $MR \equiv P'x + P$ is the marginal revenue in the regulated market and the primes indicate derivatives. The concavity of R^x (as a function of x) implies $MR' < 0$ and $x_{LL} \equiv t \cdot f_{LL} < 0$ because of the diminishing returns to labor assumption. The term in brackets is positive since (A3) can be rewritten as $x_L[MR + m\left(\frac{1-t}{t}\right)] = w$. Thus, the denominator of (A6) must be negative.

Expanding the bracketed terms in the numerator of (6) yields

$$\left[MR + m\left(\frac{1-t}{t}\right)\right] \cdot \left\{-x_L x_{LK} + x_K x_{LL}\right\}.$$

DIVERSIFICATION AND REGULATED MONOPOLY

Since capital is an noninferior input, we must have the slope of the expansion path $\frac{dK}{dL}$ be positive, so that $\frac{\partial}{\partial L}\{-\frac{x_L}{x_K}\} > 0$, which implies the negativity of the term in braces. Thus, $\frac{dx}{dm} > 0$.

Q.E.D.

Proof of Corollary 1.

To allow the choice of t by the firm, the Lagrangean (A1) must be modified to allow $0 \leq t \leq 1$, so that

$$G = \pi + \lambda[(s-r)K - \pi] + \mu(1-t) \quad (A7)$$

which, for an interior solution in (K, L, t) yields conditions (A2), (A3) and, in addition,

$$\frac{\partial G}{\partial t} = (1 - \lambda)f(K, L)[MR(x) - m] - \mu = 0. \quad (A8)$$

If the firm is not allowed to diversify, then $m = 0$ and (A8) implies that $\mu > 0$, so that $t = 1$ and the firm is selecting the x-intensive production technology. The level of output which solves this problem is denoted $\hat{x}$.

Now, consider the problem facing the firm which is permitted to sell y in the competitive market ($m > 0$) and chooses to do so ($\mu = 0$ and $t < 1$). Letting $\bar{x}$ denote the post-diversification output of the regulated product, the firm selects t so that $MR(\bar{x}) = m$. If $MR(\hat{x}) > m$, then $\bar{x} > \hat{x}$ and diversification increases output. On the other hand, suppose we had $MR(\hat{x}) < m$. Then, as long as $MR(0) > m$, the firm can always select t sufficiently small to allow $MR(\bar{x}) = m$, which implies $\bar{x} < \hat{x}$.

Q.E.D.

Proof of Theorem 2.

First, we demonstrate that a movement along the undiversified firm's binding rate of return constraint toward the efficient expansion path (from R to α in figure 2) increases x. Totally differentiating the rate of return constraint when $\theta = 1$ yields

$$dK = -dL\left(\frac{R_L^x - w}{R_K^x - s}\right).$$

Then, since $dx = x_L dL + x_K dK$, we obtain

$$dx = \frac{dL}{R_K^x - s}(x_L(R_K^x - s) - x_K(R_L^x - w))$$

which reduces to

$$dx = \frac{w x_L dL}{R_K^x - s}\left(\frac{x_K}{x_L} - \frac{s}{w}\right).$$

The denominator is negative by (3) and the fact that $\pi_K < 0$ at a (constrained) solution. Since the regulated firm operates under a capital bias, we know $\dfrac{x_K}{x_L} < \dfrac{r}{w}$, so that

$$dx > \frac{x_L dL(r-s)}{R_K^x - s} > 0 \text{ when } dL > 0.$$

Thus, by alleviating the capital bias ($dL > 0$), but maintaining the rate of return constraint, output of x increases.

Now, when $\lambda = 0$ postdiversification, the unconstrained profit maximum must satisfy $R^x \leq \theta(sK + wL)$ which also implies that $R^x \leq sK + wL$. Thus, M_D lies outside of the prediversification rate of return frontier, as depicted in figure 2, and a movement from α to M_D along ϕ increases output still further.

Q.E.D.

Proof of the Lemma.

Letting $F \equiv R^x - (wL + sK)$, the rate of return constraint is written as $F(K, L) = 0$. Then

$$\frac{dK}{dL}\bigg|_R = -\frac{F_L}{F_K} = -\frac{R_L^x - w}{R_K^x - s}$$

so that

$$\frac{d}{dL}\left\{\frac{dK}{dL}\bigg|_R\right\} = -\frac{d}{dL}\left\{\frac{R_L^x - w}{R_K^x - s}\right\}$$

$$= -\frac{1}{\left(R_K^x - s\right)^3} \cdot [R_{LL}^x (R_K^x - s)^2 - 2R_{KL}^x (R_L^x - w)(R_K^x - s) + R_{KK}^x (R_L^x - w)^2]$$

The term in brackets is a negative definite quadratic form as long as R^x is strictly concave. So the sign of the expression is that of $R_K^x - s$.

Along the negatively sloped portion of the rate of return frontier in figure 3 (the segment RV not inclusive of endpoints), a reduction in both K and L (and, hence, x since neither output is inferior) would permit an increase in profit. Therefore, we must have $R_L^x < w$ and $R_K^x < r$ which implies $R_L^x - w < 0$, and, since $s > r$, $R_K^x - s < 0$. Therefore, the expression above must be negative, as was to be shown.

Q.E.D.

Notes

We have benefited greatly from the constructive criticism provided by Paul Kleindorfer, David Salant, and the participants in the Rutgers University Advanced Workshop in Public Utility Economics. Also, we thank Eileen Moran for her comments as discussant.

1. This is apparent from the controversy over the "line-of-business" restrictions placed on the Regional Holding Companies which preclude entry into markets other than traditional tariffed local telephone service. The Regional Holding Companies have attempted to have the "line of business" restrictions relaxed to allow subsidiaries to offer services such as software programs, equipment leasing, foreign business ventures, office equipment, real estate and cellular radio systems. (U.S. vs. AT&T et al., Civil Action No. 82-0192 Misc. No. 82-0025, July 26, 1984). More recently, *Geodesic Network: 1987 Report on Competition in the Telephone Industry*, U.S. Justice Department, Antitrust Division, January 1987, and the FCC's *Report and Order*, "In the matter of Separation of costs of regulated telephone service from costs of nonregulated activities," C.C. Docket no. 86-111, have proposed some significant relaxations of the line of business restrictions subject to stringent accounting and separation procedures.

2. Baumol and Willig (1985, 31) have argued strongly that "under the separation rules, AT&T is prevented from efficiently organizing its efforts to bring innovative services to the marketplace . . . the separation rules deprive AT&T of the full benefits of its own innovations, and dull the incentives to generate them." In a similar vein, MacAvoy and Robinson (1985, 257) argue ". . . to reduce the line of business restrictions on diversification by the [Bell Operating Companies] contemporaneously with the expansion of local service competition. If the [Bell Operating Companies] can generate revenues from new business ventures, they will have less need for protection from competition in local markets."

3. These concerns were evident in the strict separation required between regulated and non-regulated ventures in the AT&T divestiture agreement, and previously in the Bell System-Western Electric relationship. There is a history of litigation on whether Western overcharged the Bell Operating Companies covering the period from the late 1940's to divestiture. Usually the results were favorable to Western. For example, "Western's prices to Bell System companies are substantially less than those of other suppliers for comparable items" (*Re Southern Bell Tel. and Tel. Co.*, 4 P.U.R. 3d 195, (Ala. P.S.C. 1954)). Less typical but hardly insignificant was the situation in California where disallowances were made and Pacific Telephone's contention that prices were reasonable was rejected (*Re The Pacific Tel. and Tel. Co.*, Dkt. No. 43145, 80 P.U.R. (ns) 355, 364 (Cal. P.U.C. 1949); 77 P.U.R. 3d 1, 9 (Cal. P.U.C. 1968)). In 1965 the state Supreme Court upheld the California Commission (*The Pacific Tel. and Tel. Co. v. California Public Utilities Commission et al.*, Dkt. No. 21788, 21793, 21794, 58 P.U.R. 3d 229 44 Cal. Rptr. 1 (Cal. 1965), aff'd 53 P.U.R. 3d 513 (Cal. P.U.C. 1965)). Although much legal talent was brought to bear on the problem of whether Western overcharged, the issue was never fully resolved.

4. A few examples include congeneration of heat and electricity (see Crew and Crocker (1986)), integrated telephone and computer information services (Baumol and Willig 1985) and local access and long distance telephone service (MacAvoy and Robinson 1983).

5. If the "competitive" market for y were a source of profit, and if the capital used in the production of y were omitted from the regulated firm's rate base, then ratepayers would benefit from diversification since they would be subsidized by that profit. But to implement such an argument would require one to justify where the "profit" comes from—market power or a superior technology—and why those conditions might obtain. The most justifiable source of technical superiority is the existence of economies of scope arising from joint production—the case discussed below.

6. If the market into which the firm diversifies is truly competitive, the predation argument does not seen very compelling for the usual reasons (see, for example, McGee (1980)).

7. Averch and Johnson (1962) provide a clear statement of this argument.

8. The import of this assumption is that the output expansion path of the firm has a strictly positive, but finite, slope.

9. Note that we are assuming that products x and y are not vertically related in the analysis which follows, so that economies resulting from such a relationship are not considered (see Crocker (1983)).

10. This is also the rate of return constraint faced by a partially regulated firm (examined in the next section) where the proportion of common costs allocated to the regulated part of the firm is $R^x/(R^x + R^y)$. This issue is considered in more detail below.

11. The proof of the corollary is simplified by the assumption that $MR(0) > m$, which is sufficient to guarantee an interior solution for t.

12. This problem has been of particular concern where electrical utilities diversify into cogeneration, investing in heat-intensive technologies. The result is often a technology choice favoring low cost

(competitively sold) heat production over efficient (regulated) electricity generation. Similar questions may arise where local telephone companies invest in enhanced-services-intensive technology for local service.

13. The "marginal revenue equals competitive price" rule is a result of the one-to-one substitution of x for y assumed in the production technology. In a more general (i.e., nonlinear) specification, the optimal choice of t would equate the marginal revenue product of t in each market.

14. Implicitly regulators have accepted this type of argument when allowing telephone companies to enter new markets. The quid pro quo for relaxed regulation and freedom to diversify has been an agreement to maintain existing prices of regulated services for a period of time. For example, see the Rate Stability Plan of New Jersey.

15. Similar arbitrary procedures have a long history in regulation, for example, the Jurisdictional Separation Procedure which was used before divestiture to allocate common costs between AT&T's local and long distance businesses. MacAvoy and Robinson (1983, 4) provide the following description: "Initially, the costs directly allocable to intrastate and interstate services are assigned .... The joint and common costs of providing these services are then arbitrarily divided between the interstate and the intrastate categories .... Average price levels for each class of service is then set to satisfy a 'revenue requirement' that covers the assigned portion of these joint and common costs."

16. Alternative allocators include lump sums and percentages of revenue. When common costs are fully distributed in proportion to revenues, so that $\theta = R^x/(R^x + R^y)$, then the rate of return constraint reduces to $R^x + R^y - wL - rK \leq (s - r)K$, which is identical to that of the totally regulated firm.

17. In particular if f exhibits increasing returns, then MR must decline sufficiently to guarantee that R^x is concave. This assumption is a sufficient, but a not necessary, condition for the results which follow.

18. Note that the case of diversification with $\theta = 1$ is illustrated since the post-diversification rate of return constraint in the discussion below is $\pi_D \leq (s - r)K$. For $\theta < 1$, the relevant rate of return is $\pi_D \leq (\theta - 1)wL + (\theta s - r)K$, which is not depicted.

19. Note that those points bounded by the frontier (such as the unconstrained profit for the undiversified firm M_R) violate the rate of return constraint, whereas those outside (such as M_D) satisfy $R^x - (wL + sK) < 0$.

20. Braeutigam (1980) examines the effects of these rules on a multiproduct regulated monopoly, providing a clear discussion of how these rules are applied.

21. If the rate-of-return constraint does *not* bind post-diversification, output (for fixed t) increases by Theorem 2 (proved below).

22. See Zajac (1972) for a general proof. Contrary to earlier results (such as Takayama (1969)), this does not require strict concavity of the revenue function.

References

Averch, H., and L. Johnson. 1962. "Behavior of the Firm Under Regulatory Constraint." *American Economic Review* (December): 1052-69.

Bailey, E.E. 1973. *Economic Theory of Regulatory Constraint*. Lexington: D.C. Heath and Company.

Baumol, W.J., and R.D. Willig. 1985. "Telephones and Computers: The Costs of Artificial Separation." *Regulation*, American Enterprise Institute, (March/April): 23-32.

Baumol, W.J., and A.K. Klevorick. 1970. "The Averch-Johnson Thesis." *Bell Journal of Economics and Management Science* 1 (Spring): 162-90.

Braeutigam, R. 1980. "An Analysis of Fully Distributed Cost Pricing in Regulated Industries." *Bell Journal of Economics* 11 (Spring): 182-96.

Crew, M.A., and K.J. Crocker. 1986. "Vertically Integrated Governance Structures and Optimal Institutional Arrangements for Congeneration." *Journal of Institutional and Theoretical Economics* (June): 340-59.

Crew, M.A., and P.R. Kleindorfer. 1986. *The Economics of Public Utility Regulation*. Cambridge, MA: MIT Press.

Crocker, K.J. 1983. "Vertical Integration and the Strategic Use of Private Information." *Bell Journal of Economics* (Spring): 236-48.

Klevorick, A.K. 1973. "The Behavior of a Firm Subject to Stochastic Regulatory Review." *Bell Journal of Economics and Management Science* 4 (Spring): 57-88.

MacAvoy, P.W., and K. Robinson. 1983. "Winning By Losing: The AT&T Settlement and Its Impact on Telecommunications." *Yale Journal of Regulation* 1:1-42.

MacAvoy, P.W., and K. Robinson. 1985. "Losing By Judicial Policymaking: The First Year of the AT&T Divestiture." *Yale Journal of Regulation* 2:225-62.

McGee, J.S. 1980. "Predatory Pricing Revisited." *Journal of Law and Economics* (October): 289-330.

McKie, J.W. 1970. "Regulation and the Free Market: The Problem of Boundaries." *Bell Journal of Economics* (Spring): 6-26.

Posner, R.A. 1968. "Natural Monopoly and Its Regulation." *Stanford Law Review* 21:548-643.

Sweeney, G. 1982. "Welfare Implications of Fully Distributed Cost Pricing Applied to Partially Regulated Firms." *Bell Journal of Economics* 13 (Autumn): 525-33.

Takayama, A. 1969. "Behavior of the Firm under Regulatory Constraint." *American Economic Review* 66 (June): 255-60.

Zajac, E.E. 1972. "Lagrange Multiplier Values at Constrained Optima." *Journal of Economic Theory* 4:125-131.

4
PREDATORY PRICING SAFEGUARDS AND TELECOMMUNICATIONS REGULATION

Alexander Larson

Telecommunications regulation frequently employs safeguards against anticompetitive practices, usually in the form of price floors, cost allocations, nondiscrimination obligations, unbundling requirements, or line-of-business restrictions. Historically, structural separation also was used extensively as a safeguard, and persists in the *Computer III* environment, being mandatory for cellular services. The issue of predatory pricing continues to surface in most major Federal Communications Commission (FCC) dockets and in many state regulatory proceedings. The ensuing discussions usually raise the dilemma of how regulation may allow large established carriers some measure of downward pricing flexibility while maintaining safeguards against anticompetitive pricing practices.

This paper takes a critical look at this dilemma by reviewing some of the recent antitrust court cases. It is argued that with increasing competition, efficiency gains from regulatory policy would more likely be achieved by price flexibility, with a greater reliance on the courts to address the issue of below-cost pricing.

1. Introduction

1.1 What Is Predatory Pricing?

Despite the extensive literature in this area (e.g. Brodley and Hay (1981), Calvani and Lynch (1982), Liebeler (1986), and Phlips (1987)), the question "What is predatory pricing?" is a difficult one to answer. Neither legal and economic scholars nor the antitrust courts have arrived at a consensus regarding its definition. A useful working definition used in a recent court decision is:

> To be predatory, it is generally agreed that a price must be below the short-run profit maximizing level and must discipline or destroy rivals such that the

predator thereafter gains sustained excess (that is, monopoly) profits larger than those lost during the rival-bashing period. The uncertain future gains must greatly exceed the present actual losses to overcome the uncertainty that rivals will be destroyed or disciplined and that monopoly profits can be reaped in the face of future entry. If rivals survive or entry occurs, not only will predation be unsuccessful, but that very prospect reduces the likelihood that a challenged low price is in fact predatory.[1]

In court proceedings, in the law and economics literature, and in public utility regulation, it is usually assumed that predatory objectives are met by somehow pricing services at levels below their relevant economic costs, however these "costs" are defined. Once competitors have been driven from the marketplace, prices are then raised above competitive levels. When discussed as a concern of public utility regulation, the predation scenario usually involves cross-subsidization, using regulated services (for which the firm has market power) as a means of financing a strategy in which competitive services are priced below cost.

Despite this apparent simplicity of the concept of predatory pricing, it raises many troubling questions. What should be the basis of costs if predation is "pricing below costs?" What should be the relative importance of predatory intent? Is the price-cost relationship the primary indicator of predatory behavior (and hence the best underlying concept for a safeguard)? What is the role of market structural variables (e.g. barriers to entry, relative shares of network capacity) in predatory pricing strategies?

1.2. Schools of Thought on Predatory Pricing

This section outlines the competing schools of predatory pricing: the "cost-based" predation benchmark school of thought, the "no rule" school of thought, and the "game-theoretic" approach (Larson and Sievers 1988).

The cost-based school states that the price-cost relationship is the primary tool in predatory pricing detection. These writers argue that predatory pricing is a rational strategy to pursue, and that a cost-based "brightline" predation standard should be applied to detect predatory behavior. Professors Phillip Areeda and Donald Turner wrote the paper that is the key to this school of thought (Areeda and Turner 1975). Though they were not the first writers to suggest the use of cost-based tests in predatory pricing rules, they were the first to formulate a comprehensive *per se* rule on predation based on price-cost relationships. Basically, the *Areeda-Turner test* considers prices above short-run marginal cost to be *per se* lawful; those below are considered predatory. Areeda and Turner suggested that average variable cost be used as a workable proxy to marginal cost in practice.[2] This standard is followed by many antitrust courts, and in fact, many predation safeguards in telecommunications regulation emulate this test.

The competing "no rule" school states that predatory pricing is either rare or irrational, hence there should be no antitrust laws against it. These writers argue that predatory pricing as a business strategy is unlikely to succeed, and that even if it were successful, there are more profitable strategies that would achieve the same ends. As a consequence, instances of firms' adopting predatory strategies are likely to be quite rare. Other writers in this camp argue that predation exists, but because it does not occur often enough to matter, having laws against predatory pricing is more likely to impede vigorous price competition than provide any safeguards to the public. In both cases, the conclusion is that no predation rules are needed. This school of thought is usually identified with the writings of McGee (1958, 1980), Bork (1978), and Easterbrook (1981).

The game-theoretic school, composed of theoretical economists such as Fudenberg and Tirole (1986), Roberts (1986), Kreps and Wilson (1982), and Milgrom and Roberts (1982), states that under certain conditions, predatory pricing may be a rational strategy, but has little or nothing to do with marginal cost. These economists represent a literature that has developed since 1982. This literature applies the rigorous analysis of game theory and the assumptions of *asymmetric information* to the analysis of predation strategy. It develops arguments that a predator firm can enjoy the same benefits as in the classical predation model without actually violating price floors suggested by writers like Areeda and Turner. Thus, this strand of the literature is not supportive of price floors based on marginal cost, nor does it suggest a cost-based alternative. It is supportive of the "no rule" school, but for differing reasons. This approach states that predation may be anything but rare, but that the informational requirements for meaningful predation detection may impose more social costs than the predation itself.

The primary innovations of this literature are that it (1) incorporates the information asymmetries present in real product markets, (2) incorporates strategic interactions among competing firms (unlike the static analysis implied by the Areeda-Turner test), and (3) examines the role of sunk costs in entrants' decisions to enter a market. Because this literature calls into question the Areeda-Turner test, it also raises the same questions regarding the cost-based predation safeguards we see so pervasively in regulation. It is fair to say that this literature is still in the evolutionary stage and is not free of problems such as multiple equilibria or underlying assumptions that may not necessarily be plausible in real industrial markets. Further, these models do not as yet incorporate regulatory constraints.

1.3. Conditions for Proof of Predation in Antitrust Court

When predatory pricing is discussed in public utility regulation, it is often assumed that a price that is below some relevant benchmark of "costs" is automatically of a predatory nature. Certainly, this is the context in which regulators, intervenors, and commentors in state and federal regulatory proceedings implicitly define "predatory pricing," often using the term "cross-subsidization" interchangeably. This is somewhat understandable, as regulation is more of an economic supervisory function, as opposed to antitrust, which is more sanction oriented. Thus, the relationship of prices to costs is usually the most important aspect of any predation safeguard used in current telecommunications regulation, embodied typically by some type of price floor or cost allocation scheme. Because of this virtually exclusive reliance on the price-cost relationship in regulation, it is instructive to examine the determinants of predatory pricing used by the antitrust courts under Section 2 of the *Sherman Act*. As it turns out, the trend in antitrust courts is the recognition that other ingredients of an "attempt to monopolize" (which implicitly includes "predatory pricing") must be examined besides the relationship of prices to costs.

To establish that an "attempt to monopolize" has taken place, a plaintiff must establish:
- The defendant's specific intent to control prices or destroy competition in a relevant market.
- The defendant's predatory or anticompetitive conduct directed to accomplishing the unlawful purpose.
- A dangerous probability of success.

The "specific intent" and "dangerous probability" elements only apply to an "attempt to monopolize" case, which can be levied against a firm that currently does not have a high (70% or more) market share. A "monopolization" claim, however, can under section 2 be based solely on large market shares and predatory pricing. If a plaintiff in an "attempt to monopolize" case cannot prove all of these ingredients, then it cannot establish that such an attempt (which includes "predatory pricing") has taken place.

What is interesting here is that in an "attempt" case, the "dangerous probability of success" ingredient can be examined first and, if it is lacking, the other items need not be examined in detail. Determining if a dangerous probability of success exists need not involve a detailed examination of the price-cost relationship. Instead, it can rely on market structural variables (e.g. entry barriers or other variables that bear on the ability of the predator firm to recoup the short run losses that predation requires) whose absence or presence would make predation impossible regardless of the price-cost relationship. Further, even in a "monopolization" case, a court has some ability to examine structural issues like barriers to entry under the guise of assessing whether the defendant has market power.

This is in stark contrast to public utility regulation, in which the price-cost relationship is preeminent and market structural variables, definitions of the relevant market, and the dynamic intertemporal aspects of a predation strategy never even enter the discussion.

2. Predatory Pricing Safeguards in Public Utility Law

Safeguards against anticompetitive practices in telecommunications regulation usually can be classified in one of six ways: (1) explicit or implicit price floors, (2) cost allocation methods, (3) restrictions on the lines of business in which a telephone company may participate, (4) nondiscrimination obligations, (5) unbundling requirements such as open network architecture (ONA), and (6) structural separations (which applies today only to cellular services). Predatory pricing is usually handled using price floors of some kind. There are several examples of predation safeguards currently in use, or proposed, in telecommunications regulation. This section discusses several of them.

2.1. Predation Safeguards Used by the FCC

The FCC's Net Revenue Test. In the FCC's *OCP Guidelines Order*, it proposed a general guideline for the flexible pricing of message toll service (MTS).[3] This guideline applied to the offering of message toll service (MTS) price reductions from an *optional calling plan* (OCP). The FCC defined an optional calling plan in this docket as "a supplemental or additional MTS offering which allows customers to purchase MTS under an alternative, non-traditional pricing mechanism."[4] For example, the FCC meant that an OCP may offer service on a distance-insensitive basis or in bulk at a reduced rate. An OCP was not to involve changes to the rates or rate structure of the underlying basic MTS service.

The basic objective of the FCC in setting out these guidelines was to constitute a policy statement designed to prevent anticompetitive behavior while allowing dominant carriers increased pricing flexibility. The FCC attempted to strike a balance between the competitive dangers of "predatory" pricing by dominant firms and, on the other hand, the danger of stimulating economically inefficient entry by maintaining an artificially high pricing "umbrella" (which serves to protect inefficient competitors and inflate prices to consumers).

In setting out some reasonable and workable guidelines, the FCC proposed what it termed a *net revenue test*. This test required a carrier to demonstrate that when it offered price discounts on MTS using an OCP, it increased its net revenues (gross revenues minus costs) by doing so. This would ensure that an OCP price reduction was not simply a method for setting prices below costs for anticompetitive purposes. In effect, the net revenue test was set up as a comparison of the incremental revenues and costs resulting from the addition of an OCP. If the additional revenues from an OCP exceeded the additional costs it caused, the net revenue test was passed and the rates/cost relationship of the OCP was acceptable to the FCC. The conditions of the net revenue test and a detailed economic critique of it may be found in Larson, Monson, and Nobles (1989).

Thus, the FCC addressed whether the rates proposed by a dominant carrier were low enough to be predatory. The FCC specifically referenced the process in which a dominant carrier deliberately sacrifices current revenues to drive competitors out of the market, recouping its losses through higher prices and profits earned in the absence of competition. It also referenced a similar practice called *pricing without regard to cost*, which is discussed by Noll and Owen (1989) and Brock and Evans (1983).

The Price Caps Docket. In 1989, the FCC announced a fundamental revision in its method of regulating common carriers, choosing to replace rate of return regulation with an alternative known as *price caps*. The purpose of price caps is to prevent excessive prices in markets in which the FCC is not certain that competitive forces are sufficient by themselves to prevent overpricing, while avoiding the substantial social costs of standard rate of return regulation coupled with fully distributed cost pricing.

Essentially, price cap regulation applies an indexed, aggregate average price constraint on market "baskets" of federally regulated access services. In addition to such upper limits on both prices and allowed price changes, the FCC sought to provide lower limits on prices to prevent the possibility of predatory pricing. In the recent regulatory proceedings on price caps, predatory pricing safeguards were proposed as a part of this alternative form of regulation. In its *Notice of Proposed Rulemaking*, the FCC acknowledged that the standard "Section 208" complaint process and the antitrust laws provide for a for airing claims that rates for a particular service were priced in a predatory manner.[5] It also acknowledged that price caps would reduce, if not eliminate, the ability of a carrier to raise its rates to reap the benefits of predation.[6]

The FCC also raised the possibility that, for example, predation under price caps could take place if (1) price caps were set too high, or (2) cross-subsidization of some services within a basket were performed using revenues from other services for which the firm had market power.[7] The FCC thus solicited comments on three proposed remedies for this eventuality: (1) retention of its existing bar on resale restrictions, (2) a minimum duration requirement on any proposal that would reduce rates, and (3) price floors for certain services (e.g. long run incremental cost, marginal cost, average variable cost, the net revenue test).[8]

In the *Further Notice of Proposed Rulemaking*, the FCC referenced price "bands," which were ranges within which a carrier could raise or lower any individual rate element in any year and still be entitled to streamlined review. With respect to rate reductions, the band also was to mark the range within which reductions would be credited for purposes of measuring compliance within the aggregate cap.[9] The FCC never intended for such bands to be a *per se* test for predation, but nevertheless believed the manner in which they were formulated (together with the antitrust laws, the Section 208 complaint process, and other safeguards) would contribute to deterring any predatory activity.[10] The FCC declined in the *Further Notice* to adopt any exclusive standard for price floors in conjunction with price caps.[11]

In the *Report and Order and Second Further Notice of Proposed Rulemaking*, the FCC proscribed rate reductions greater than 5% for a service category unless AT&T could support such a proposal by cost materials "demonstrating that the proposed reduction is not predatory."[12] The FCC adopted the average variable cost standard as the standard for determining whether a proposed rate decrease must be suspended pending investigation.[13] The FCC acknowledged, however, that predatory pricing is "generally uncommon, and proven cases are rare."[14]

The Joint Cost Order. Another tacit predation safeguard due to federal regulation of telecommunications is the FCC's *Joint Cost Order*.[15] On Feb. 6, 1987, the FCC released the *Report and Order* on CC Docket No. 86-111, now incorporated in *Part 64* of the FCC's Rules and Regulations.[16] This order allows all carriers to use nonstructural accounting procedures rather than structural separation to separate costs of *regulated* and *nonregulated* activities. It became effective on Jan. 1, 1988 for all telephone companies using shared resources to provide regulated services and nonregulated activities for interstate business. Essentially, all

Tier I local exchange carriers (those with over $100,000,000 in annual operating revenues) and AT&T were required to file and implement a Cost Allocation Manual (CAM) by Sept. 1, 1987 and before selling customer premises equipment (CPE) without following *Computer II* structural separation conditions.[17] Once this CAM was approved by the FCC, regulated carriers would be allowed to offer enhanced and other nonregulated services. Carriers would then be allowed to use plant, operations, marketing, and administrative resources for both regulated and nonregulated services.

The stated purpose of *Part 64* is to safeguard against cross-subsidies and ensure that economies of joint production are not sacrificed. The FCC's general goal was to choose rules that cause regulated markets to produce results as close as possible to the results of unregulated markets that are subject to a high degree of competition.[18] Implicit in this is a safeguard against predatory pricing in unregulated markets. The *Part 64* rules are an integral part of the FCC's *Computer Inquiry III* proceeding, replacing structural separation with nonstructural accounting safeguards.

The basis of *Part 64* is an FDC method with emphasis on direct assignment of costs and cost causation. Wherever possible, the directly assignable costs of a service are directly assigned to it.[19] Costs are directly assigned to either regulated or nonregulated categories or cost objectives whenever it is possible to do so. The procedures adopted will not be used to apportion costs among specific regulated or nonregulated products or services, only to categories.[20]

2.2. Examples of State Predation Safeguards

Missouri's recently enacted House Bill 360 specifically prohibits the cross-subsidization of "competitive" services using the revenues of one or more "monopoly" services.[21] House Bill 360 does not mention "predation" or "predatory pricing" specifically, but it provides safeguards against it. Its provisions seek to ensure that services for which there is active competition are not priced at levels below cost, with the revenue shortfalls made up with the revenues from local exchange service, or some other service for which there is virtually no competition.

Section 392.400.3 of House Bill 360 deals with the concept of predatory pricing, requiring that the Commission establish appropriate methods for: (1) calculating the costs of providing any telecommunications service by a noncompetitive company, and (2) determining whether rates for the service are equal to or above costs:

> The commission shall establish ... appropriate methods for calculating the costs of providing any telecommunications service offered by a noncompetitive or transitionally competitive telecommunications company and for determining whether the rates ... for such telecommunications service are at a level equal to or greater than such cost. The commission may order any noncompetitive or transitionally competitive telecommunications company to conduct a cost study and to provide the results thereof to the commission.[22]

It goes on in Section 392.400.5 to state that:

> It shall be unjust, unreasonable, and unlawful for a noncompetitive or transition-

ally competitive telecommunications company to offer or provide a competitive or transitionally competitive telecommunications service *below the cost of such service* as determined by the commission if the commission finds that such offering or provision of service constitutes conduct which is not consistent with the promotion of full and fair competition [*emphasis added*].[23]

Thus, House Bill 360 specifically addresses the issue of cross-subsidization in this latter passage, prohibiting the setting of prices of competitive or transitionally competitive services at levels below their costs.

Similarly, the Texas Public Utilities Regulatory Act (PURA) specifies that rates shall not be "subsidized either directly or indirectly by regulated monopoly services; or ... predatory or anticompetitive."[24]

Another recent example is State Senate Bill No. 2320 from the State of North Dakota (a/k/a "State Price Caps"), effective July 1, 1989:

Revenues obtained from regulated services ... may not be used to subsidize or otherwise give advantage to a telecommunications company in its unregulated services, and revenues from essential services may not be used to subsidize or otherwise give advantage to a telecommunications company in its nonessential services. ... The price charged for an unregulated service or a nonessential service must cover the cost of providing that service.[25]

3. Useful Analytic Criteria from the Courts

Recent antitrust court decisions offer some valuable lessons regarding the design of predatory pricing safeguards in telecommunications regulation. The recent trend in the courts is to downplay the price-cost relationship in deference to other structural aspects of the market that bear on the viability of a predation strategy (for example, the ability to recoup short-run losses incurred during the rival-bashing period). Recent court activity has seen the emergence of significant reliance on economic theory to resolve antitrust issues. This reliance on economic theory has spawned (1) a new standard for summary judgement of predation cases, and (2) the judicial repudiation of standard cross-subsidization arguments.

This section discusses several important predatory pricing cases and their implications for predation safeguards in telecommunications regulation.

3.1. Northeastern Telephone Co. v. American Telephone and Telegraph Co.

In *Northeastern Telephone Co. v. American Telephone & Telegraph Co.*,[26] a supplier of telephone terminal equipment argued that AT&T engaged in a form of predatory pricing and cross-subsidization caused by setting the price of its equipment below its fully distributed cost. The court of appeals reversed judgement for the plaintiff on its claim that AT&T had engaged in predatory pricing to maintain its monopoly of sales of business telephone equipment.

This case is instructive for several reasons. First, the court argued that the relationship of price to reasonably anticipated marginal cost (or average variable cost as its surrogate) is the proper test of predatory pricing.[27] The court rejected the plaintiff's argument that pricing below FDC created a situation of anticompetitive cross-subsidization.

> Northeastern seems to believe that whenever a product's price fails to cover fully distributed costs, the enterprise must subsidize that product's revenues with revenues earned elsewhere. But when the price of an item exceeds the costs directly attributable to its production, that is, when price exceeds marginal or average variable cost, no subsidy is necessary. On the contrary, any surplus can be used to defray the firm's non-allocable expenses.[28]

The court concluded that LRIC is the appropriate cost standard for judging whether pricing is predatory:

> This is not an economist's quibble or theoretical musing; it is a matter of principled analysis and practical reality in the market place. Pricing at or above long-run incremental cost in a competitive market is rational and profitable business practice. Because there are legitimate, and in fact compelling, business reasons for pricing products at or above their long-run incremental cost, no predatory intent should be presumed or inferred from such conduct.[29]

What is a bit more novel about this case is that it rejected a *reverse-subsidization* argument (i.e. it rejected the argument that low prices in one market force the predator to raise them in another market), though it did not reject this concept using mainstream economic analysis. The defendant's low prices were found to be above "cost" (i.e. long run incremental cost) and thus not in need of some source of revenues for subsidies. Thus, the court implicitly accepted the concept of cross-subsidization by suggesting that subsidization would have occurred if prices were below cost. As will be demonstrated subsequently, two other landmark cases went much farther into the economic analysis required to address the cross-subsidization issue.

3.2. Matsushita Electric Industrial Co., Ltd. v. Zenith Radio Corp., et al

One of the most important predatory pricing cases since the Areeda-Turner test was developed is the case of *Matsushita Electric Industrial Co. v. Zenith Radio Corp*. Not only does it offer key judicial insights into determinants of predation beyond the price-cost relationship, it offers an analysis on cross-subsidization.

In this case, Japanese manufacturers of televisions were charged with conspiring to charge predatory prices for televisions sold in the United States. The case was born in 1970 when National Union Electric Corporation brought suit against a number of Japanese firms. Four years later Zenith Radio Corporation also brought suit against the same Japanese firms and the two actions were consolidated (Elzinga 1989).

The basic predation allegation against the Japanese firms was that they engaged in a global conspiracy over a period of more than two decades with the objective of destroying the American television industry. The predation allegations were two-fold: (1) charging monopoly prices in Japan through a price-fixing conspiracy, and (2) using the monopoly profits made in Japan to subsidize a predatory pricing campaign in the United States (Elzinga 1989).

In reversing the Court of Appeal's refusal to grant the defendant summary judgement, the Court recognized the difficulty of successfully undertaking a strategy of predatory pricing, stating:

> A predatory pricing conspiracy is by nature speculative. Any agreement to price below the competitive level requires the conspirators to forego profits that free competition would offer them. ... [T]he success of such schemes is inherently uncertain: the short run loss is definite, but the long-run gain depends on successfully neutralizing the competition. Moreover, it is not enough simply to achieve monopoly power, as monopoly pricing may breed quick entry by new competitors eager to share in the excess profits. The success of any predatory scheme depends on maintaining monopoly power for long enough both to recoup the predator's losses and to harvest some additional gain. [Cites omitted][30]

The court thus found that even if the defendants could later raise prices to monopoly levels, they could not realistically expect to recoup the enormous loss that had occurred during a two-decade period of alleged predation. Entry of other firms would probably occur in response to monopoly prices, in the absence of entry barriers, and if so it would be difficult to maintain an alleged conspiracy of "predators" after they became monopolists. The Court found that this improbability of predation under such circumstances must be taken into account when deciding motions for summary judgement in predation cases. Further, it found that the plaintiff must not only prove that the defendant's prices were below some relevant measure of costs, but also that the defendant had a reasonable expectation of recovering, in the form of later monopoly profits, more than the losses incurred during the predation period.

Prior to *Matsushita Electric Industrial Co. v. Zenith Radio Corp* an explicit rejection of cross-subsidization did not appear in case law. In *Matsushita*, the court held that a conspiracy to charge high prices in one market is not evidence of a conspiracy to engage in predatory pricing in another market. The court concluded that, first, conduct in one market has little bearing on conduct in another market because rational firms independently maximize profits in each separate market. Second, it concluded that high profits in one market do not suggest a willingness to engage in predatory conduct in another market. Both of these conclusions essentially reject the notion of cross-subsidization (Rasmussen and Glazer 1988).

From a purely legal perspective, the *Matsushita* case addresses the suitability of summary judgement in an antitrust case, i.e. avoiding a full trial on the merits. It accomplished this, however, by an uncharacteristic reliance on economic theory. In effect, *Matsushita* tells us that economic theory serves as the role of a filter, capable of sorting out inappropriate cases from those worthy of a court's full consideration (Elzinga 1989). The predatory allegations dismissed by the Supreme Court in this case by relying on economics are, in concept, the same allegations given virtually automatic credence in the regulatory arena.

3.3. Cargill, Inc. v. Monfort of Colorado, Inc.

The antitrust court decision in *Cargill vs. Monfort of Colorado* offers some valuable lessons for policymakers involved in predation safeguards in public utility regulation.[31] In this case, a firm challenged the merger of two rivals, claiming that the newly merged firm could engage in predatory practices by lowering its prices to some level at or slightly above its costs to compete for market share. The plaintiff claimed that for it to remain competitive, it would have to lower its prices (resulting in a loss of profitability), but not exit from the market.

This case and its resulting decision is of great importance for its analysis of market structure issues related to predatory pricing. The Court observed that a firm's possession of the financial resources necessary to absorb losses over an extended period of time from below-cost pricing is not sufficient to support a claim of predatory pricing. Rather, the firm's share of market capacity and the barriers to entry after competitors have exited the market must be considered. The reasons for exploring the market structure were stated as follows:

> In order to succeed in a sustained campaign of predatory pricing, a predator must be able to absorb the market shares of its rivals once prices have been cut. If it cannot do so, its attempts at predation will presumably fail because there will remain in the market sufficient demand for the competitors' goods at a higher price, and the competitors will not be driven out of business when the alleged predator is incapable of successfully pursuing a predatory scheme.

> It is also important to examine the barriers to entry into the market, because "without barriers to entry it would presumably be impossible to maintain supracompetitive prices for an extended time." *Matsushita* .... In evaluating entry barriers in the context of a predatory pricing claim, however, a court should focus on whether significant entry barriers would exist *after* the merged firm had eliminated some of its rivals, because at that point the remaining firms would begin to charge supracompetitive prices, and the barriers that existed during competitive conditions might well prove insignificant.[32]

The Court's analysis of the market structure in this case led it to conclude that the merged firm lacked the capacity necessary to pursue predatory pricing and that the record did not support the district court's finding of high barriers to entry. On the other hand, the court found that predatory pricing is inimical to the antitrust laws and can inflict antitrust injury on a competitor. Moreover, the court did not cite the academic literature challenging the concept of predatory pricing and recommending that low prices be treated as *per se* lawful.

3.4. Clamp-All Corp. v. Cast Iron Soil Pipe Institute et al

In *Clamp-All v. Cast Iron Soil Pipe*[33] the court also rejected a theory of cross-subsidization, as it did in *Matsushita*. In this case the plaintiff, Clamp-All Corporation, sued the Cast Iron Soil Pipe Institute and several of its members, claiming that they behaved unlawfully by agreeing to charge high prices on some products as a means of financing a below-cost pricing strategy. The First Circuit rejected this claim, stating:

> [T]he only important element here for a court to examine at the request of a competitor is the *low* price. If that price is unlawfully low, if, for example, it is a predatory price, it does not ordinarily matter whether the money to pay for the

resulting temporary loss comes from a bank account, a legacy, a lottery prize, or the proceeds of a price-fixing conspiracy in respect to another product; regardless of financing source, the practice would be unlawful .... We do not see how a dubious kind of "financing source" could, in and of itself, convert a lawful low price into an unlawful one.[34]

Thus, the court rejected the notion that a high price in one market is necessarily evidence of predatory pricing in another market. Though this is an antitrust case, not public utility regulation, it has significant implications for predation safeguards as provided by telecommunications regulation, since the economic concepts are the same: The alleged source of financing of a predatory pricing strategy has no bearing on whether low prices are *unlawfully* low. This would also be true even if the source of financing turned out to be "high" prices paid by "captive" ratepayers with few or no service alternatives.

Not surprisingly, the court supported the concept of incremental cost as the cost-based benchmark for predatory pricing:

[T]he measure of a "predatory price" is price below "incremental cost." That is to say, the addition to total cost (to the firm) of producing and selling additional output would exceed the return from selling that additional output. [Cites omitted][35]

3.5. Analysis

These predatory pricing cases and the decisions resulting from them have a great deal to contribute to the way in which policymakers should formulate predation safeguards in telecommunications regulation. Preeminent here is the *Matsushita* case, for it eased the standard for granting summary judgement, and forces one to question the very reason for predation safeguards (and the way they are constructed) in telecommunications regulation. It is clear that virtually all predation safeguards in telecommunications rely only on the relationship of prices to costs. Yet *Matsushita* and the logic employed in its decision calls all of this into question. Liebeler's thesis is that almost all of the predatory pricing cases that have come before the courts since 1975 could have been decided summarily for the defendant under the standards set forth in *Matsushita* (Liebeler 1986). This could have been done without examining the price-cost relationship relied on so heavily as the standard in telecommunications regulation. The lesson to be learned here is that predation detection does not depend exclusively on the price-cost relationship, if at all. Further, other factors, such as market structural issues, should be given more weight than the price-cost relationship. It is extremely costly to discover the defendant firm's costs, and if other necessary ingredients for a predation strategy are absent, there is no need to examine the price-cost relationship and hence incur the heavy expense of doing so.

Similarly, *Cargill vs. Monfort of Colorado* increases the difficulty of a plaintiff proving predatory pricing, or a likelihood of such conduct, because the alleged predator must have the capacity to serve most of the market, and there must be high post-predation entry barriers. In interstate telecommunications, for example, a predatory scheme probably would leave the lines and switches of a bankrupt competitor in the same position as the shut-down plants in *Cargill*—facilities that could readily be reactivated by a new entrant, thereby suggesting low post-predation entry barriers. In this case, suppose that a large established carrier like AT&T had the capacity necessary to engage in the rival-bashing part of predation, but that its rivals had installed substantial capacity (even if their share of actual sales was still small). Then, low post-predation entry barriers would lead an antitrust court to find a low likelihood of predation under the standard used in *Cargill*. The very validity of predation safeguards as used in telecommunications regulation must be questioned seriously under the standard set in *Cargill*.

Regarding the issue of cross-subsidization, the courts traditionally have been receptive to cross-subsidization arguments. *Matsushita* and *Clamp-All*, however, have laid the groundwork for the judicial *repudiation* of this concept, which has been unpopular among economists and antitrust scholars for a long time (Rasmussen and Glazer 1988).

Matsushita holds that a conspiracy to charge high prices in one market is not evidence of a conspiracy to engage in predatory pricing in some other market. The Court stated first that conduct in one market has little bearing on conduct in another market because rational firms independently maximize profits in each separate market. Second, it stated that high profits in one market do not suggest a willingness to engage in predatory conduct in another market. Both of these points essentially reject the notion of cross-subsidization.

The decision in *Clamp-All* also soundly rejected the notion that a high price in one market is necessarily evidence of predatory pricing in another market. Although the related argument of reverse-subsidization was rejected in the *Northeastern Telephone* case, the economic analysis was not as in-depth as in *Matsushita* or *Clamp-All*. The former case implicitly accepted the concept of cross-subsidization by suggesting that it would have occurred if prices did not exceed costs. *Matsushita* and *Clamp-All* go farther into the economic analysis, basically contending that a predatory pricing strategy must stand on its own as a "sound" strategic move. The *Matsushita* and *Clamp-All* cases essentially close doors opened in past cases like *Northeastern Telephone*.

4. Conclusion and Policy Recommendations

A test for the usefulness of any regulatory policy is whether it identifies bad practices that would otherwise be legal, without adding to the set of legitimate business practices that are inappropriately condemned. Do predation safeguards built into telecommunications regulation pass this test? Unfortunately, the answer to this question is most likely to be "No."

Public utility regulation in general is oriented toward economic supervision, in contrast to antitrust law. Because of this, it must employ tools that will prevent predatory pricing *before* it is allowed to occur. This in itself is not objectionable. Regulation's economic supervision function in telecommunications, however, has led to an almost exclusive reliance on simple, mechanical, cost-based rules as the primary means of addressing predatory pricing concerns. In light of recent antitrust court decisions and the economic logic they employed, this tendency toward such simple mechanical rules based only on costs must be questioned seriously. Predatory pricing depends on several variables, the price-cost relationship being but one of these (and not necessarily the most important). Thus, any simple rule based on the cost-price relationship exclusively can only go so far in preventing price-based predatory behavior.

The decisions in *Cargill* and *Matsushita* tell us that the role of barriers to entry and other aspects of market structure can be far more important, and less costly, than the price-cost relationship in making the judicial determination of predatory pricing. Yet no mechanical cost-based rule can address such complex market structure issues. *Matsushita* is particularly important to this analysis, for all predatory pricing cases that came before the courts between 1975 and 1986 could have been decided summarily for the defendant under its standards (Liebeler 1986). This could have been done without examining the price-cost relationship employed virtually exclusively as the relevant benchmark in regulation. Essentially, the tools employed in regulation to prevent predatory pricing are the very tools *Matsushita* and *Cargill* tell us we do not need, to solve a problem that probably does not exist in the first place. Such simplistic tools ignore more complete analyses that would make the automatic reliance on the price-cost relationship (and the possibly erroneous inferences from it) unneccessary.

As regulated telephone companies face more and more competition in various markets, the best regulatory policy may be to have significantly *lessened* oversight on downward pricing flexibility of carriers currently considered "dominant." This seemingly paradoxical objective could be accomplished by using very loosely defined price floors (or preferably none at all), and by encouraging many of the flexible pricing plans now being proposed in the industry. These include: (1) the ability to lower prices relatively quickly with limited regulatory scrutiny, (2) pricing new services using incremental cost-based regulatory methods like the FCC's net revenue test, (3) allowing nonregulated activities to be priced on the incremental cost standard using standard discounted cash flow analyses and other financial and economic tools in lieu of regulation-mandated CAMs, and (4) allowing customer-specific proposals by large carriers, which also could be based on the net revenue test (Larson, Monson, and Nobles 1989). This would facilitate efficient pricing of telecommunications and would allow large carriers to compete fairly, while allowing customers to benefit from economies of scope and other efficiencies enjoyed by large established carriers. In essence, large carriers would be allowed to set prices that are simply lower, yet still subsidy-free.

Further, in the more competitive environment, a trend away from asymmetric regulation would be beneficial in markets where incumbent carriers must compete with new market entrants. In markets where economies of scale and learning-by-doing result in cost reductions, economic theory teaches us that prices will trend downward. Frequently such trends are led by the newer firms who are seeking to use low prices to help gain brand recognition, goodwill, and company reputation (Elzinga 1989). Under such circumstances, price reductions by the incumbent carriers may be necessary to foster competition and ensure that the least cost provider becomes the least price supplier.[36]

The important unifying thread in all of this is in allowing large carriers to have flexibility in lowering their prices so as to compete, without being hampered unnecessarily by predation safeguards based only on some ex ante "correct" basis of cost and its relationship to price.

If increased pricing flexibility is allowed in regulation and predation concerns remain, such concerns can be dealt with by the courts in much the same way they are dealt with in other, unregulated industries (Besen and Woodbury 1983). Thus, our conclusion is that reduced regulatory oversight and increased pricing flexibility, coupled with the traditional role of the courts in dealing with predatory pricing behavior, may be preferable to continuing current regulatory practices.

This conclusion is based on several considerations. First, the courts offer a greater ability to deal with alleged below-cost pricing episodes than regulation has to offer. Predation is a complex subject requiring extensive findings of fact that the courts were set up to handle. In the courts, improper conduct can be challenged directly by injured private persons. In addition, the courts offer a flexible arsenal of antitrust remedies capable of dealing not only with predatory pricing but other types of anticompetitive practices. In place of injunction, private damages, and criminal sanctions, regulation's simplistic rules by themselves may offer relatively little. Further, antitrust's general and comprehensive proscription of unreasonable agreements and/or anticompetitive exercises of power seems better suited to handling predatory pricing concerns than regulation's rather more specific, rigid catalog of permitted and prohibited behavior (Areeda 1972). Finally, let us not forget that regulation does not necessarily lead to immunity from the antitrust laws, meaning that the *Sherman Act* applies to many regulated services anyway.

Second, regulation's predation safeguards may unwittingly allow unregulated firms to use regulation to subvert competition, in the form of a "cost raising" strategy. It is well known that in antitrust cases, discovering the defendant's costs is among the largest expenses to the defendant. This is in part why the standard for summary judgement set in *Matsushita* is so valuable, for it largely prevents the use of antitrust (and its expensive, protracted proceedings) to subvert competition and impose costs. Yet current regulation, which relies on the supervision of the price-cost relationship, makes it relatively easy for unregulated firms to impose costs on their large, regulated competitors. Showings of costs are expensive to produce and defend in regulatory hearings. To make a proceeding even more protracted, a competitor at relatively little cost can file direct testimony that speculatively calls into question a cost study, a methodology, or some other aspect of the underlying price-cost relationship. Further, it is possible for competitors of RBOCs to argue successfully for a full cost-of-service docket at the state level, in which definitions of costs, subsidy flows, and other familiar topics are discussed ad nauseum, forcing the RBOC to expend significant resources, and forestalling any actions it may have planned to pursue in the marketplace. Thus, the reliance on the price-cost relationship in regulation makes it relatively easy to impose costs on large regulated carriers, forestall their entry into profitable other markets, or forestall legitimate competitive responses.

A reliance on the courts would largely prevent this type of behavior by incumbent carrier's smaller rivals. A full court proceeding and finding of fact is much more costly and difficult to use as a cost-raising strategy than regulation, and hence may not appeal to firms not truly in earnest about antitrust damages. As noted, *Matsushita* may make frivolous antitrust claims less appealing, since there is no guarantee under its standards that a case would not be resolved rather quickly in summary judgement. *Clamp-All* may also have a chilling effect on frivolous suits in which plaintiffs try to use the standard cross-subsidization arguments as a competitive weapon. If it were viable to use antitrust as a tool to subvert competition, we'd no doubt observe *Sherman Act* activity involving the RBOCs, yet such a pattern has not been observed since the Bell System divestiture.

In sum, the increasingly competitive telecommunications industry will require that large established carriers be afforded much greater pricing flexibility. Yet regulation's current handling of predation concerns may impede this increased flexibility while offering no economic benefits. As telecommunications becomes more competitive, it would most likely be best to relax considerably the existing regulatory constraints on downward pricing flexibility and rely instead on the courts to handle below-cost pricing concerns.

Notes

The author is Senior Economist, Southwestern Bell Telephone Company. The opinions expressed in this paper are those of the author and do not express the opinions, policies, or business plans of Southwestern Bell Corporation or any of its subsidiaries. The author wishes to thank Bill Drexel, Mark Meitzen, Michael Meyer, and Pat Nobles of Southwestern Bell for helpful comments on interim drafts of this paper. Special thanks must go to Jim Green and to Professors Michael Crew, Keith Crocker, and Bill Kovacic.

1. *Indiana Grocery, Inc. v. Super Valu Stores, Inc.*, 864 F.2d 1409, 1415 (7th Cir. 1989), citing Areeda (1987).

2. The generic definition of average variable cost is the variable cost of a service at a given output level divided by that output level. Areeda and Turner, however, meant for their implied definition of average variable cost to include product-specific fixed costs (Baumol 1986), making their definition de facto average incremental cost. Thus, the original intent of Areeda and Turner for their predation safeguard turned out to be the same in concept as the one later suggested by Ordover and Willig (1981) for the multiproduct firm. Ordover and Willig recognized, however, that product-specific fixed costs are irrelevant to output decisions (and hence a predation strategy), and that cross-elastic effects belonged in the cost calculations.

3. Guidelines for Dominant Carriers' MTS Rates and Rate Restructure Plans: Memorandum Opinion and Order, CC Docket 84-1235, 50 Fed. Reg. 42,946 (hereafter cited as *OCP Guidelines Order*) (1985).

4. *OCP Guidelines Order* at para. 1.

5. This refers to Section 208 of the *Communications Act of 1934*, which allows for complaints to the FCC. 47 U.S.C. 208.

6. Policy and Rules Concerning Rates for Dominant Carriers, CC Docket No. 87-313, Notice of Proposed Rulemaking, 2 FCC Rcd 5208 (1987) at para. 48 [hereinafter cited as *Notice*].

7. *Notice* at para. 49.

8. *Notice* at para. 50.
9. Policy and Rules Concerning Rates for Dominant Carriers, CC Docket No. 87-313, Further Notice of Proposed Rulemaking, 3 FCC Rcd 3195 (1988) at para. 285 [hereinafter cited as *Further Notice*].
10. *Further Notice* at para. 290.
11. *Further Notice* at para. 291.
12. Policy and Rules Concerning Rates for Dominant Carriers, CC Docket No. 87-313, Second Further Notice of Proposed Rulemaking, 4 FCC Rcd 2873 (1989) at para. 52 [hereinafter cited as *Second Further Notice*].
13. *Second Further Notice* at para. 498.
14. *Second Further Notice* at para. 499.
15. In the Matter of Separation of Costs of Regulated Telephone Service from Costs of Nonregulated Activities, Report and Order, CC Docket No. 86-111, 2 FCC Rcd. 1298 (1987) [hereinafter *Joint Cost Order*].
16. *See,* 47 C.F.R. § 64.901 (1987).
17. In the Matter of Amendment of Section 64.702 of the Commission's Rules and Regulation, Notice of Inquiry and Proposed Rulemaking, 61 F.C.C.2d 771 (1977), Tentative Decision, 72 F.C.C.2d 358 (1979), Final Decision, 77 F.C.C.2d 384 (1979) (the F.C.C.'s *Computer II* inquiry).
18. *Joint Cost Order* at par. 111.
19. *Id.* at pars. 2, 113.
20. *Joint Cost Order* at par. 151.
21. The bill does not use this terminology; it classifies services as "competitive," "transitionally competitive," and "noncompetitive."
22. MO. REV. STAT. § 392.400.3 (1987).
23. *Id.* at § 392.400.5.
24. TEX. REV. CIV. STAT. ANN. art. 1446 c § 18(g) (Supp. 1988).
25. State of North Dakota, Senate Bill No. 2320 at § 9.
26. 651 F. 2d 76, 86 (2d Cir. 1981), *cert. denied,* 455 U.S. 943. (1982).
27. *Id.* at 87.
28. *Id.* at 90.
29. *Id.* at 1123.
30. *Matsushita Electric Indus. Co., Ltd. v. Zenith Radio Corp.,* 475 U.S. 574, 590-91 (1986).
31. *Cargill, Inc. v. Monfort of Colorado, Inc.,* 479 U.S. 104, 107 S. Ct. 484, 93 L. Ed. 2d 427 (1986).
32. *Cargill, Inc. v. Monfort of Colorado, Inc.,* 107 S. Ct. 484, 494 n. 15 (1986).
33. *Clamp-All Corp. v. Cast Iron Soil Pipe Institute,* 851 F.2d 478 (1st Cir. 1988).
34. *Id.* at 485-486.
35. *Id.* at 486.
36. The courts have acknowledged that a price below cost may have nothing to do with a predatory episode: "Trying to infer (or refute) predatory conduct from the relation between price and cost is difficult business. Often a price below cost reflects only the sacrifice necessary to establish a presence in a competitive market (for example, new magazines lose money for years as they try to increase circulation and attract advertising revenue, without creating the tiniest risk of monopoly) ... " *A.A. Poultry Farms, Inc., et al., v. Rose Acre Farms, Inc.,* 881 F.2d 1396, 1400 (7th. Cir. 1989). This, of course, has some obvious implications for the introduction of new services by telephone companies. Regulation may not allow negative cash flows for any significant period of time, even though such negative cash flows may be a normal attribute of the service's product life cycle.

References

Areeda, P. 1972. "Antitrust Laws and Public Utility Regulation." *Bell Journal of Economics and Management Science* 3 (Spring): 42-57.
Areeda, P. 1987. "Monopolization, Mergers, and Markets: A Century Past and the Future." *California Law Review* 75 (May): 959-981.
Areeda, P. and D. Turner. 1975. "Predatory Pricing and Related Practices Under Section 2 of the Sherman Act." *Harvard Law Review* 88 (February): 697-733.

Baumol, W.J. 1986. *Superfairness: Applications and Theory.* Cambridge: MIT Press.
Baumol, W.J., and R.D. Willig. 1989. "Price Caps: A Rational Means to Protect Telecommunications Consumers and Competition." *Review of Business* 10 (Spring): 3-8, 18.
Besen, S.M., and J.R. Woodbury. 1983. "Regulation, Deregulation, and Antitrust in the Telecommunications Industry." *Antitrust Bulletin* 28 (Spring): 39-68.
Brock, W.A., and D.S. Evans. 1983. "Predation: A Critique of the Government's Case in US v. AT&T." In *Breaking Up Bell: Essays on Industrial Organization and Regulation,* edited by D.S. Evans, pp. 41-94. Amsterdam: North-Holland.
Brodley, J.F. and G.A. Hay. 1981. "Predatory Pricing: Competing Economic Theories and the Evolution of Legal Standards." *Cornell Law Review* 66 (April): 738-803.
Calvani, T., and J.M. Lynch. 1982. "Predatory Pricing Under the Robinson-Patman and Sherman Acts: An Introduction." *Antitrust Law Journal* 51: 375-400.
Easley, D., R. Masson, and R. Reynolds. 1985. "Preying for Time." *Journal of Industrial Economics* 33 (June): 445-460.
Easterbrook, F.H. 1981. "Predatory Strategies and Counterstrategies." *University of Chicago Law Review* 48 (Spring): 263-337.
Elzinga, K.G. 1989. *Collusive Predation: Matsushita v. Zenith (1986).* In *The Antitrust Revolution,* edited by J.E. Kwoka and L.J. White, pp. 241-262. Boston: Scott, Foresman.
Fudenberg, D. and J. Tirole. 1986. "A 'Signal-Jamming' Theory of Predation." *RAND Journal of Economics* 17 (Autumn): 366-376.
Hovenkamp, H. 1985. *Economics and Federal Antitrust Law.* St. Paul: West.
Kreps, D., and R. Wilson. 1982. "Reputation and Imperfect Information." *Journal of Economic Theory* 27 (August): 253-279.
Larson, A.C. 1989. "Cost Allocations, Predation, and Cross- Subsidies in Telecommunications." *Journal of Corporation Law* 14 (Winter): 377-398.
Larson, A.C., C.S. Monson, and P.J. Nobles. 1989. "Competitive Necessity and Pricing in Telecommunications Regulation." *Federal Communications Law Journal* 42 (December): 1-49.
Larson, A.C., and M.P. Sievers. 1988. "On the Ineffectiveness of Price Floors in Telecommunications Regulation." *Willamette Law Review* 25 (Winter): 89-133.
Liebeler, W.J. 1986. "Whither Predatory Pricing? From Areeda and Turner to Matsushita." *Notre Dame Law Review* 61: 1052-1098.
McGee, J.S. 1958. "Predatory Price Cutting: The Standard Oil (N.J.) Case." *Journal of Law and Economics* 1 (October): 137-169.
McGee, J.S. 1980. "Predatory Pricing Revisited." *Journal of Law and Economics* 23 (October): 289-330.
Milgrom, P., and J. Roberts. 1982. "Predation, Reputation, and Entry Deterrence." *Journal of Economic Theory* 27 (August): 280-312.
Milgrom, P., and J. Roberts. 1987. "Informational Asymmetries, Strategic Behavior, and Industrial Organization." *American Economic Review* 77. Papers and Proceedings (May): 184-193.
Noll, R.G., and B.M. Owen. 1989. "The Anticompetitive Uses of Regulation: United States v. AT&T." In *The Antitrust Revolution,* edited by J.E. Kwoka and L.J. White, pp. 290-337. Boston: Scott, Foresman.
Ordover, J.A., and D.M. Wall. 1987. "Proving Predation after *Monfort* and *Matsushita*: What the 'New Learning' Has to Offer." *Antitrust* 1 (Summer): 5-10.
Ordover, J.A. and R.D. Willig. 1981. "An Economic Definition of Predation: Pricing and Product Innovation." *Yale Law Journal* 91 (November): 8-53.
Phlips, L. 1987. "Predatory Pricing." Unpublished Document, Center for Operations Re-

search and Econometrics.

Rasmussen, G.G, and K.L. Glazer. 1988. "Antitrust Implications of Cases Rejecting Cross-Subsidization Arguments." *Antitrust* 3 (Fall): 28-32.

Roberts, J. 1986. "A Signaling Model of Predatory Pricing." *Oxford Economics Papers* 38. Supplement (November): 75-93.

Roberts, J. 1987. "Battles for Market Share: Incomplete Information, Aggressive Strategic Pricing, and Competitive Dynamics." In *Advances in Economic Theory: Fifth World Congress*, edited by J-M Grandmont and C.F. Manski, pp. 157-195. Cambridge: Cambridge University Press.

Sievers, M. 1987. "The Transition to Antitrust Regulation in the Telecommunications Industry: A Comparison of Public Utility Law Regulation and Antitrust Law Regulation." Paper presented at the National Association of Regulatory Utility Commissioners, San Francisco, CA, July 19-20.

Tirole, J. 1988. *The Theory of Industrial Organization*. Cambridge: MIT Press.

Wall, D.M. 1989. "Predatory Pricing: Are Cost Tests on the Way Out?" *Antitrust* 4 (Fall/Winter): 40-43.

5

OIL PIPELINE RATES: A CASE FOR YARDSTICK REGULATION

Jordan Jay Hillman

1. Introduction

Oil pipeline rates are currently regulated by the Federal Energy Regulatory Commission (FERC) under provisions of the Interstate Commerce Act. This reflects the differing views of such regulation as mainly a matter of transportation or energy policy. The impetus for the administrative regulation of oil pipelines arose, however, from antitrust concerns. During 1906-1977 the task fell to the Interstate Commerce Commission (ICC) under the basic statutory standards applied to railroads. In 1977, it was transferred to the Department of Energy (DOE) and FERC.[1]

Whoever regulates, oil pipelines today operate in a mix of competitive and monopolistic markets. Individual oil pipelines are sometimes characterized as "natural monopolies" because of significant scale economies in the operations of a single pipeline up to the point of full capacity. On this basis, the classic case for public utility regulation is often made. However, where current or anticipated demand warrants additional pipeline capacity, the usual rationale for "protecting" a natural monopoly may not apply. As regards added capacity, the existing pipeline often enjoys no cost advantage over new market entrants. Such an advantage may exist where feasible expansion within an existing right of way is uniquely available to the original operator. That operator could also initially benefit from lower capital costs based on past successful operations and "throughput" guarantees by shipper/owners. But, in general, with sufficient demand and the initial pipeline at full economic capacity, entry is not barred by scale economies unique to the incumbent firm.

Where the capacity of a single pipeline is sufficient to handle all demand in its market, a "true" natural monopoly may exist. In many markets, however, intramodal and low cost water operations (sometimes with connecting short haul truck movements) offer effective competition. Such competition may deprive affected pipelines of greater scale economies. (Where pipelines compete, however, any scale economy loss by one may be offset in the gain by another.)

In assessing the benefits and costs resulting from open competition or protected natural monopolies, Congress has chosen not to restrain competition in oil pipeline markets.[2] In particular, it has never sought to limit capacity through use of certificates of convenience and necessity.[3] The benefits of unrestricted competition have been deemed more important than those realized from added scale economies.

This view is consistent with the origins of oil pipeline regulation. The aim in 1906 was not to protect Standard Oil's scale economies. It was to provide independent shippers with competitive access to the pipelines of this vertically integrated monopoly.

The 1977 transfer of oil pipeline rate regulation to FERC decisively severed the basic symmetry of the regulatory regime governing railroad and oil pipeline rates.[4] Under FERC, the standard of reasonableness is strongly influenced by the public utility rate-of-return model applied to natural gas and electric power firms. The FERC experience has reinvigorated efforts to end or lessen oil pipeline rate regulation. This article supports use of a noncost based "yardstick" alternative to the public utility model.

2. Some Pertinent Regulatory History

2.1. The Hepburn Act of 1906

Among its other railroad provisions, the Hepburn Act of 1906 empowered the ICC to prescribe maximum rates for common carrier services.[5] Neither the House nor Senate bill initially proposed any form of pipeline regulation.[6] On April 16, Senator Henry Cabot Lodge submitted an amendment to include them as "common carriers" under the 1887 Act. This was possibly coordinated with President Theodore Roosevelt's May 4 message to Congress transmitting "A Report by the Commissioner of the Bureau of Corporations in the Department of Commerce and Labor on the Subject of Transportation and Freight Rates in Connection with the Oil Industry."[7]

The message and report focused on a system of secret rebates and railroad rate discrimination on oil, from which Standard was said to have "benefited enormously." In alluding to Standard's ownership of oil pipelines, the report set out a rationale for their regulation.

> The advantages of a pipeline over a railroad in the transportation of oil can hardly be overstated. A liberal estimate of the cost of piping crude oil from ... western Pennsylvania to the Atlantic seaboard, for instance, would not be more than 10 cents a barrel, including interest and depreciation, whereas the railroad charge is more than four times that amount.
>
> ... while the pipe lines of the Standard in the Northeastern States are nominally common carriers, the independent refiners can not avail them-

> selves of these pipe lines to transport crude oil to strategic points... because of prohibitive charges. The pipage rates to outside shippers are several times the actual cost of shipment to the Standard.

The Lodge amendment was promptly adopted.[8]

As common carriers, oil pipelines would be required to (1) provide non-discriminatory service to all shippers; (2) charge just and reasonable rates, subject to specific maxima prescribed by the ICC; (3) comply with the rate discrimination and tariff filing provisions of the Act; and (4) establish reasonable through routes and joint rates. Of greater significance to the structure of the oil pipeline industry, however, was its exclusion from the so-called "commodities clause" of the Hepburn Act.

The Commodities Clause amendment was introduced by Senator Elkins of West Virginia on May 7, 1906, following earlier adoption of the Lodge amendment. Its aim was to bar common carriers from transporting commodities in which they held a beneficial interest. It addressed the circumstance that where the actual cost of hauling a commodity is less than the transport charge, a common carrier with an ownership interest in the commodity enjoys an advantage over competitive shippers.[9]

Because the Lodge amendment preceded the Elkins amendment, the Senate had no prior occasion to consider the likely consequences of applying the Commodities Clause to oil pipelines: namely, that as common carriers, pipelines would likely be barred from transporting the crude oil or refined products of their corporate parents or affiliates. Stated conversely, as a condition of being able to use the pipelines now so vital to their operations, Standard Oil and other integrated oil companies could be required to divest themselves of ownership. In the struggle which followed, the oil industry prevailed.

This 1906 decision by Congress to permit operation of oil pipelines as components of vertically integrated oil companies remains intact.[10] While the issue continues to resurface,[11] the current legislative scene offers no evidence of likely reconsideration.

2.2. Implementing the Competitive Access Goals of the Hepburn Act
2.2.1. The Interstate Commerce Commission: 1906-1977

The inclusion of oil pipelines as common carriers under the Hepburn Act reflected no particular intent to subject them to rate-of-return regulation. The main purpose of the Hepburn Act was to permit the ICC to fix maximum rates. The relevant context was the ICC's prior concentration on individual rates, rather than on overall earnings.

In 1911, five years after the Hepburn Act, the railroads sought to justify their first general rate increase on overall revenue needs. Even at that late date, the ICC questioned its authority to determine the question.

> We have no authority, as such, to say what amount these carriers shall earn, nor to establish a schedule of rates which will enable them to earn that amount. Our authority is limited to inquiring into the reasonableness of a

particular rate or rates and establishing that rate or practice which is found lawful....[12]

Sharfman, in his treatise on the ICC, observed that "During these earlier years," preceding the 1906 Hepburn and 1910 Mann-Elkins Acts, "the Commission . . . permitted itself only rarely to deal with issues other than those raised in the attacks of shippers on individual rates."[13] In sum, the focus of regulation known to Congress in 1906 was on the individual rate, not total earnings. The first pipeline decision involving individual rates was not until 1922.

a. *Brundred Bros. v. Prairie Pipeline Co., 68 I.C.C. 458 (1922)*

In *The Pipeline Cases*, 234 U.S. 548 (1914), the Supreme Court had upheld the constitutionality of regulating oil pipelines as common carriers. In this first reported case following that decision, the complaint alleged that joint rates over through routes between particular origins and destinations were unreasonably high, as were the minimum tender requirements of 100,000 barrels. Complainant's proof on the rate issue consisted of the ratios of pipeline operating income to investment over four recent years.

The ICC rejected the rate complaint on the following principle: "But where, as here, only individual rates are assailed, the fact that in the past defendants' operations have been profitable is not of controlling importance." Related to this was the fact that the "gallonage" involved was "but a small percentage of the total gallonage transported by defendants." It also found the rates reasonable in comparison to "other rates for pipeline service" which had been submitted by the defendants. It noted, however, the possible relevance of overall earnings where the general rate level was put in issue. On the minimum tender complaint, the ICC reduced the 100,000 barrel requirement to 10,000.

b. *Reduced Pipe Line Rates And Gathering Charges, 243 I.C.C. 115 (1940); 272 I.C.C. 375 (1948)*

This decision resulted from an ICC crude oil rate investigation begun in 1934. It followed complaints by independent refiners located near the oil fields against recent crude oil rate reductions to distant refineries.

The initial respondents were 37 pipelines, only 27 of which served nonaffiliated shippers. The ICC described these shippers as "relatively few in number" and "in large part or wholly" interested in other common-carrier pipelines. It ascribed the absence of rate complaints to this mutuality of interest. It also viewed as "evident" that rates were not made "with any relation to the cost of service." Benefits to pipeline owners from such rates were described as "ultimate" rather than "directly derived from common carrier operations." The ICC did not identify these "ultimate" benefits. However, it may have implied the use of rate barriers to independent crude oil refining in its observation that "the general measure of [many] rates . . . is excessive, and it is no answer . . . that independent shippers are few, or that they are not using the services offered, when the rates demanded are excessive."

As for monopoly and competition, the ICC noted the rate uniformity among pipelines serving major origins and destinations, such as the Mid-Continent field and Chicago. It concluded, however, that unlike the case of intramodal competition among "rail, highway and water carriers," rate changes by one or any group of pipelines "have no compelling effect on the level of the rate schedules of others...."

Despite the initial complaints against rate reductions, the ICC saw its primary task as the prevention of excessive overall earnings. Just and reasonable rate levels were set by requiring the same rate of return for all respondents on their respective Section 19a "fair value" valuations.[14] The ICC's rationale for 8% was brief. Due to relative traffic instability, a higher return was warranted than for "industries of a more stable character...." With no further explanation, 8% was characterized as "ample".

The returns of 21 respondents were found to exceed 8%. These were directed to show cause why the total revenues of each should not be reduced by a percentage resulting in a return of 8% on rate base value. With no regard for demand, this tentative reduction was to be applied "equally to the rates severally stated" in the filed schedules.

The principal dissent from the order reflected a different view of competitive conditions. It ascribed the currently equalized 38.5 cent rate from Mid-Continent origins to Chicago to the force of intramodal competition. It noted that varying percentage reductions imposed on each pipeline would result in rate maxima of 33.5, 30.5, 29.5, and 17.5 cents. Competition would then compel the rates to be equalized at 17.5 cents without permissible increases in other markets. The dissent concluded by asserting the impracticability of an "individual net earnings" standard under conditions of competition. In its second report on further hearing (delayed in part by World War II), the ICC affirmed the earlier report.

c. *Petroleum Rail Shippers' Assoc. v. Alton & S.R.R.*, 243 I.C.C. 589 (1941)

This proceeding began with a more usual complaint of excessive rates on refined petroleum products from Mid-Continent oil fields to Midwest markets. Defendants included both railroads and pipelines. The pipeline practice was to maintain rates on refined petroleum products at the corresponding rail rates. Complainants claimed that excessive profits realized by the low cost pipelines were used by the integrated oil companies to provide price concessions to jobbers and retailers. Contrary to its majority view on the essential absence of competition in crude oil movements, the ICC found growing competition for refined products from barge and lengthening truck hauls.

Having thus discerned added financial risk in carrying refined products, the ICC, without further discussion, noted that its calculations of prescribed reasonable rate maxima included "an amount to add for return on value at 10 percent." As for minimum tenders, 25,000 barrels was found reasonable for normal service on single shipper tenders. For smaller shipments awaiting an aggregation of 25,000 barrels, a 5,000 barrel minimum was found reasonable.

d. Minnelusa Oil Corp. v. Continental Pipe Line, 258 I.C.C. 41 (1944)

The significance here is in the ICC's adherence to an 8% return for crude oil pipeline operations. While the earlier decision involved pipelines east of the Rockies, the defendants in *Minnelusa* operated within this territory. Defendants argued that the "hazards and risks" in carrying crude oil in mountain territory were closer to those encountered in carrying petroleum products than in carrying crude oil east of the Rockies. The ICC's only stated rationale for applying the same 8% return to these pipelines was the absence of "concrete evidence to support the contention that any lower rate of return than 10% would be confiscatory." The only choice considered was between 10% or the presumptively correct 8%.

e. Petroleum Products, Williams Bros. Pipe Line, 351 I.C.C. 102 (1975); 355 I.C.C. 479 (1976)

This case began with the pipeline's 1971 filings for increased local and joint rates. Because the proposed increases were system-wide, the ICC focused on overall earnings. Technical issues included depreciation, the allowance of certain affiliate payments and litigation expenses, and the use of "normalization" or "flow through" tax treatment. However, the core issues of rate base and rate of return were again disposed of by precedent. A 10% return was found reasonable solely on the 1941 authority of *Petroleum Rail Shippers' Association*. As its only stated rationale, the ICC declared that "until the principles underlying the determination of a fair rate of return for pipelines can be formulated in a proper proceeding, it would be unwarranted for us to hold that a rate of return which was considered reasonable in 1941 is unreasonable today."[15]

As for rate base, shippers argued for original cost, and the pipeline, for net investment (reflecting the purchase price paid the previous owner). In turn, the ICC held to its customary Section 19a valuation formula. The ICC found the following rate base values (as of December 31, 1966, in millions): net original cost, $101.1; Section 19a valuation, $167.6; net actual investment, $287.8. That the ICC's financial analysis did not contemplate a need to adapt an allowed return to the wide variances among the proposed rate bases is strongly implied in the following statement: "If a 10-percent return standard were applied to each of [the foregoing] bases, the allowed earnings would be about $10 million, $16.8 million, and $28.8 million, respectively." No further comments in mitigation of this clear implication is offered by it.[16]

2.2.2. The Elkins Act Consent Decree

The 1941 Elkins Act consent decree, having been vacated in 1982, has no current regulatory impact.[17] But it forms an interesting episode in the use of system-wide financial constraints to encourage reasonable oil pipeline rates. Rather than imposing a limit on earnings, the decree barred dividends from pipelines to shipper-owners in excess of "[an owner's] share of 7 percentum of the valuation" of the pipeline's common carrier properties. While there was no limit on retained earnings, their use was limited to debt retirement or new construction (which was then excluded from the valuation base). In 1959, the Supreme Court upheld the pipelines' position that the 7% limit was to be calculated on total valuation rather than on equity alone (*U. S. v. Atlantic Refining Co.*, 360 U.S. 19 (1960)). The Elkins Act complaint had been part of a broader Department of Justice (DOJ) antitrust effort seeking pipeline divestiture by shipper-owners. Its theory was that the payment of any dividends by pipelines to shipper-owners constituted an illegal rebate of rates. The decree adopted the view that only "excessive" dividend payments were illegal rebates. Whether the dividend restriction would have encouraged lower rates by reducing higher profit incentives is uncertain in view of the Supreme Court's holding. The decree was largely shorn of substance through widespread replacement of equity by lower cost debt.[18]

2.2.3. The 1977 Transfer of Oil Pipeline Rate Regulation to FERC

The 1977 transfer to FERC of ICC jurisdiction over oil pipeline rates and valuation appears unrelated to the ICC's performance. It was one of several energy-related transfers proposed by President Carter in recommending a new Department of Energy. The stated aim was to "place under one roof the powers to regulate fuels and fuel distribution systems, powers which are now shared by the FEA and the FPC along with the [SEC] and the [ICC]."[19]

In the hearings, the Association of Oil Pipelines (AOPL) opposed the transfer of jurisdiction on the stated grounds that FERC regulation would impede transport coordination in view of continued ICC regulation of rail and motor carriage of petroleum products. It argued also for retention of a current value component in the rate base. In reply to these and similar objections, the Administration characterized energy pipelines as "exclusively a mode of conveying energy resources, as opposed to the railroads, which has [sic] multi-purpose objectives."

In resolving these issues, Congress sought to accomodate the AOPL. To FERC, as a reconstituted Federal Power Commission within the Department of Energy, was transferred all ICC "functions and authority" over oil pipeline rates and valuation. These included the Section 19a obligation to determine "cost of reproduction new and cost of reproduction less depreciation" as well as "original cost." This may have reassured the oil pipelines initially, but Section 19a did not actually compel ICC or FERC to give weight to this vestige of *Smyth v. Ames*.[20]

The Senate Report offered assurance of stability. In noting that ICC regulation had provided a "stable regulatory framework" and in recognizing "the importance of regulatory continuity," the Senate Committee purported to make "no substantive changes in the existing method of regulation under the Interstate Commerce Act."[21] While not repeating this point, the Conference Report said nothing to dispel it.

2.2.4. Oil Pipeline Rate Regulation Under FERC
a. Williams Pipe Line—Continued

The shippers' appeal from the ICC's decision was not argued and decided until 1978, following passage of the DOE Act. The Act provided for judicial review of pre-transfer litigation "as if this Act had not been enacted." While adhering to the directive, the Court found (among other substantive criticisms) that the ICC's approach to rate base valuation and rate of return were artifacts of a "bygone [pre-*Hope*] era."[22] The case was remanded to FERC on its counsel's assurance that the prolonged litigation would be moved "with dispatch."

FERC's commitment of "dispatch" was honored more than four years later by its opinion and order of November 30, 1982.[23] In its baptismal encounter with oil pipelines, FERC acted on two major insights. First, that "Oil pipeline rate regulation is not a consumer protection measure . . . . It is and was a producer-protection measure." Thus, it "neither requires nor warrants the strenuous regulatory efforts long deemed appropriate . . . in consumer protection." FERC then noted the total absence of consumer intervention in this or previous ICC proceedings.[24] Second, it emphasized the minor impact of oil pipeline rates on the ultimate delivered product price. In respect to intermediate crude oil prices, it traced a declining ratio in pipeline revenues per barrel to the cost of a barrel of crude from 64.7% in 1931 to 1.92% in 1981.[25] In asking whether "the substantial costs of rigorous oil pipeline regulation justify an incremental consumer benefit of a fraction of 2%," FERC's answer was "a clear no." FERC characterized "the case for aggressive Federal intervention in oil pipeline ratemaking" as "flimsy," but also recognized that its administrative discretion was "not broad enough to encompass deregulation or nullifcation of the statute . . . ." Its aim then was "to define a regulatory procedure which makes some sense in the contemporary economic environment."[26]

In accommodating that aim to the "just and reasonable" standard governing the rate base, FERC decided "For the present at least . . . [to] adhere to the formula we inherit . . . ," subject to the "tentative" conclusion that this status quo be kept until Congress provides "a better guide to its regulatory treatment . . . ."[27]

What FERC could not abide, however, was the ICC's simplistic use of an industry-wide rate of return based on stale precedent. It adopted instead a rate-of-return formula comprised of the actual debt service requirement; a suretyship premium to a parent-guarantor of the pipeline's debt; and an entrepreneurial rate of return on the equity portion of the valuation rate base.[28]

The novelty here was in the method of determining an "entrepreneurial" rate of return. The "social need" was for "returns high enough to induce the construction of new pipelines and to avert the premature abandonment of old ones." To this end, pipelines were given a choice of the "most favorable" among eight standards, reflecting a variety of alternative investment opportunities. These included "realized nominal rates of return" on shareholders' book equity "in American industry generally" over the past five years, or over the past year; or in the oil industry generally for the same periods; or the parent's non-pipeline returns over the same periods; or total returns on a "diversified common stock portfolio" for the past five years, or "over the long run." These options were not intended to equate returns with actual equity costs, but to provide a cap on "gross abuse." Returns no higher than those "in a roughly comparable segment of the economy's unregulated sector" were neither "extortionate or abusive."

To avoid "the need for refined inquiries into the allocation of costs . . . essential to segment-by-segment regulation," FERC opted for "System-Wide" rather than "Point to Point" regulation. Internal "averaging," or discrimination, would give "free play to competitive factors in the industry."[29]

The order was reversed on appeal.[30] More important than the resolution of various technical issues was the court's systemic approach to the "just and reasonable" standard, under which rates must fall within a "zone of reasonableness." In determining zonal bounds "the most useful and reliable starting point ... is an inquiry into costs." Where a noncost factor is given weight, FERC is obliged to "offer a reasoned explanation of how the factor justifies the resulting rates." The court found that FERC' "largely undocumented reliance on market forces as the principal means of regulation" failed to meet this obligation. The court saw as FERC's "fundamental flaw" an equity return based on other investment opportunities. By failing to ascertain the particular risks of oil pipeline operations, FERC had not determined the actual return required for viability.[31] While competition might drive prices down to the "zone of reasonableness," FERC's regulatory scheme provided no monitor or constraints.[32]

As for the rate base, the court found that FERC's rationale for adopting the ICC formula fell short of "reasoned decisionmaking." It admonished FERC that "original cost ..., a proven alternative, enjoys advantages that should not be underestimated."[33] The court also took a more benign view toward the use of cost allocations in developing segment costs. It urged FERC to be "cognizant of the ICC's past cost allocation practices."[34]

On remand, FERC took as its "evident" guideline "that oil pipeline rates as a general rule must be cost-based."[35] Although the *Williams* litigation had been settled, FERC decided to continue Phase I of the original dual purpose proceeding "to devise generic principles for the purpose of setting just and reasonable oil pipeline rates." While not binding rules, these principles were intended to fulfil the court mandate to fashion "a proper ratemaking method ...."

The rate base was now to reflect net depreciated original cost, with the equity portion trended by an appropriate case-specific inflation index. Rate of return was to reflect the individual pipeline's embedded cost of debt and a cost of equity derived from its particular risk. One factor in assessing risk would be "competition faced by the pipeline." The inflation component of this cost of equity would then be subtracted to arrive at a "real" deflated cost. This would then be applied to the inflation trended equity component of the rate base.[36] CPI and the GNP inflator were noted as possible indices. In general, capital structures were to be actual rather than hypothetical. Where a parent provided, issued, or guaranteed pipeline debt, its capital structure would be used; otherwise the pipeline's. Parties in a given case would also be able to urge another capital structure.[37]

b. Post-Williams Developments

The first case to reach initial decision under these "generic principles" revealed the complexities in their application. The rates involved were newly filed by Southern Pacific Pipe Lines (SPPL) on refined petroleum products.[38] Settlement was reached between SPPL and the only shipper-protestant. On staff request, however, FERC directed the ALJ to reject the settlement absent proof of "close correlation" between cost-of-service and projected revenue stream. As aviation fuel consumers, ten major airlines serving the southwest then intervened.[39]

The ALJ rejected the new rates solely on SPPL's failure to allocate total costs and revenues between interstate and intrastate services.[40] SPPL had no previous need for this allocation, and its records would not permit a timely determination. As an alternative, SPPL proposed including intrastate revenues as a setoff. This was rejected by the ALJ because longer-haul interstate movements had no significant competition, while shorter haul intrastate movements faced motor carrier competition. Since intrastate revenues were "disproportionately low," their inclusion with intrastate costs would burden interstate financial results.

While finding this single issue dispositive, the ALJ addressed other points. A second cost allocation issue involved SPPL's contention that the legality of its rates should be determined on a company wide basis. In addition to the required inter/intrastate allocation, the ALJ held that (1) the more distant North Line must be treated as a separate rate-making entity from the Southern System and (2) the physically disconnected East and West Lines of the Southern System must be similarly separated. This would require a multi-tiered allocation of total common costs.

The capital structure issue is also of interest. The pipeline had a 100% equity ratio (reflecting its exclusion from the Elkins Act decree), while that of its railroad parent was 79%. Contrary to the "generic principles," the ALJ rejected the use of either. The parent had guaranteed the original debt issued to build the system, but more recently the debt had been converted to equity. The 100% equity ratio would result in a starting rate base of $225.8 million, or $39 million more than the $186.6 million ICC valuation base. The ALJ conceded, however, that the pipeline's equity conversion (irrelevant to any result under ICC standards) had preceded its sudden new ratemaking relevance under FERC. Thus, there was no issue of "manipulation."[41] The ALJ also rejected the parent's actual capital structure (which would produce a starting rate base of $11.6 million over ICC valuation) on grounds of differing parent and pipeline risks. For support, the ALJ drew on natural gas precedents.[42]

These various rulings, if adopted by FERC, could greatly complicate future oil pipeline rate regulation. Increased reliance on cost allocations would be required; and FERC's rich store of public utility precedents could increasingly find favor as a handy means of deciding oil pipeline regulatory issues. Moreover, a pipeline's failure to move to a prescribed hypothetical capital structure could mean financial loss. With FERC's approval of a second settlement, however, the need for its own decision on these issues was deferred.[43]

Buckeye Pipe Line, involving an independent carrier of refined products, posed a practical problem of how regulators should respond to competition in regulated markets.[44] Otherwise faced with summary rejection of its rate filings, Buckeye honored the ALJ's order to file cost of service data on all point to point rates. In its appeal to FERC, Buckeye sought to avoid disclosure of the data pending final decision on its relevance. As FERC noted in reversing the ALJ, disclosure would be to "competing oil pipelines and unregulated competitors such as barges, private truck fleets, private pipelines and refineries . . . not required to file either cost or price information."[45]

FERC then drew on a potentially significant dictum from *Farmers Union II*: "Moving from heavy to lighthanded regulation within the boundaries of an unchanged statute can . . . be justified by a showing that under current circumstances the goal and purposes of the statute will be accomplished through substantially less regulatory oversight."[46]

Given this possibility of "lighthanded" regulation, FERC concluded that an absence of "market power" in relevant markets might lessen the need for strict cost based regulation. The required proof would be:

> . . . that [the pipeline's] shippers have alternate ways to ship their product, that buyers have alternate ways of obtaining supplies, or the existence of other constraining factors which would restrain its prices to ensure that they are just and reasonable . . . . From such a showing the Commission could conclude that . . . competition in the relevant markets will operate as a meaningful constraint . . . .[47]

The matter was remanded for further evidence on "whether Buckeye lacks significant market power in the market or markets where it seeks less strict ratemaking scrutiny . . . ." The newly designated ALJ thereupon found that "[B]uckeye . . . lacks significant market power in each of its relevant markets at the present time."[48] To determine "significant market power" the ALJ applied a standard agreed on by all parties—that over a two-year period "Buckeye could not lose 15 percent of its transportation volumes as a result of a 15 percent rate increase."

2.2.5. Epilogue: The Regulatory Frustrations of the Public Utility Model

The ICC's lack of resolve in applying a public utility model to oil pipeline regulation was epitomized in its cavalier treatment of rates of return. In technical terms, the *Farmers Union I* reversal of the ICC's *Williams Bros.* decision was richly deserved. The ICC's perplexing indifference to its task, however, was more likely rooted in a continuing institutional sense of the irrelevance of that task, based on the insights of its initial 1922 *Brundred Bros.* decision. Where "individual rates are assailed," it had said, the past profitability of overall operations is not of "controlling importance." A better test of reasonableness could be found in comparisons "to other rates for pipeline services."[49] In its original Opinion 154, FERC articulated (at too great length) what the ICC had implied—that cost based public utility regulation was ill suited to oil pipeline markets. Its duty, however, was to accommodate the law and reality. The court found the accommodation excessive and FERC now continues the struggle. Query: Is the better solution not outright repeal of the public utility model?

3. Competition, Monopoly, and Industry Structure

Six recent major studies of competition and monopoly in oil pipeline markets differ in the details of their conclusions. All but one, however, agree that pipelines lack market power in a large portion of their markets.

Of the six studies, three had sponsors with direct interests in the outcome. Although these might be suspect, the competence and professional standing of the researchers justify evaluations on their merits. These consist of two separate studies by Edward J. Mitchell and David J. Teece sponsored by AOPL and one by the Robert E. Anderson and Richard T. Rapp of National Economic Research Associates (NERA) sponsored by a group of independent refiners.[50]

Two studies were by government agencies, DOE and DOJ (the latter through its Antitrust Division).[51] Another study by an independent scholar, John A. Hansen, was based on data and research compiled and undertaken during the author's service as a staff economist at FERC.[52]

In determining the presence of market power, the matter of market definition is obviously critical. In defining product markets, there was substantial accord on use of a four category definition comprised of crude origin, crude destination, product origin, and product destination markets. The studies differed notably, however, in their definitions of geographic markets. A published summary of four of the studies shows the following lows and highs in the number of geographic markets used: crude origin, 17 states (Hansen) to 182 largest oil fields (NERA); crude destination, 39 refinery markets (Hansen) to 181 BEAs (DOJ); product origin, 27 states (Hansen) to 181 BEAs (DOJ); and product destination, 59 "niches" (Mitchell) to 183 BEAs (NERA).[53] Despite the wide variance in geographic market definitions, five of the six studies found competition sufficiently effective and pervasive to warrant some measure of deregulation.[54] Of these five, the DOJ report warrants special comment because of its detailed and conservative analyses of the competitive status of individual markets.[55]

DOJ used the four category definition of product markets noted above and 181 BEAs as presumptive geographic markets for all product categories. Individual BEAs were adjusted as required for better market definition. The Herfindahl-Hirschman Index (HHI) was used to measure market concentration. Markets with an index of 2500 or below were deemed sufficiently competitive for deregulation.[56] An index above 2500 indicated a "high risk" market suggesting "a strong likelihood of noncompetitive behavior . . . in the event of deregulation of all the pipelines serving it."

The DOJ report presents a notable anomaly. Although the analysis of market concentration was by individual product and geographic markets, the unit for recommended deregulation or continued regulation was the pipeline.[57] The following explanation was offered.

> It may seem sensible at first blush to regulate all high-risk markets and deregulate all non-high-risk markets; however, that is not a practical policy. Most costs of serving one market cannot easily be separated from those of

serving another; thus, partial regulation would raise difficult cost allocation problems.

Accordingly, "[I]n deciding whether a particular pipeline should be regulated, it is therefore necessary to balance the high-risk against the non-high-risk markets."

In any case, the extent of deregulation recommended by DOJ was noteworthy. It included all crude oil pipelines in the lower 48 states and all but five product pipelines: Colonial, Williams, Chevron (Salt Lake-Spokane), Southern Pacific, and Calnev.[58] Six others were deemed too close to call on current information: Wyco, Badger, Yellowstone, West Shore, Kaneb, and Texas Eastern. As set out in DOJ's Report, in 1983 the five pipelines recommended for continued regulation carried 26% of total barrel-miles (in the lower 48 states), of which 22.6% were carried by Colonial. Pipelines recommended for immediate deregulation carried 70.9%. The six requiring further study carried 3.1%.

In 1988, AOPL reported "over 138" pipelines in service.[59] In 1983, the various modes carried the following ton-mile market shares of refined products in the United States petroleum transport market: pipeline-45.49%; water-51.57%; rail-0.96%; and truck-1.98%.[60]

The pattern of ownership in the oil pipeline industry includes four basic forms: (1) single ownership of a pipeline by an integrated oil company; (2) single ownership by a non-oil company; (3) joint ventures in which several owning firms, usually oil companies, own a percentage of pipeline stock, often based on anticipated proportional usage; and (4) undivided joint interest ownership, under which each participant owns directly an undivided percentage interest of pipeline capacity and each is responsible for a fixed portion of capital costs and for variable operating costs based on actual throughput.

Under monopoly conditions, the differing ownership patterns raise different aspects of the regulatory problem. Particularly where the pipeline operates as part of a single integrated oil firm, the preponderance of its traffic may in substance be its own. Here the problem goes back to regulatory origins. As in the case of Standard Oil in 1906, the aim is to assure independent competitors economic access to their natural markets. Overall earnings have secondary relevance at most to the problem of non-discriminatory access. Of more direct concern is the point-to-point rate.

At the other extreme is the pipeline totally independent of oil industry ownership. Where all traffic derives from nonaffiliated shippers, the concern is not for non-discriminatory competitive access. Here, overall earnings may be more relevant to the reasonableness of the rate level, but they remain a secondary and indirect proxy for market prices. Joint ventures and undivided joint interest ownership will ordinarily fall between the extremes of independent or integrated single company ownership.

Under varying market conditions of competition and monopoly, the issues arising from different conditions of ownership tend to merge. The common concern is whether a given rate so exceeds a market norm as to deny a shipper fair economic access to the desired market.

4. Toward A More Economic Regulatory Regime

An AOPL supported bill in 1988 purported to "eliminate regulation of the levels of oil pipeline rates and charges . . . ."[61] Consistent with the continuing status of oil pipelines as common carriers, however, "undue discrimination" in rates and services was prohibited.[62] Rate discrimination was to be governed by the standards of Sections 2 and 3(1) of the Interstate Commerce Act.[63]

Section 2 requires the same rate for "like and contemporaneous service in the transportation of a like kind of traffic under substantially similar circumstances." Given its application to carriage of the same commodity over the same route between the same points, Section 2 has special relevance to pipeline affiliates of integrated oil companies. Even with identical rates for affiliated and independent shippers, the usual claims of discrimination based on excessive earnings would remain. Their resolution could again require recourse to the cost-based standards of the public utility model.

Section 3 more broadly bars "undue discrimination" against a "person, place, port or type of traffic." Its coverage is commonly described as locality or commodity discrimination. The 1988 AOPL bill, however, contained two remarkable exceptions to the customary scope of Section 3. Thus, "undue discrimination" was defined to exclude transportation of "different commodities" or over "different routes." These exceptions do offer the important advantage of largely eliminating a need for rate/cost comparisons in determining the existence of any discrimination (apart from the issue of its justification). But they also virtually nullify the asserted ban on Section 3 discrimination.

AOPL now supports the current Administration proposal, which would control market power through rate maxima, adjusted by a competitive rate index rather than by costs and earnings.[64] Its principal provisions, which follow, offer a useful model for considering regulatory reform.

1. Sixty days following the effective date of the Act, FERC's existing jurisdiction over oil pipeline rates ends and the revised system of maximum rate regulation begins. Within 120 days of the effective date, the Attorney General may, by petition, mandate the Secretary of Energy to "adjudicate" whether rate regulation for pipelines designated in the petition should continue. The Attorney General's selection of markets must be guided by the "methods, assumptions, standards, and definitions" used in DOJ's May 1986 Report. In the adjudication, however, the Secretary is not bound by the Report.

Comment: It is odd that the Secretary is free to use his own analytical methods in accepting or rejecting DOJ recommendations, but not in the critical stage of identifying markets for possible future regulation. The problem is exacerbated by the designation of these Attorney General recommendations as "an agency action committed to agency discretion . . . not . . . subject to judicial review . . . ." While this anomaly is mitigated by the procedures described below in (2), it is not eliminated.

2. Within 180 days of the effective date, any person substantially affected by

the deregulation of any pipeline market may file a similar petition. Without need for any given methodology, the petition must provide "a reasonable basis" for concluding that rate regulation is in the public interest. In these cases, adjudication by the Secretary is discretionary rather than mandatory, except where, after consultation, the Attorney General recommends adjudication.

Comment: This procedure for considering additional markets for continued regulation is useful, but the permitted consultation with DOJ would relate to markets not designated by it. DOJ may prove protective of its own methodology by not recommending additional markets for adjudication, except in cases of change. *Ex Parte* consultation with DOJ could give undue weight to its methodology or current orientation.

3. Within 270 days of the effective date, the Secretary must identify all pipeline markets for which future regulatory status is to be adjudicated. Rate regulation under the Act then ends in all other markets.

4. Following adjudication, rate regulation continues only in pipeline markets where the Secretary finds it necessary in the public interest "to constrain the exercise of substantial market power in the supply or demand of products transported . . . ." In all other adjudicated markets, regulation terminates within sixty days. Decisions of the Secretary not to adjudicate and decisions following adjudication are subject to judicial review.

5. "Interested persons" may thereafter petition for reconsideration of pipeline regulatory status, but only as to markets under continuing regulation. Subject to judicial review, the Secretary has discretion as to whether such a petition is to be adjudicated. In so deciding, the Secretary may consult with the Attorney General, who may be a party in any subsequent adjudicatory proceeding. The status of deregulated pipeline markets is then final. New pipelines are not subject to rate regulation.

Comment: It is realistic to assume that conditions of competition and monopoly will change in pipeline markets. While the general trend may be toward greater competition, individual markets may experience reduced competition. This might occur through permitted mergers of otherwise non-competitive pipelines, or the withdrawal from markets of competitors. In theory, reconsideration of regulatory status should be available in all markets. The argument against any reimposition of regulation is based on the legitimate consideration of avoiding the financial uncertainties of a vacillating regulatory status. The failure to balance these countervailing concerns is a weakness in the Administration's proposal.

6. Continuing rate regulation is limited to maximum rates. An initial period for setting "base" maximum rates extends from the commencement of the revised rate regulatory regime until one year following the Secretary's publication of the rates subject to adjudication (see, Pars. 1. and 3.). During this period the base maxima are essentially those in effect on a specified date, as periodically adjusted by the Producer Price Index (PPI).

Comment: The purpose of the PPI adjustment is to reflect estimated changes in actual internal cost levels. In theory, the index serves as a proxy for changes in industry-specific cost levels (thus excluding productivity/efficiency changes). The PPI is used more for its general credibility and availablility than as an accurate measure of changes in oil pipeline cost levels. If this were a permanent index, serious disparities might develop between changes in the index and actual pipeline cost levels. But for temporary use, the PPI provides a practical balance.[65]

7. Pipeline markets still subject to continuing regulation following the Secretary's adjudication (see, Par. 4.) are also subject to possible rate reductions. Within 120 days of the Secretary's adjudications, the Attorney General may petition the Secretary to determine whether base rates should be reduced in designated markets. Within 180 days any interested person may file a similar petition stating a "reasonable basis" for proposed reductions. The Secretary must adjudicate the former, but has discretion in deciding to adjudicate the latter.

8. The standard of judgment for rate reductions is whether "the pipeline's market power has resulted in a base rate that is significantly higher than the rate would likely be if the relevant market were not subject to market power." In so deciding, the Secretary is expressly limited to "statistical evidence of rates charged by that pipeline in competitive markets." Statistical significance is to be determined under "commonly accepted standards."

Comment: The limitation of rate comparisons to competitive rates of "that pipeline" is unduly restrictive. If "that pipeline" has enough competitive markets to permit credible comparisons, it may be workable. The section-by-section analysis makes no reference to the limitation or to the possibility that a single pipeline may lack sufficient competitive markets for such comparisons. However, the proposed adjustment of base rates by competitive prices rather than cost constructs, is the right approach.

9. Following the PPI adjustment period, maximum rates would be adjusted periodically by a Competitive Pipeline Price Index (CPPI). Its purpose is "to reflect relative changes in prices charged by pipelines in competitive markets not subject to [FERC] rate regulation." The Secretary must derive the CPPI "from the average revenue per barrel-mile of a sample of pipelines in such markets." Should the CPPI calculation prove "unduly burdensome," the Secretary may substitute an existing index, if it "accurately reflects increases in prices in competitive markets."

10. Maximum rates so determined are "presumed conclusively to be lawful" *and* "not . . . subject to . . . challenge or inquiry under [FERC] rate regulation." Rates below the maxima charged by a pipeline to affiliate shippers must be extended to all shippers. Otherwise, "[N]othing in the Act" makes it unlawful to charge rates below the maxima.

Comment: Under "Applicability of Antitrust Laws," the section-by-section analysis states that the Act "is not intended to affect in any manner the applicability of the antitrust laws to transportation of oil or products." Accordingly, rates below the maxima are subject to antitrust jurisdiction with regard to predation. The section-by-section analysis indicates intended application of antitrust laws to "irrational price discrimination" in all markets.

11. All interstate oil pipelines remain common carriers required to provide "fair,

equitable and non-discriminatory" transportation service on reasonable demand; establish through routes; maintain just and reasonable practices and reasonable classifications.[66] Rates are expressly excluded, however, from the requirement of "fair, equitable and non-discriminatory terms and conditions."

12. Pipeline/shipper contracts which vary from the published schedules governing basic common carrier services are "conclusively . . . presumed to be in the public interest, as long as in regulated markets, the regulated service is available at no more than the maximum rate."

Comment: This conclusive presumption, covering the full range of "public interest" rather than mere lawfulness under "the Act," could conflict with the antitrust savings clause. (See, comment on (10)). It could also be construed to supercede the general rule of rate equality where affiliate shippers pay below maximum rates. (See, (10)). Query: Would it also validate collusive contracts which "restrain trade" by conferring significant competitive advantages on affiliates or other favored shippers. The discussion of "Contracts" in the section-by-section analysis ignores the issue. The Act needs clarification.

5. A Modified Proposal For Yardstick Regulation

Market power has been aptly described as the ability "to raise price above a competitive level without losing so many sales so rapidly that the price increase must be rescinded."[67] The recent studies of market power in oil pipeline markets discussed above reach the following consensus: (1) the absence or presence and degree of market power varies among markets and (2) in some significant portion of these markets, there is an absence of market power in any pipeline. If this consensus offers a reliable premise for developing regulatory policy, the Administration proposal rests solidly on two sound principles.[68]

The first is that the best economic yardsticks for judging regulated prices are, if available, prices generated by competition. Regulated prices derived from inherently arbitrary cost allocations, or the vagaries of marginal cost analysis (even if theoretically preferable), generally fail in their aim to replicate competitive prices.

The second is that regulation, where required, should operate directly on "problem" markets and their prices, rather than indirectly on firms and their earnings. With regard to their wide variances in market power, railroad and oil pipeline markets are much alike. In the case of railroads, Congress has already acted to regulate markets rather than firms. In 1976 and 1980, the Interstate Commerce Act was amended to limit railroad maximum rate regulation to markets in which a carrier has "market dominance."[69]

There are, however, differences in the markets of the two industries. The greater variety and distinctiveness of product and geographic markets in the railroad industry render the development of competitive rate yardsticks from comparable markets less feasible. Accordingly, reliance on cost based proxies for competitive rates persists. In the oil pipeline industry, however, the greater commonality of products and traffic flows should permit development of credible competitive rate yardsticks. The Administration proposal properly seeks to utilize these market characteristics. The following modifications address some previously noted problems in its proposal.[70]

1. The initial purpose of market classification should not be to select markets for deregulation or continued regulation. It should be to identify markets sufficiently competitive to provide reliable competitive rate yardsticks. The resulting market divisions should be much the same, but not necessarily identical. Selection would be made through an expedited DOE rulemaking process with participation open to governmental, shipper, consumer, and oil pipeline interests. To provide a useful focus, DOJ's delineation of markets could be treated as a rebuttable presumption. DOE's determination of "yardstick" markets would be published within one year. Either its decision should stand as a non-reviewable action committed to agency discretion; or judicial review should be limited to "arbitrary or capricious" error. Petitions for changes in market designations could be filed periodically.

2. DOE would then proceed to calculate Competitive Pipeline Price Yardsticks (CPPYs) from among prevailing rates in "yardstick" markets. The first task would be to classify product and geographic markets for comparability. Market groupings should be broad enough to include a sufficient number of rates for a reliable sample. They should also be narrow enough to reflect similarities of cost and demand factors among geographical and product sectors. To suggest the obvious, rates on aviation fuel should not be judged by yardsticks derived from competitive crude oil rates. Developing suitable classifications will not be simple. The process should allow for representations and recommendations from all interests entitled to participate in step (1). "Yardstick" rates would be derived from average revenues per barrel-mile in suitable samples of product and geographic markets. Judicial review and periodic reconsideration of CPPY markets would be as in (1). The determination of CCPYs and their applications would occur no later than a year after DOE's decision in step (1).

(iii) During the two "decisional" periods of one year each, or less, required under (1) and (2), lawful maximum rates will be determined as follows. Current FERC jurisdiction with regard to maximum rates would continue during the first period. (However, regulation of rates below the lawful maxima would be limited to the principles described below in (5)). During the second period, in which CPPYs are being determined following selection of "yardstick" markets, maximum rate regulation in these markets would be suspended. Non-yardstick markets would be subject during this period to existing lawful maxima (including subsequent decisions on rates in litigation). Thereafter, rate maxima in all markets would be governed by their CPPY rates. These yardsticks, and the resulting rate maxima, would be revised periodically to reflect prevailing rates in current yardstick markets.

While competitive yardstick markets will technically remain subject to maximum rate regulation, in practice these would operate as if unregulated. This would result from the use of actual rates in these markets as the legal maximum rates. Complications in defining yardstick rates, or legal maxima, could arise, however, in yardstick markets where prevailing rates exceed bare marginal costs. The idiosyncratic demand factors of some shippers may lead to rates below the prevailing level, but still above marginal costs. The determination of the proper yardstick, or maximum rate, might involve a melding of various rates. Or rates shaped by general and idiosyncratic demand factors could be separately identified to permit use of the former.

4. Even though yardsticks will constitute the basic statutory standard for lawful maxima, economic and constitutional considerations require added flexibility in responding to market conditions. Here the entire pipeline must be considered. As for economics, an enterprise must meet its total costs. If proportional contributions to overheads cannot be realized in its most competitive markets, some added contribution must be sought in other markets. In constitutional terms (market conditions permitting), *Hope* guarantees earnings sufficient "to assure confidence in [the regulated firm's] financial integrity . . . so as to maintain its credit and attract capital."[71] On both economic and constitutional grounds rate maxima require the ultimate safety valves of cost and earnings standards. To minimize their use, while protecting "captive" shippers, the following procedures would apply. For rates no more than ten percent (or some other reasonably determined percentage) over the lawful maximum, an affected shipper could petition for a reduction to a rate no lower than the legal maximum. The needed proof would be that the increment above the maximum imposes a competitive disadvantage which precludes commercially justified market access. If such proof is offered, the pipeline may or may not find it profit maximizing to reduce the rate. Where it deems the reduction unnecessary to hold the traffic, it may seek to refute the shipper's claims. It may also be required to demonstrate that, given its overall rate structure and costs, the rate is necessary to realize a "constitutional" return; that it operates with reasonable efficiency and that any of its other rates below lawful maxima would not contribute to higher earnings if increased. For rates more than ten percent over the maximum, interested persons could petition for similar justification without actual proof of specific injury.

Comment: Since the need for recourse to a cost-based earnings standard may be unavoidable, the effort should be to minimize the possibility, while protecting legitimate shipper interests. This proposal is intended to encourage negotiated solutions to disputes over the impact and need for rates above the maxima. Note also that under the principles of (5), below, the pipeline could offer nonaffiliated shippers selective reductions from wider rate applications, if necessary to hold the traffic. The aim is to permit and thereby encourage market-oriented prices in all markets.

5. Subject to an "affiliate" exception, rates below the lawful maxima would not be regulated other than by applicable antitrust law. The principles of Section 2 of the Interstate Commerce Act would apply to below maximum rates charged by a pipeline to affiliate shippers. Accordingly, rate equality would generally be

accorded nonaffiliate shippers of the same products between the same points over the same route. Where affiliate rates below maxima are based on volume minima, Section 2 type equalization could be avoided only by proof of cost reductions commensurate with rate reductions. Subject to antitrust constraints, pipeline contracts with individual nonaffilate shippers varying from general common carrier tariff schedules would be valid. Contracts with affiliates would require adequate notice to the firm's nonaffiliate shippers operating in its markets affected by the contract. Such shippers could request investigation of these contracts on grounds of substantial competitive disadvantage not justified by costs or other commercial considerations. Section 2 rate equalization principles would also apply to affiliate contract rates absent specific cost justification.

Comment: With the exception of volume differences, it is reasonable to presume that shipments qualifying for Section 2 coverage are carried under similar cost conditions. Rate equalization between affiliates and nonaffiliates seems warranted to prevent discrimination, where the motive for it is greatest. A special case can be made, however, for volume discounts based on valid cost factors. The problem of Section 3 is more difficult. Proof of discrimination, justified or not, will often require complex cost studies. Moreover, the constraints of Section 2 principles could operate to lessen the incentives for unfair pricing under Section 3 principles. The need for application of Section 3 principles to below-maximum rates charged affiliates should be left to experience. If need be, provision could be made for Statements of Concern as to below-maximum rates to affiliates not covered by Section 2 principles. DOE could conduct investigations, as warranted. After a specified period, it could recommend to Congress whether, in addition to antitrust coverage, a need exists for applying Section 3 principles to below-maximum rates extended to affiliates.

6. Conclusion

The proposed system of yardstick regulation is directed to the two historic concerns of oil pipeline regulation. These are: (1) to remove competitive disadvantages imposed on independent shippers through the ownership of pipelines by integrated oil firms and (2) to constrain monopolistic pricing wherever market power is exercised by integrated or independent pipelines. Given the mix of competitive and monopolistic oil pipeline markets, the prime justification for any regulation is the desire to maintain prices at competitive levels wherever and whenever market power comes into play. The traditional public utility cost based model has either focused on a secondary standard of overall earnings or has sought illusory cost based proxies for competitive prices. Competitive price levels can be replicated more accurately at less cost through yardstick prices derived from competitive markets.

The prospect of widening the spread between revenue levels and costs will reinforce managerial efficiency incentives in all markets. The instant proposal will also provide greater flexibility in adjusting prices to changing market conditions.

Price discrimination would be subject to the same antitrust constraints as in other industries. Only where below maxima rates are accorded to pipeline affiliates would the regulation of price discrimination require equalization or cost justification.

Notes

1. The following materials offer a background of varied views on the oil pipeline industry. Books: Johnson (1967); Wolbert (1951, 1979); Mitchell (1979). Articles: Adams and Brock (1983); Coburn (1988); Navarro and Stauffer (1981). Legislative Materials: "Oil Company Ownership of Pipelines," Staff Report of the Subcommittee on Antitrust and Monopoly, Sen. Judiciary Committee, 95th Cong., 2d Sess. (1978); "Oil Pipeline Regulation," Hearings on H.R. 4488 and 6815, Subcomm. on Fossil and Synthetic Fuels, House Comm. on Energy and Commerce, 97th Cong., 2nd Sess., May 10 and Sept. 23, 1982; "Oil Pipeline Deregulation," Hearing on Title IV, Subtitle D, of H.R. 1155 and H.R. 2734, Subcomm. on Energy and Power, House Comm. on Energy and Commerce, 100th Cong., 2nd Sess., March 30, 1988. Misc.: Office of Economic Analysis (1980); GAO Report to Congress (1979); Department of Justice (1986).

2. Technically, however, together with railroads and other common carriers, oil pipelines were made subject to minimum rate regulation under Sec. 418, Transportation Act, 1920. 41 Stat. 456, 484 (1920).

3. These are typically used to restrict entry in "natural monopoly" markets to protect scale economies, or to constrain "destructive" competition in other markets. Since natural monopoly theory imputes some unique "essentiality" to the regulated activity, certificates are often required for market abandonment as well as entry. In addition, a "certified" public utility may be required to expand services and facilities. Oil pipelines are free as well, however, from these added requirements.

4. The link was notably weakened, however, in the "Railroad Revitalization and Regulatory Reform Act of 1976", 90 Stat. 31. It provided for the elimination of railroad maximum rate regulation except in markets served under conditions of "market dominance." See, Secs. 202 (b) and (c) of the Act, 90 Stat. 35-36, codified as amended in 49 USC Sec. 10709; and *infra*, n. 69 and related text.

5. 34 Stat. 584 (1906), as amended, 49 U.S.C. Secs. 10102 and 10501 (1988).

6. An "oil pipeline" history of the Hepburn Act is found in Johnson, *supra*, n. 1, at 23-32. This recap draws on his work and, more directly, on relevant legislative materials.

7. The message, titled "Transportation and Freight Rates in Connection with the Oil Industry," with Report attached, is printed as Sen. Doc. No. 428, 59th Cong., 1st Sess. For House proceedings involving oil pipelines see, 40 Cong. Rec. 9336-40.

8. 40 Cong. Rec. 6358 *et seq*. (May 4, 1906). The amendment established as "common carriers" under the Act to Regulate Commerce (as then titled) any entity engaged in "The transportation of oil or other commodity, except water and except natural or artificial gas, by means of pipelines . . . ."

9. 34 Stat. 585, 49 U.S.C. Sec. 10746. As originally enacted the clause barred railroads from transporting "any article or commodity, other than timber and the manufactured products thereof, manufactured, mined or produced by it, or under its authority, or which it may own in whole or in part, or in which it may have an interest, direct or indirect . . . ." Pipelines are also free from other forms of "industry structure" controls such as those governing mergers and coordinations.

10. Subsequent decisions involving railroad subsidiaries of large shippers put in question the premise that application of the clause to oil pipelines would effectively prohibit carriage of the traffic of parents or close affiliates. See, *U.S. v. South Buffalo Ry*., 333 U.S. 771 (1948).

11. See, Sen. Judiciary Comm. 1978 Staff Report and Adams and Brock (1883).

12. *Advances in Rates-Eastern Cases*, 20 I.C.C. 243, 247-8 (1911). Nevertheless, because the proposed general class rate increases would "affect the entire rate fabric within this territory" the ICC considered the evidence on revenue needs as an element of reasonableness. The evidence was found wanting, largely due to the absence of credible valuation information. *Id.*, 305.

13. Sharfman (1936).

14. Enacted in 1913, Section 19a called for the ICC to determine "fair value" elements in connection with its valuation of common carrier properties. (37 Stat. 701) At the time Congress had reason to believe that "fair value" rate bases were constitutionally required under *Smyth v. Ames*, 169 U.S. 466

(1898). Section 19a is codified as 49 U.S.C. Secs. 10781-5. See also, *infra,* nn. 20 and 22 and related text.

15. The following data (from Federal Reserve Board Bulletins) on average market rates for corporate bonds in 1941 and 1976 provides a broad measure of comparative interest rates: Aaa (Moody's, all classes)—2.77 and 8.43%; Public Utility (recently issued)—3.11 and 8.49%. In basing a 1976 rate of return on a 1941 precedent the ICC ignored the differences.

In defense of the ICC it might be suggested that a suitable adjustment for a near trebling of interest rates was effected through the inclusion of reproduction cost in the fair value rate base. The ICC itself, however, offered no such rationale. (See text immediately preceding this note.) Moreover, the fair value rate base included a significant original cost component. Navarro and Stauffer (1981, 298) note that " . . . as a consequence of the weights in the valuation base, the 'valuation' cannot be expected to track the true replacement value even if the cost escalation index is otherwise exactly correct." The partial use of reproduction costs to compensate for ignoring changes in market interest rates over time is even more tenuous. For example, in relating the identical statutory standards and fair value rate base formula to railroad rates of return the ICC recognized the relevance of current capital markets. "A fair rate of return at any given time depends upon the opportunities of investment and business conditions generally." *Increased Railway Rates, Fare, and Charges,* 1946, 266 I.C.C. 537, 546 (1946). See also, the comparative yield analysis at p. 547.

16. 355 I.C.C. 483. The controversies in *Williams Bros.* did prompt the ICC to initiate rulemaking proceedings in 1974 to consider possible changes in valuation methodologies and related accounting rules. *Ex Parte No. 308, Valuation of* Common Carrier Pipelines, 39 Fed. Reg. 32333, Sept 6, 1974. This was later expanded to include the question "what is the proper rate of return for crude petroleum and petroleum products." 41 Fed. Reg. 2100, Jan. 4, 1976. The quoted language and the ICC's refusal in *Williams Bros.* to determine a company-specific cost of capital suggests a continuing intent to prescribe industry wide returns. The 1977 jurisdictional transfer to FERC mooted the proceeding.

17. *U.S. v. Atlantic Refining Co.,* No. 14060 (D.D.C. Dec.23, 1941), vacated per settlement, (D.D.C., Dec. 13, 1982).

18. The history of the broader "Mother Hubbard" litigation and the consent degree is set out from varying perspectives in Johnson (1967), see "Consent Decree" entry, Index; Wolpert (1951), see "Consent Decree" entry, Index; and Sen. Judiciary Comm. Staff Report, *supra,* n. 1, at 119-24. Johnson best describes the many interpretive problems spawned by the loosely drafted decree.

19. The President's "Message to the Congress on Proposal to Create a Department of Energy," House Doc. No. 95-91, at 1. The following brief legislative summary of the transfer is based on the following items. 1. "Department of Energy Organization Act," Hearings on H.R. 4263, Subcomm. of the House Comm. on Government Operations, 95th Cong., 1st Sess., Mar. and Apr., 1977; 2. "Department of Energy Organization Act," Hearings on S. 826, Sen. Comm. on Governmental Affairs, 95th Cong., 1st Sess., Mar. and Apr., 1977; 3. House Rep. No. 95-346, Part 1; 4. Sen. Rep. No. 95-164; and 5. Sen. Rep. No. 95-367, (Conf.Rep. on S. 826).

20. See, *supra,* n. 14 and *infra,* n. 22 and related text. Other ICC functions relating to oil pipeline transportation were transferred to the Secretary of Energy. The "Department of Energy Organization Act" is at 95 Stat. 565. The relevant transfer provisions are found in Sections 306 and 402(b) of the Act, 95 Stat. 581 and 584. These are codified in 42 U.S.C. Secs. 7155 and 7172(b).

21. Sen. Rep. No. 95-164, at 35.

22. *Farmers Union Cent. Ex. v. FERC,* 584 F.2d 408, 413 (D.C. Cir. 1978); cert. den. 439 U.S. 995 (1978). (*Farmers Union I*) The Supreme Court's "end result" earnings adequacy test in *FPC v. Hope Natural Gas Co.,* 320 U.S. 591 (1944) had ended any need under *Smyth v. Ames,* for a "fair value" rate base. The Court also confirmed that the 1913 Valuation Act imposed no such requirement. See, *supra,* nn. 14 and 20 and related text.

23. *Williams Pipe Line Co., Dock No. OR-1-000, et al,* Opinion 154, 21 FERC Par. 61,620 (1982); reh'g den., Opinion 154-A, 22 FERC Par. 61,086 (1983).

24. 21 FERC 61,584 and 61,602.

25. *Id.,* 61,606-7. The decline reflected increases over 50 years in pipeline revenue per barrel from 44 to 61 cents and in the cost of a barrel of crude from $0.68 to $31.77.

26. *Id.,* 61,585.

27. *Id.,* 61,632.

28. *Id.,* 61,644-6. To avoid double counting inflation, this rate of return was to be reduced to the

extent that the valuation rate base reflected its inflation component.

29. *Id.*, 61,651. FERC described cost allocations as "metaphysical, inconclusive and barren." In noting the potential abuse under cost-based regulation of inter-affiliate asset transfers, FERC put the burden of justifying transaction prices on the pipeline. The decision is treated more broadly in O'Neill and Knapp (1983).

30. *Farmers Union Central Exchange,et al v. FERC*, 734 F.2d 1486 (D.C. Cir. 1984).

31. 734 F.2d 1522.

32. *Id.*, 1502-04, 1508-09.

33. *Id.*, 1512, 1530.

34. *Id.*, 1529. Other issues less pertinent here were also considered. See Coburn (1984).

35. *Williams Pipe Line Co.*, 31 FERC Par. 61,377 (1985). Opinion 154-B., at 31 FERC 61,833.

36. *Id.*, 61,834. FERC explained its choice of trended original cost rather than the rate of return to reflect inflation as an effort to "help newer pipelines with higher rate bases to compete with older pipelines with lower rate bases ... because TOC mitigates the front end load problem for new pipelines." See, *Id.*, 61,835 for FERC's discussion of the issue.

It was also necessary to determine a starting rate base for regulatory purposes. The pipelines argued for the ICC valuation rate base; shippers, for net depreciated original cost. FERC split the difference by basing the debt portion of the starting rate base on net depreciated original cost and the equity portion on ICC valuation reduced by the percentage of book depreciation to original cost. However, parties could argue a lack of entitlement to this formula.

37. 31 FERC 61,836. Rehearing of Opinion 154-B was denied in principal part. 33 FERC Par. 61,326. Opinion 154-C. For further detail see Coburn (1985).

38. *Southern Pacific Pipe Lines, Inc.*, Init. Dec., 39 FERC Par. 63,018 (1987).

39. This may have been the first direct non-shipper consumer intervention in an oil pipeline rate case. The substantial use of aviation fuel by these major corporate consumers might commercially justify intervention if the total cost of fuel were in fact materially affected by the pipeline rates.

40. 39 FERC 65,077-8, citing *Panhandle Eastern v. FPC*, 324 U.S.635 (1945).

41. *Id.*, 65,084.

42. *Id.*, 65,082-6.

43. *Southern Pacific Pipe Lines, Inc.*, Order Approving Offer of Settlement, 45 FERC Par. 61,242 (1988). Meanwhile, the ALJ's rulings belie the non-substantive "housekeeping" rationale stated by the President and accepted by Congress as reason for the jurisdictional transfer to FERC.

44. *Buckeye Pipe line Co.*, Order Granting Interlocutory Appeals, 44 FERC Par. 61,066 (1988); Order Denying Rehearing, 45 FERC Par. 61,046 (1988).

45. 44 FERC 61,186. In recognizing "the likelihood of competitive injury" to Buckeye, the ALJ had in fact stayed his order pending appeal.

46. 734 F.2d 1510. While the dictum offered a possibility of greater regulatory flexibility, it gave no assurance that the "unchanged statute" would permit significant departures from the established cost based methodology.

47. 44 FERC 61,186.

48. *Buckeye Pipe Line Co.*, Dock. No. IS 87-14-000, Initial Decision, Feb. 12, 1990. The relevant geographic markets for analysis were "the transportation or delivery of refined petroleum products to the BEAs Buckeye services." BEAs are economic areas defined by the U.S. Department of Commerce, Bureau of Economic Analysis. See, *infra*, n. 53 and related text.

49. *Supra*, Part II. B. 1. a., *Brundred Bros.*

50. See Mitchell (1982); Teece (1986); NERA (1983).

51. Coburn (1982); U.S. Department of Justice (1986).

52. Hansen (1983).

53. A summary is in Griese (1985). BEAs are economic areas developed and used by the Bureau of Economic Analysis, U.S. Department of Commerce. (See, *supra*, n. 48.) "Niche" is a term used by Mitchell to describe a suitable geographic area for analyzing market concentration. These varied in each of the four product areas. Both Hansen and Mitchell used U.S. Standard Metropolitan Statistical Areas (SMSAs) in defining product destination markets or niches.

54. The exception was the NERA study in which markets were characterized as presenting high, medium or low risk of market power due to a lack of effective competition. Its conclusion was that overall risk was too high to warrant deregulation. Nevertheless, risks were found to vary among markets.

Only 50% of production in crude origin markets fell into the high or medium risk range (12 and 38%, respectively); in crude delivery markets about two-thirds of deliveries were found to be made into low risk refinery markets. The highest risks were found in product origin and destination markets in which 85 and 90% of collections and deliveries, respectively, were termed medium or high risk.

The studies are generally compared and evaluated in Coburn (1985; 1987). See also, Griese (1985).

55. The term "conservative" seems warranted by the following considerations: (i) the use of actual water competition only, without regard to any price constraints from potential water competition; (ii) the measurement of market share by pipeline capacity rather than actual shipments and (iii) the relatively small size of geographic markets.

56. An HHI is calculated by summing the squares of the market shares of all firms in the market. Thus, in a market of four competitors with equal shares of 25%, the HHI would be four times 625, or 2500. For a discussion of the HHI and its uses see Griese (1985, 119-120).

57. "Pipeline" was not necessarily defined, however, as an entire corporate entity. A single pipeline company may operate separate non-contiguous systems (cf. SPPL, *supra*). For its purposes DOJ viewed the pipeline unit as "a contiguous set of physical properties that forms a proper unit for regulation or deregulation."

58. Reference is to the "lower 48 states" because of the exclusion of the Trans Alaska Pipeline System (TAPS). The current Administration deregulation proposal, now supported by AOPL, continues to exclude TAPS. Thus, its early deregulation is not likely. See, S. 1471, 101st Cong., 1st Sess.; Cong. Rec., Aug. 2, 1989, S 9755, 9756, *infra*, n. 64 and related text. The creation and initial regulatory history of TAPS following discovery of the Prudhoe Bay oil resevoirs are noted in *Trans Alaska Pipe Line Rate Cases*, 436 U.S. 631 (1978).

59. See, 1988 House Hearings, "Oil Pipeline Deregulation," *supra*, n. 1, at 192.

60. Griese (1985, 119-120).

61. The text of this bill (H.R. 2734, 100th Cong., 2nd Sess.) is in 1988 House Hearings, "Oil Pipeline Deregulation," *supra*, n. 1.

62. AOPL supports the common carrier status of oil pipelines as the necessary basis for eminent domain authority in some 22 states.

63. These are now codified as 49 U.S.C. Secs. 10741(a) and (b).

64. "Oil Pipeline Regulatory Reform Act of 1989", S. 1471 and H.R. 3092, 101st Cong., 1st Sess. The bills are identical. For the text and a section-by-section analysis of S. 1471, see Cong. Rec., Aug. 2, 1989, S. 9755-61. As noted, *supra*, n. 57, the bills exclude TAPS. The two principal sponsors of H.R. 3092 also sponsored H.R. 2734, 100th Cong., 2nd Sess., the bill supported by AOPL in 1988.

65. For a general introduction to price level regulation, including the selection of an "inflation" index see Hillman and Braeutigam (1989).

66. These provisions may present problems of interpretation beyond the scope of this article. In particular, the term "transportation" may require clarification in regard to such ancillary functions as the provision of storage and terminal facilities.

67. Landes and Posner. (1981).

68. FERC Conmmissioner Charles G. Stalon began the weaning of DOJ from its 1986 recommendations to deregulate pipelines rather than markets and to continue cost based regulation. See, House Hearings (1988). The gist of the infectious wisdom offered by Commissioner-Economist Stalon to a responsive DOJ was that the "cost-of service" model for oil pipeline regulation be replaced with "price caps on a market-by-market basis using the prices that are created in the competitive markets to establish those in the noncompetitive markets . . . ." *Id.*, at 112. See also, 48-90.

69. For citation of the 1976 legislation and current codification see, *supra*, n. 4. The 1980 amendments were included in the Staggers Rail Act of 1980, 94 Stat. 1985, 1900.

70. The use of "yardstick competition" as a standard for determining reasonable cost allowances for regulated utilities is proposed in Shleifer (1986). His proposal relates to firms rather than markets, and he notes the problem of controlling collusive strategies. Yardstick prices derived from competitive markets, as distinguished from yardstick costs generated under conditions of market power, are not subject to such collusion.

71. Ordinarily, if market conditions do not permit the regulated firm to realize "constitutional" earnings, it may be entitled to abandon all, or some portion, of its markets. *Brooks Scanlon Co. v. Railroad Comm.*, 251 U.S. 396, 399 (1920). Unlike public utilities, however, oil pipelines have never been constrained from abandoning markets at will.

References

Adams, W., and J.W. Brock. 1983. "Deregulation or Divestiture: The Case of Petroleum Pipelines." *Wake Forest Law Review* 19:705.
Coburn, L. L. 1982. "Petroleum Pipeline Deregulation: A Competitive Analysis." *U.S. Dept. of Energy*. Reprinted in 1983 House Hearings, "Oil Pipeline Deregulation." 1:57.
Coburn, L. L. 1984. "Farmers Union II: Sisyphus Starts Up The Hill Again." *Energy Law Journal* 5:309.
Coburn, L. L. 1985. "Is There Sufficient Economic Analytic Justification for Oil Pipeline Deregulation?" *Transportation Research Forum* 26:110
Coburn, L. L. 1985. "Oil Pipeline Regulation: Has The FERC Finally Slain The Minotaur?" *Energy Law Journal* 6:209.
Coburn, L. L. 1987. "Petroleum Pipeline Deregulation: A Critical Analysis of the Primary Analytic Justifications for Deregulation." *Transportation Research Forum* 28:346.
Coburn, L. L. 1988. "Eighty Years of US Petroleum Pipeline Regulation," *Journal of Transport History* 9:149.
GAO Report to Congress. 1979. "Petroleum Pipeline Rates and Competition—Issues Long Neglected By Federal Regulators And In Need Of Attention." (July 13).
Griese, N.L. 1985. "Current Trends in Defining Oil Pipeline Markets for the Purpose of Measuring Competitiveness." *Transportation Research Forum* 26:116.
Hansen, J.A. 1983. *U.S. Oil Pipline Markets: Structure Pricing and Public Policy*. MIT Press.
Hillman, J.J., and R.R. Braeutigam. 1989. *Price Level Regulation for Diversified Public Utilities*. Boston:Kluwer Academic Publishers.
House Hearings. 1988. "Oil Pipeline Deregulation." 1:112-13, 116-17.
Johnson, A.M. 1967. *Petroleum Pipelines and Public Policy*. Harvard University Press.
Landes, W.M., and R.A. Posner. 1981. "Market Power In Antitrust Cases." *Harvard Law Review* 94:937.
Mitchell, E.J. 1882. "A Study of Oil Pipeline Competition." Reprinted in 1983 House Hearings, *"Oil Pipeline Deregulation,"* 1:479.
Mitchell, E.J., ed. 1979. *Oil Pipelines and Public Policy*. American Enterprise Institute Conference.
Navarro, P., and T.R. Stauffer. 1981. "The Legal History and Economic Implications of Oil Pipeline Regulation." *Energy Law Journal* 2:291.
NERA. 1983. *Competition in Oil Pipeline Markets: A Structural Analysis*. Washington, DC
Office of Economic Analysis. 1980. "Federal Pipeline Regulation." *Department of Energy* (August).
O'Neill, B.D., and G.M. Knapp. 1983. "Oil Pipeline Regulation After *Williams*: Does The End Justify The Means?" *Energy Law Journal.* 4(61).
Sharfman, I. 1936. *The Interstate Commerce Commission*, vol. III-B (14). New York: The Commonwealth Fund.
Shleifer, A. 1985. "A Theory of Yardstick Competition." *Rand Journal of Economics* 16:319
Teece, D.J. 1986. *Oil Pipeline Rate Deregulation*. Association of Oil Pipelines (November 20).
U.S. Department of Justice. 1986. "Oil Pipeline Deregulation." *Antitrust Division* (May).
Wolbert, G.S., Jr. 1952. *American Pipelines*. University of Oklahoma Press.
Wolbert, G.S., Jr. 1979. *U.S. Oil Pipelines*. American Petroleum Institute.

6

TELECOMMUNICATIONS SERVICES AS A STRATEGIC INDUSTRY:
Implications for United States Public Policy
Robert G. Harris

1. Emergence of Strategic Telecommunications Policies

Although there was little or no thought given to the implications of the AT&T divestiture for international competition at the time, there has been a growing recognition that the Modified Final Judgement has had considerable consequence for international trade and, possibly, the competitiveness of United States telecommunications equipment manufacturers, service providers, and users in information intensive industries. More generally, United States telecommunications policy has traditionally been based on an extremely parochial view of the world, especially considering what was happening elsewhere.

Simply put, by the late 1980s the United States no longer had a telecommunications sector far superior to that of other nations, in the quality or extent of the network, in the range of communications or information services available through the network, or even in underlying technological prowess. In a recent study of international trends in telecommunications technology, Schnoring found that in 1979 the United States was the world leader in "technological capacity."[1] By 1986, however, Japan had moved dramatically ahead, having "taken the lead in telecommunications development activities and accumulated the largest stock of proprietary technology," as measured by the issuance of significant international patents to companies of Japanese origin (Schnoring 1989, 17).

This growing awareness of the global implications of domestic telecommunications policy has shifted the terms of the public policy debate, as well it should. The change in orientation is due largely to two factors, one general to the United States economy, one specific to telecommunications. At the general level, there is substantial evidence that the performance of the United States economy has lagged behind some of our major competitors and trading partners. Although there is much dispute over the causes of this relative decline in productivity and economic growth rates, "competitiveness" has become a central concern of policymakers in Washington and state capitals. This concern has in turn generated a recognition that, in a global economy, it is relative performance that counts. Both the reality of United States economic welfare and people's perceptions of their economic well-being increasingly depend on how well they are doing compared to others.

At the specific level, it has been readily apparent that the leading nations of Europe and the Pacific Rim have targeted telecommunications, or, more broadly, information technologies, as a central element in their national economic strategies (Rothwell 1986, 102). In the Pacific, Japan, Korea, Hong Kong, and Singapore have developed and begun implementing national telecommunications initiatives; in Europe, the United Kingdom, France, Germany, and the Nordic countries have developed explicit national strategies for information technologies.[2] Moreover, the European Economic Community "has chosen the telecommunications sector as the *leading industry* of its strategy for achieving regional integration—"1992" (Thimm 1989, 57).

It is not surprising that many of the nations which have implemented a "strategic telecommunications policy" have traditions of economic planning. Even in the United Kingdom, though, which of late shares American hostility toward "industrial policy," the government has taken a number of "neo-corporatist" policy initiatives intended to promote information and communications development (Cawson 1987).

But it is the Japanese whose targeting of information technologies—including telecommunications, computers, and information services—as the engines of economic growth is most explicit and most consequential for their national telecommunications policy. In the Japanese view, these are leading or strategic industries which will play a vital role in promoting the competitiveness of Japanese enterprises and continued growth of the Japanese economy. According to official documents[3] (and in the privately expressed views of many Japanese officials interviewed by the author), the "informatization" of Japan will have sweeping social, political, and cultural implications as well (Harris 1989).

In distinct contrast to the United States, Japan has developed and is implementing a coherent national telecommunications policy intended to place Japanese telecommunications companies and intensive users of telecommunications services in global leadership positions in their respective industries. The key elements of that policy include the use of competition in local and long-distance telephone service to spur efficiency (especially through staff reductions at Nippon Telephone & Telegraph (NTT)); acceleration of the introduction of new information services through liberal entry policies and no line-of-business restrictions on NTT; provide for stable funding of research and development through the dedication of revenues received by the Ministry of Finance from NTT dividends and continuing sale of stock to support "Advanced Telecommunications Research;" and stimulation of investment in the telecommunications infrastructure through national commitments to expedite widespread adoption of Integrated Services Digital Network

(ISDN) in this decade and broadband fiber optics in the next.[4]

In an increasing number of countries, national policies are premised on the idea that *telecommunications is a strategic industry, with economic characteristics that require or deserve special consideration in assessing policy alternatives.* That premise, and its implications for United States telecommunications policies, are the subjects of this paper.

While the term "strategic industry" is often used indiscriminately (i.e., meaning that an industry is *important*), there is a rapidly growing literature analyzing the economic conditions and characteristics of an industry that make it strategic.[5] In Section 2, we briefly review the origins of the concept and some of the recent empirical work attempting to substantiate the effects of strategic industries on economic development and national economic performance.

In Section 3, we identify the economic characteristics of a strategic industry as exceptions to the assumed characteristics of a "perfectly competitive" industry and demonstrate that telecommunications services has all of these characteristics to a very substantial degree. By telecommunications services, I mean the public telephone network, including switched and dedicated ("private line") services. The telecommunications *infrastructure* is the physical and technical capacity required to provide telecommunications services. While concerned primarily with telecommunications services, there are strong linkages between the telecommunications services and telecommunications equipment industries, linkages, which are a crucial aspect of the strategic character of telecommunications services. It has been argued—and Japanese and European policies assume—that telecommunications equipment is itself a strategic industry. But since our interest is in telecommunications services, we will look at telecommunications equipment only in terms of the vertical linkages between the two industries.

Having shown the characteristics of telecommunications services that make it a strategic industry, Section 4 addresses some of the implications for telecommunications policies in the United States. While the strategic industry analysis points mainly to competition and regulatory policies that are similar to those derived from comparative statics, strategic industry analysis does shift the tradeoffs between policy criteria in some cases, and often strengthens the case for efficiency-oriented outcomes over equity concerns (especially those which are very short-run in character). The central message is that United States telecommunications policies must—in order for the United States to be internationally competitive in the "information age"—explicitly acknowledge and incorporate the broader economic developmental benefits of telecommunications services. We can no longer regulate telecommunications as if it were a purely domestic industry, when other nations have chosen telecommunications as a leading instrument of national economic development and competitive advantage.

2. Origins of the Concept of Strategic Industry

Although the term "strategic industry" is of fairly recent vintage, the concept has historic antecedents beginning at least with Schumpeter, who emphasized the importance of dynamic competition, with new industries uprooting entrenched positions of dominant firms or even replacing entire industries through the "gales of creative destruction." In this dynamic process of change and technological advance, Schumpeter stressed the role of "leading industries," which, in his definition, were the engines of economic growth and technical progress (Nelson 1984). Commentators since Schumpeter have used the terms "vital," "developmental," or "transformational" to describe such industries.

The term strategic industry has been used for some time in reference to industries whose goods or services were deemed essential to meeting national security objectives. The range of industries covered, at one time or another in public debates, is quite considerable, including raw materials (oil, metals), transportation (the interstate highway system), education (the post-Sputnik Federal aid to higher education and teacher training), and, of late, "high-tech" industries (high definition television). These industries are argued by some to have important military applications and generate significant contributions to technological development. While this paper will not address the issue of strategic *military* value, there is a growing recognition that national security depends heavily on the economic performance of strategic industries in a *commercial sense*, which is the purpose of the paper.

For our purpose, the origins of the concept of strategic industry lie in the field of economic development and Albert O. Hirschman's seminal work of 1958, *The Strategy of Economic Development*. Hirschman introduced the notion of backward and forward linkages from a sector (e.g., transportation, communications) to supplier and user industries and argued that high investment in sectors with strong linkages will lead to more rapid economic growth. He also coined the concept of "Social Overhead Capital"—infrastructure industries that (1) provide services that are basic to a great variety of economic activities; (2) exhibit a high degree of "publicness" (and are therefore usually provided by public agencies or private firms under public control); (3) are immobile and therefore cannot be imported; (4) have substantial "lumpiness" or technical indivisibilities; and (5) have very high capital/output ratios, with large fixed investment required to achieve an economically viable level of output. Given these characteristics, Hirschman argued that investment in social overhead capital was not only essential, but also required a national strategy for economic development.

In one of the most important empirical tests of Hirschman's ideas, Fishlow's 1965 study of the railroad industry found that substantial positive backward linkages to supplier industries induced substantial demand and technological gains in iron and machinery. Forward linkages had dramatic effects in agriculture and food processing and the "opening of the West," with less discernible effects in the manufacturing or industrial sectors.

More recently, Cohen and Zysman (1987) have employed the Hirschman-Fishlow approach to argue that "manufacturing matters"—that there are substantial forward and backward linkages across manufacturing industries (e.g., semiconductors to computers), and from manufacturing to services (e.g., manufacturing stimulating demand for services and manufactured goods as an essential input to service industries).

Much of the latest work in strategic industries comes from trade theory and has been influenced by the increasing use of game theory to model the interactions among nation states. This work challenges the implicit assumptions of neo-classical trade theory, namely (1) decreasing returns (or at least no significant increasing returns); (2) competitive market structures (no firm or national set of firms has the power to extract rents); and (3) no positive externalities or spillovers of technology into other industries. Once one allows for "market failures," neither the neo-classical explanation of trade as being determined by comparative advantage nor the policy prescription of "free trade" necessarily holds. One of the leading developers of "strategic trade theory," in reviewing and synthesizing these developments, has argued that these "changes in trade theory have strengthened the view that nations are competing over who gets to realize these externalities" (Krugman 1987, 138).

As one would expect, trade theorists have been concerned primarily with "tradeable goods," but they often recognize that the characteristics of a strategic industry may also apply to non-tradeable goods, i.e., goods whose transportation costs are so high relative to value that the relevant markets are local or services produced with fixed, immobile physical plants (Krugman 1987). Since our interest is primarily in telecommunications services, the analysis in Section 3 will concentrate on non-tradeable services, recognizing the backward vertical linkages to telecommunications equipment, which has become a global industry in recent years.

3. Characteristics of a Strategic Industry

3.1. Introduction

In classifying the characteristics of a strategic industry,[6] I have attempted to identify each of the individual economic factors which might cause an industry to differ from the model of "perfect competition" in ways that would increase its strategic value to a national or regional economy.[7] In reality, these characteristics rarely occur in isolation; in some industries, all or most of these characteristics apply. Likewise, each of these characteristics is a matter of degree in any given industry (e.g., positive externalities can be large or small). I define a strategic industry as one with a substantial number of these characteristics, and to a substantial degree. In addition to identifying the generic characteristics of a strategic industry, I will show that telecommunications services has virtually all of these characteristics, and to a very great extent.

There are two classes of strategic industry characteristics, internal and external:

3.2. Internal Economies

Internal economies generate increasing returns to firm size: as output of the firm increases, costs increase less than proportionately.[8] If these internal economies are large,[9] there are two main consequences. First, firms in the industry can generate excess profits (economic rents) because the scale advantage may limit rivalry and entry sufficient to charge prices above average costs. In tradeable goods industries, these rents can accrue to "national firms," thereby improving national economic performance (Krugman 1987). Second, given these economies, average costs decline with output, so increased demand reduces the cost of producing the service to all other buyers. Depending on the nature of the economies, there may be a high degree of indivisibility (i.e., a large initial investment prior to production), in which case the service may have the attributes of a "public good."

Scale economies: increasing returns to scale at the plant or company level, due to indivisibilities (initial fixed cost can be spread over more units of production) or the use of more efficient, more capital intensive, modes of production at higher output levels. Economies occur not only in production, but also at pre- and post-production stages. Most importantly, in R&D intensive industries, firms may incur a large sunk cost in research and product development before bringing products or services to market. At the post-production level, the most important economies are typically associated with distribution channels and brand name loyalty.

Scope economies: increasing returns across multiple products or services, due to improved utilization of shared resources or the use of more efficient but more capital intensive modes of production. A good example of such scope economies is the dual use of transportation systems for passengers and freight, a characteristic which is critical to understanding the economics of railways, highways, and airways. Similarly, a communications network can be used for voice, data, and video services, thereby spreading fixed costs across a larger volume of usage.

Network economies:[10] increasing returns through the joint operation of multiple links and/or nodes in a network industry (transportation, communications, energy transmission and distribution). These include:

(1) economies of traffic density (lower unit costs as throughput over a link increase);

(2) routing economies (more efficient utilization of links (by optimal traffic routings) and vehicles (by improved scheduling capabilities); and

(3) inter-temporal economies (offsetting temporal incidence of demand across customers to improve capacity utilization).

Learning economies: increasing returns to scale over total production (i.e., lower unit costs as cumulative production increases) due to "learning by doing" (Rosenberg 1982a, 121-122). These economies are often product-specific (as in the "learning curve"), but there is the potential for learning that transcends specific products. Workers who learn skills in one product line can transfer them to others; organizations that develop product development capabilities in developing one product can apply those capabilities to other, related products.[11]

In addition to these individual internal economies, their ultimate impact may be magnified by compounding over time due to *positive feedback effects* (Arthur

1989). Whether due initially to these economies or historical accident,[12] positive feedback effects can leverage a small, temporal advantage into a long-term sustainable advantage. Early entrants into an industry might realize sufficient scale and learning economies to generate a competitive price advantage, gain market share, feed revenues into R&D and product development and thus gain continuous improvements in competitive position (the so-called "first mover" advantage). If substantial, these feedback effects cause "path dependency" in the development of an industry, such that early entrants have a long-term advantage over later or potential entrants (David 1988). When that happens, the national identity of the early moving firms has consequences for national economic performance.

3.3. Internal Economies in Telecommunications Services

The telephone network exhibits very substantial scale and scope economies in the use of central office switches to provide exchange and inter-exchange services (Shin 1988, 64-69) or local calling and custom calling services. There are also substantial network economies, including economies of traffic density in inter-office trunks and long-distance networks; routing economies from moving traffic over lesser used circuits to increase capacity utilization; and inter-temporal economies from using facilities to serve asynchronous customer demands (e.g., business daytime use, residential evening use of central offices and inter-exchange circuits). Telecommunications services companies have realized substantial learning economies, as in the dramatic improvements in the productivity of engineers and technicians due to increasing experience with digital switching technology or optical fiber transmission equipment.

Beyond these individual economies, the telecommunications services industry has enjoyed very significant positive feedback effects. With rapidly growing demand over a long period of time, carriers were able to further exploit scale, scope, network, and learning economies. These economies in turn produced three major benefits within the telecommunications services industry:

(1) lower costs, which translated into falling real prices for telecommunications services, thereby further stimulating demand;

(2) sufficient revenues to finance major investment to expand capacity largely through internal financing, which lowered the cost of capital and allowed firms to make large, lumpy investments and further realize internal economies; and

(3) extensive deployment of the network and achievement of virtually universal service.

In addition to the internal economies in telecommunications services, there are substantial economies of scale and scope in telecommunications equipment. Consequently, the induced demand for telecommunications equipment from national investment in telecommunications infrastructure has important effects on the competitiveness of domestic equipment suppliers in international equipment markets.

3.4. External Economies

The principle and implications of *negative externalities* has become well-known and widely appreciated in the past two decades. Though there is substantial disagreement over the remedies, there is strong consensus that public policies must protect consumers, workers, and the environment from negative externalities, hence the increased regulation of consumer products, workplace safety, and environmental pollution. The principle of *positive externalities* is less well-known or widely appreciated.[13] Yet these externalities are almost certainly growing in magnitude and consequence for firm, industry, and national economic performance.

Public policies have been used to internalize these benefits in some cases.[14] Intellectual property rights, for example, are designed to internalize the benefits of invention, innovation, creativity, and brand loyalty, through patent, trade secrets, trademark, and copyright protection. Firms also attempt to appropriate returns through the ownership of "co-specialized" assets (Teece 1986). But there are many instances in which such schemes do not exist or would be infeasible—i.e., when there is a weak "appropriability regime." When that is the case, the existence of positive externalities means that the social return on investment exceeds the private return, which reduces the externalities-generating activity below the socially optimal level.

The following classification attempts to identify and define specific types of positive externalities, recognizing that one would typically observe these externalities in combination.

3.4.1. Horizontal Externalities

Horizontal externalities cast benefits on other firms in an industry or to producers or consumers of complementary goods and services. Horizontal externalities include:

(1) *Network externalities*: economic benefits that accrue to other consumers or producers within an industry. The classical example is a telephone network, in which the value of the service to any one customer depends on the number of other customers. Network externalities also occur in industries in which standards, compatibility, and/or interoperability are important, because the number of users of a given standard (e.g., MS.DOS microcomputers) increases interoperability.

(2) *Complementary externalities*: economic benefits that accrue to consumers or producers of complementary goods and services. The standardization and widespread adoption of personal computer operating systems has been a boon to PC software producers, and vice versa. Similiarily, France Telecom's Minitel initiative has stimulated literally thousands of suppliers of enhanced information services.

(3) *Technology externalities*: technological developments in one industry spillover into related industries. These occur in part because of the uncertainty in the research and development process, i.e., researchers set out looking for one thing, but discover another. They also occur because innovations often can be applied to

other products with little or no modification (Rosenberg 1982b).

(4) *Learning externalities*: In knowledge-intensive and other skilled industries, learning often spills over into related industries. Researchers trained and experienced in one industry migrate to other, related industries. As noted by Reich (1990), given the relative international immobility of labor, compared to capital, positive externalities can best be captured by a national economy through the increased skill, knowledge, and productivity of labor in any given nation, rather than ownership of capital.

3.4.2. Backward Vertical Externalities

In industries that are vertically linked, there are powerful interactive effects from growth and development in the user industries to supplier industries (Rosenberg 1982b; Porter 1989). Of greatest importance typically is the induced demand for inputs, which enables supplier firms to realize scale, scope, and learning curve economies. These linkages may be especially significant when the supplier industries produce tradeable goods for a user industry that produces non-tradeable goods or services. In that case, stimulated demand in the supplier industry by expansion of the national user industry can provide a domestic "platform" to accelerate R&D, product development, share of national producers in global markets, and, perhaps, sustainable advantage.[15] The induced demand effect in vertically linked industries can be characterized as an externality or as a vertical economy. There are two other types of vertical externalities:

(1) *Technology externalities*: technologies that spillover vertically across industries. Backward linkages occur when technology developed at one level can be used, or stimulates technological developments, in supplier industries.

(2) *Learning externalities*: In knowledge-intensive and other skilled industries, learning also spills over into vertically related industries. Researchers trained and experienced in one industry migrate to upstream or downstream industries. Rapid expansion at one level generates a pool of human resources which over time migrates to other levels (Porter 1989). Moreover, in tightly linked vertical industries, technology does not merely spillover from one level to the other, there are also potential synergies from working together (Von Hippel 1988; Rosenberg 1982a). Innovation occurs through learning together, the supplier bringing knowledge of one kind, the user, knowledge of another kind. Through the interaction of people from the two industries, the performance of both is improved.

3.4.3. Forward Vertical Externalities

The same types of vertical linkages that travel upstream also travel downstream, when developments in a supplier industry generate economies or benefits to user industries. These effects are especially significant when the supplier industry produces non-tradeable goods and the user industries, tradeable goods. Then, stimulating development of the supplier industry can improve the competitiveness of user industries. The more widespread are the forward vertical linkages (so long as they are national or less than national in their incidence), the greater the potential national benefit.

3.4.4. Substitutes For Goods With Negative Externalities

The final class of "positive externalities" refers to goods or services which compete with, by substituting for, other goods and services that generate negative externalities. Then, negative externalities can be reduced by increasing the production of the goods with no (or lower) negative externalities. For example, when mass transit reduces congestion on highways and reduces air pollution directly (auto emissions), or indirectly (oil refinery emissions), there are positive benefits to those who would have suffered from the congestion or pollution.

3.5. Scope of Externalities, Degree of Linkages

In addition to the *magnitude* of positive externalities created by an industry, there are two attributes of those externalities which are important to strategic industry analysis: their geographic scope or incidence and the degree to which they are linked to the firms or industries they impact.

The geographic scope of positive externalities can be local, regional, national, supra-national, or international in scope. In order to be an effective instrument of national economic policy, externalities should be national or intra-national in scope. Even if externalities are large in magnitude, they have no strategic value for a nation if they are international in effect. For example, one of the limits on the use of basic research to promote economic development is that it is very difficult for a nation to capture or appropriate the positive externalities for itself.

One should also distinguish between tightly linked and loosely linked industries (Rosenberg 1982a; Cohen and Zysman 1987). The more tightly linked the industries are, vertically or horizontally, the more the industries are able to isolate the externalities. If there are very tight relationships between users in industry x and suppliers in industry y, then the induced demand effects of expansion by firm x_1, would specifically benefit suppliers to x_1. In loosely linked industries, even large externalities may not matter much because they are so widely diffused in their incidence. R&D intensive industries tend to be more tightly linked, with externalities falling on national firms (Nelson 1984).[16]

3.6. External Economies in Telecommunications Services

Before assessing the magnitude of each of the external economies, consider first the geographic scope of those economies and the degree of linkages with other affected industries. Looking forward to users, telecommunications services are immobile and non-tradeable. To be competitive, a nation must therefore have a first-class telecommunications network—there is no other option. Whatever the strategic value of manufactured goods, there is never a question of availability of supply. There may be competitive advantages to domestic supply over imports, but it is not a matter of doing without. Moreover, as the number and sophistication of telecommunications services increases, the linkage between suppliers and users is growing tighter.

Looking vertically backward to the linkages with telecommunications equipment, these range from very loose (e.g., simple Customer Premises Equipment (CPE) sold directly to the end user or through telecommunications services companies as a channel of distribution) to very tight (sophisticated central office switching equipment). In the former instance, any spillover effects on suppliers are international in scope, since suppliers anywhere could enjoy the benefits of induced demand, internal economies, and positive externalities.

In the latter instance, the linkages are extremely tight, and growing tighter (Harris 1990). If one observes how long it takes for a switch maker to develop a relationship with a potential customer and how many of the foreign telecommunications equipment manufacturers have located major R&D and manufacturing facilities in the United States, it is quite evident that many of the external economies from telecommunications services to telecommunications equipment are national in scope. The most important horizontal externalities in telecommunications services, especially for complementary services, are also national in their incidence. The French investment in a packet switching network and Minitel terminals has induced over 10,000 suppliers of complementary information services in France; it has had virtually no spillover effects into the United States.

3.6.1. Horizontal Externalities

For fifty years, telecommunications policy in the United States was driven largely by the goal of universal service, which was in turn based on a recognition of the positive externalities of additional customers on the network. Having achieved that goal, it seems we have forgotten the principle, which is as applicable to the next generation of telecommunications services as it was to the last. Much of the value of ISDN or broadband integrated services to any given user will depend on how many others have access to them.

There are also powerful horizontal externalities on complementary industries, especially information services. Capabilities built into the public switched network could greatly facilitate access to—and thereby demand for—enhanced communication and information services.

3.6.2. Backward Vertical Externalities

The backward vertical externalities to manufacturers of sophisticated telecommunications equipment are also quite strong, with important second-order effects as well. The first-order effects include the induced demand for equipment, which provides incentives and revenues to support research and development and enables suppliers to realize economies of scale and scope in equipment manufacturing. There are also significant externalities upstream in technology (especially in software), and learning by doing, and using (witness the large number of joint R&D ventures between telecommunications services providers and telecommunications equipment manufacturers). Upstream second-order effects include the horizontal spillovers from telecommunications equipment manufacturers to related industries, including the electronics, semiconductor, computer, and software industries (e.g., the development of the transistor and semiconductors at Bell Labs) (Shooshan & Jackson 1989).

3.6.3. Forward Vertical Externalities

The most significant externalities, and therefore the greatest potential strategic advantage, of telecommunications services are those that benefit users. In the past decade or so, telecommunications services have literally revolutionized many industries; in virtually all industries and sectors, telecommunications services have generated or have the potential to generate major productivity gains.

Two recent studies of the role of telecommunications services in regional economic development have concluded that telecommunications services are playing an increasingly important role, especially in the high-technology, knowledge-intensive industries that generate skilled jobs and a high degree of learning on the job. Coopers and Lybrand (1987) found that purchases of telecommunications services by business in the United States were growing at the rate of 11.8% per year, compared with GNP growth rates averaging 2.5%. Employment is growing fastest in "telecom-intensive" industries. Even though unit costs are declining, purchases of telecommunications services are a growing share of business costs. Consequently, business users are more price-sensitive and mobile, so the local cost and quality of telecommunications services play an increasingly important role in business location decisions. The OECD study (1988) found extraordinarily rapid growth in the importance of telecommunications services to business users, with crucial effects on international competition in telecommunications-intensive industries.

In his study of the impact of information technologies on service industries (financial services, health care, insurance, and publishing), Quinn (1987) found substantial forward linkage economies and externalities, including realization of economies of scale and economies of scope (the capacity to provide entirely new service products through the same service network); output complexity (an enormous increase in the quantity and quality of services); a blurring of industry boundaries through functional cross-competition; and improved international competitiveness, through the locational decisions of manufacturers who use these services.

One of the most critical downstream benefits of telecommunications services is the increased geographic extensiveness of user industries. In urban areas, this extension improves accessibility and enhances competition among goods and service providers (e.g., Automated Teller Machines competing with branch banks; telemarketers competing with local retailers). In rural areas, this often means a substantial improvement in the quality of service available, or even the difference between having service or not (e.g., remote health care services).

In observing the growing linkages between telecommunications services suppliers and users, it is evident that the vertical economies and externalities are, if anything, growing over time. For an increasing number of industries, access to advanced telecommunications services will be essential to competitive advantage—possibly even competitive survival—in global markets.

3.6.4. Reduce Negative Externalities

Although the greater potential may lie in the future, telecommunications services are, generally speaking, a substitute for transportation. From telecommuting to the use of on-line classified advertising and direct marketing services, telecommunications has the potential to reduce urban congestion and air pollution, two of our most serious national problems. In the future, widespread availability of affordable teleconferencing facilities may reduce the demand for inter-city travel and thereby ease congestion in airports and the air traffic control system.

When taken together, the internal economies and positive externalities of telecommunications services afford a significant opportunity for improving the economic performance of the United States economy. Other nations—developed and developing—have been and will be devoting considerable attention to devising policies that exploit these opportunities to improve the quality of life and the competitiveness of their economies and enterprises. In the next section, we will examine the implications for United States telecommunications policy, of telecommunications services as a strategic industry and of the growing use of telecommunications as an instrument of national and supra-national economic strategy.

4. Public Policy Implications

One of the main problems with the term "strategic industry" is that it immediately conjures up images of "industrial policy," of targeting large public subsidies for investment or R&D in the industry in question and/or of trade protectionism. That is not what I have in mind. The question is not, however, whether we will have industry policies, but what those policies will be (Patrick 1986). We have, and will continue to have, public policies with very significant effects on telecommunications services, its suppliers, and its users. Antitrust, regulation, government procurement, taxation, and trade policies directly affect the evolution of the telecommunications industries, the dynamics of competition and technological change in those industries, and the competitiveness of telecommunications equipment suppliers and users in their respective markets.

The chief implication of the strategic nature of telecommunications is that policymakers should take far greater account of the dynamic consequences of policy and implementation decisions. The United States cannot have a unified "national telecommunications policy"—the industries are too complex and the policy making process too complicated. However, when specific policy issues are addressed, though, the strategic industry perspective could inform the policy debate and shift the weights given to various policy criteria. It would cause policymakers to explicitly incorporate some of the more important internal economies and external benefits of telecommunications services into their analyses and decisions. While there is little systematic, quantitative evidence of these effects, it is better to use qualitative information than to ignore these factors altogether.

The objective of this section, then, is to consider some specific examples of telecommunications policies and how they might be affected by the strategic industry perspective.

4.1. Tax and Investment Policies

One of the most striking characteristics of traditional telecommunications policies in the United States can best be seen in contrast to policies toward public infrastructure industries, including:

Transportation Infrastructures: highways, roads and streets; airports & airways; inland waterways & ports; the postal system;

Electric Power: Large scale power generation, transmission (hydroelectrics, TVA), municipals (generation, distribution), REA;

Water Supply & Distribution: dams, reservoirs, distribution;

Education/Knowledge Infrastructure: elementary, secondary schools; state colleges and universities; public libraries, publications and data sources.

Privately provided infrastructure industries in the United States include:
Transportation: railways,[17] and oil and gas pipelines;

Electric power: investor-owned electric utilities in generation, transmission and distribution;

Communications: wireline telephone network, cable TV, and mobile/cellular telephone.

The general recognition of the economic developmental effects of investments in public infrastructure provided the economic rationale for major public funding commitments. The economic rationale is no less true of private sector infrastructure industries, but, because they have been privately provided, there has been much less public awareness and discussion of these benefits. Consequently, public policies have treated infrastructure industries very differently, depending on whether they are public or private. The differences in treatment of public and private infrastructure industries include direct and indirect subsidies:

(1) For some public infrastructure services, users pay no fees (e.g., elementary, secondary education), or fees which do not cover the full costs of service (higher education; airports, highways, and waterways). In contrast, users of private infrastructure services pay prices that cover the total cost of those services.

(2) Most public infrastructure investment are financed by debt with tax-free interest, which greatly reduces the capital costs of those large investments compared to private infrastructure investments, which are financed with taxable-interest debt;

(3) Public infrastructure is exempt from state and local property taxes. Because private infrastructure industries are also capital intensive (land, buildings, right-of-way structures, and equipment), their property taxes are very substantial.

(4) Public entities pay no Federal, state, or local corporate income tax, which significantly reduces their effective cost of capital. Private infrastructure providers, in contrast, pay enormous amounts of corporate income taxes.

(5) Gasoline or airline excise "taxes" are actually user charges which cover some, but not all, of the costs of the services consumed by auto owners or air passengers. Telecommunications users pay excise and gross receipts taxes, which, for the most part, are not used to recover the costs of telecommunications service.

Table 1 shows the taxes paid by telecommunications common carriers, as reported to the Federal Communications Commission, over the past 25 years. Although taxes as a percentage of total operating revenues have decreased from 21% to 13%, that still represents a substantial share, especially in comparison to public infrastructure industries, which pay none of these taxes. The imposition of these taxes discourages investment in the telecommunications network and usage of the network.

Table 1. Telecommunications Taxes: 1965-1987									
($ millions; excluding social security taxes)									
	Federal Income Taxes	Deferred Fed. Inc. Taxes	St/Local Income Taxes	Property Taxes	Gross Receipts Taxes	Other Taxes	Total Taxes*	Operating Rev.	Taxes/ Revs
1987	5420	3448	819	2459	1618	350	14115	106334	13%
1986	5050	4543	761	2327	1790	286	14758	111249	13%
1985	3326	4030	746	2227	1647	274	12251	74745	16%
1984	2453	3541	585	2183	1827	263	10851	66327	16%
1982	430	3823	586	2085	1495	250	8669	60370	14%
1981	891	2867	513	1978	1322	251	7822	52041	15%
1980	496	2459	417	1839	1164	237	6612	44141	15%
1975	189	1486	236	1488	747	120	4266	27919	15%
1970	1535	76	141	960	417	64	3194	16987	19%
1965	1456	0	49	608	227	69	2409	11237	21%
Source: Statistics Communications Common Carriers—Federal Communications Commission									

The point of this discussion is not that we should convert private infrastructure industries to public ownership, nor that we should make large public subsidies to telecommunications. The point is that telecommunications investment generates tremendous social value in excess of private returns, and we should carefully design public policies that are cognizant of and promote the realization of those social benefits. That may mean targeted public subsidies in some instances (e.g., to support rural telephone infrastructure investment and service), as competition reduces the feasibility of continuing cross-subsidies through regulated rates. It may mean reducing the taxation of telecommunication services (i.e., excise and gross receipts taxes), as a means of promoting greater usage, thereby stimulating additional private investment.

4.2. Line-of-Business Policies toward Local Exchange Carriers (LECs)

From the perspective of economic growth and development, the imposition of line-of-business restrictions on a strategic industry makes very little sense. Although there are legitimate concerns about the use of market power in one line of business for anticompetitive purpose in other lines of business, the use of outright prohibitions eliminates the possibility of carriers realizing economies of scope and reduces the generation of horizontal and vertical spillovers to other industries. The use of regulatory controls to prevent cross-subsidies and predatory pricing, in contrast, enables the nation to capture these economies and externalities, while protecting against anticompetitive abuses. This argument is particularly applicable to the following line-of-business restrictions:

4.2.1. MFJ Manufacturing Restriction on the RHCs

The Modified Final Judgement (MFJ) restriction on manufacturing and manufacturing-related research and development reduces incentives for technological development of the network and inhibits learning economies between equipment manufacturing and telecommunications services (by reducing the potential for "double loop learning" and positive feedback effects in joint R&D). No other nation has imposed such onerous restrictions on their telecommunications service providers (Harris 1989). The effects of this restriction are especially harmful because upward learning economies and synergies are much greater between network-based products and services (e.g., central office switching and CLASS services) than with CPE (which is becoming a "commodity" product). In combination with the inherent conflict of interest between AT&T's dual role as a regional holding company (RHC) supplier (of equipment) and competitor (in interexchange and information services), the manufacturing restriction biases RHC supplier relations toward foreign firms (Harris 1990). Consequently, over the long-run, RHC investment in telecommunications infrastructure will improve the competitiveness of those foreign-based equipment manufacturers in global markets.

4.2.2. MFJ Information Services Restriction on the RHCs

The MFJ information services restriction (which may be subject to major change given the recent decision of the Circuit Court of Appeals overturning Judge Green's decision) greatly reduces the incentive for information services R&D and network investment. Substantial enhancements of the network such as ISDN may not be economic unless there is a large increase in the variety of services and volume of usage (and LEC's are allowed to price that usage economically). Given the network externalities, these restrictions also reduce the probability of reaching a "critical mass;" the "demand pull" of a mass market may be necessary for inducing an adequate supply of value-added and other information services, revenues from which could allow recovery of network investment.

4.2.3. Cable Cross-Ownership and Channel Service Restrictions on Local Exchange Telephone Carriers

The cable TV cross-ownership restriction, in combination with channel services regulation and local franchise monopolies in cable TV, represents a major obstacle to deployment of a broadband fiber network. Revenues from the carriage of video services is almost certainly a necessary condition to justify economic investment in fiber ISBN (Pepper 1988), analogous to the "joint use" of highways, railways, and airways for passenger and freight services and hydroelectric projects for electricity generation, flood control, and recreation. The potential upward external economies from domestic investment in a broadband network are enormous and would position equipment suppliers located in the United States to play a major role in subsequent broadband investments in other countries. In the absence of a major shift in United States policy, it seems likely that, given Japan's investment commitment to a fiber optic network, Japanese telecommunications equipment suppliers will acheive a competitive advantage in fiber optic equipment markets.

4.3. Rate of Return Regulation of Local Exchange Carriers

Given recent and pending changes in competition policy (e.g., intraLATA entry), there has been a substantial increase in the riskiness of LEC capital investment through the increased probability of stranded or underutilized investment due to loss of market share to new entrants and lower profitability due to post-entry price competition. Similarly, LEC's are experiencing, relative to the stable technological environment of prior decades, significantly increased risk due to uncertainty about the future rate of technological change. In light of those risks, LEC's face a serious asymmetry in their allowed rate of return as set by state regulators. If risky investments are successful, LEC profits will be limited to (or near) the LEC's cost of capital (even if it involves "recontracting" after a brief lag, as under a price cap regime). If the LEC investment is unsuccessful, shareholders bear the cost of failure, without a corresponding upside potential. This bias in rate-of-return regulation reduces economic incentives for modernization and expansion of local exchange telephone networks, which is directly contrary to the states' economic development interests.

4.4. Rate Regulation of Local Exchange Carriers

Virtually all telecommunications rate design questions would benefit from a strategic industry analysis, but three issues best illustrate how policymakers could explicitly incorporate the strategic consequences of pricing decisions. While one could reasonably support the following policy prescriptions solely on the grounds of static efficiency effects, the arguments are much stronger when dynamic, strategic effects are also considered.

4.4.1. Pricing of Central Office Services

Historical regulatory efforts to keep the price of "basic service" (access and local usage) as low as possible, have been accompanied by pricing of central office services (custom calling features) greatly in excess of costs. This traditional treatment of "discretionary services" reduces market penetration and the potential for cost recovery of network upgrades (e.g., digital switching in low or no growth markets can often be justified only on the basis of revenues from new, enhanced services). Likewise, the pricing of enhanced services biases the choices of large, sophisticated customers from Centrex to Private Branch Exchanges (PBX) and the choices of small users from Central Office-based services to answering machines, speed/auto dialers, and the like.

In addition to the static inefficiencies of these price distortions, there are substantial strategic consequences as well. Whereas the United States has world-class technology and manufacturing capability in central office switching and software, it has no technology lead or manufacturing advantage in small CPE or auxiliary telephone equipment. Hence, these pricing distortions and regulatory obstacles to new LEC services reduce the incidence of backward vertical externalities that would accrue to switch manufacturers in the United States.

4.4.2. Pricing of Special Services

Rapidly increasing differences among customer needs and preferences requires the widespread use of special contracts, with terms and conditions designed to meet particular situations. The lack of pricing flexibility for LECs, combined with long delays in obtaining approval of special services contracts, is a substantial competitive disadvantage in markets with demanding customers and unregulated competitors. The LEC's inability to price special contracts flexibly inhibits network utilization, thereby denying economies of scale and scope in local exchange networks.

Beyond the loss of internal economies though, are the potential loss of network externalities for other users, since large users have choices biased away from the public switched network and toward private networks. This bias reduces interoperability of the network, since private networks have a lower degree of access and interconnection than the public switched network (Bar 1987).

4.4.3. Usage Sensitive Pricing

In most states, the pricing of access and local calling is completely out of line with cost causality: a much larger share of costs are non-traffic sensitive than are revenues. The underpricing of local usage through flat rate residential rates reduces the economic incentives for local network upgrades that would facilitate access to and use of information services. Recalling the earlier discussion of horizontal externalities from telecommunications services to complementary services, usage-sensitive pricing would enable LECs to capture some share of the value they create by providing access to information services providers such as Telenet, Tymenet, or Prodigy. The additional revenues generated by such usage would provide the incentive and the resources for network upgrades. The magnitude of the problem, and the potential strategic gains of usage-based pricing, will vastly increase with the emergence of new services that will increase local usage (e.g., voice messaging services).

4.5. Federal-State Jurisdictional Issues

One of the most important implications of telecommunications as a strategic industry is jurisdictional: since many of the potential economic benefits of strategic telecommunications policy are at least regional or even national in their scope, I will argue for a declining state involvement in telecommunications regulation, through less regulation by the states and through a jurisdictional shift to the Federal Communications Commission. It is increasingly apparent that competition among the states for the economic development benefits of an upgraded network and improved information services promotes progressive regulatory policies and constrains states from ignoring some of the external economies generated by telecommunications services. Even so, because the telecommunications infrastructure is inherently national, substantial differences in public policies among the states raises the cost of doing business.

The United States is one of a few countries with substantial local involvement in telecommunications policy. The growing interest in the strategic national consequences of telecommunications regulation, when combined with the growing trend toward provisioning more telecommunications services on an interstate basis,[18] undermines the rationale for state regulation . While it is unlikely that states will accede to Federal authority without a battle, the strategic industry perspective points toward a gradual diminution of the state role in telecommunications regulatory policy. While there will continue to be an important role for states to play, it will lie mainly in promoting telecommunications services to generate and capture local economies and externalities to attract business and industry and stimulate economic development.

5. Conclusion

Historically, United States policies toward public infrastructure industries have incorporated—if implicitly—developmental benefits of internal and external economies. The United States has been an international leader in public infrastructure investment and technological development. Major public investments in the economic infrastructure have played a significant role in the nation's economic growth and global leadership over the past several decades.

Unfortunately, public recognition of similar economic benefits from private infrastructure has lagged behind. Only recently, as other nations have turned their attention to telecommunications services as a means of promoting economic growth—as an instrument of national economic strategy—have United States policymakers begun to take sufficient notice. Merely declaring that telecommunications is a strategic industry will matter very little, of course. But concerted efforts to measure the internal and external economies from telecommunications services and an honest endeavor to consider and incorporate those effects in public policy decisions can potentially improve the performance of telecommunications industries and the nation's economy.

Notes

The author gratefully acknowledges the research assistance of Joanne Oxley; the helpful comments of David Mowery, Michael Crew and Timothy Brennan; and the financial support of the Pew Charitable Trusts, through its research grant to the Center for Research in Management at the University of California, Berkeley.

1. The comparison is based on an analysis of international patents, using an index of five year accumulations of patents, excluding those of "minor" significance (Schnoring 1989, 16).
2. For descriptions of specific information technology initiatives in leading European nations, see Gassman (1985); for an analysis and comparison of European and North American industrial policies toward information technologies, see Rothwell (1986).
3. See, for example, Japanese Ministry of Posts and Telecommunications (1987; 1988; 1989); and Japan Information Processing Development Center (1987).
4. For an analysis of recent developments in Japanese telecommunications policy and its implications for the United States, see Harris (1989).
5. Although that literature is concerned primarily with international trade theory and policy, and hence addresses "tradeable goods," much of the developing theory applies to non-tradeable goods as well and is therefore relevant here.
6. For an early effort at classifying the characteristics of a strategic industry, see Gresser (1984).
7. "Regional" can mean sub-national (the San Francisco Bay area, the "Northeast") or supra-national (the European Community).
8. Economies that spillover to other firms in the industry are included under horizontal external economies.
9. Large relative to the size of the relevant market and as a percentage of total costs.
10. Strictly speaking, network economies could be expressed as a combination of scale and scope economies; I have chosen to classify and describe them separately for ease of exposition.
11. One main reason for the displacement of existing firms in an industry by new firms due to a radical change in technology is that individual and organizational learning may be technology specific. Thus, the leading vacuum tube producers were unsuccessful in the transistor industry because they had learned "too well."
12. The "choice" of an industry standard, such as the QWERTY keyboard, the 12-hour clock, or the VHS videotape format, may be a random occurence, i.e., not reflecting superior technology or economics. Once established, however, such standards can be difficult or impossible to replace, even by clearly superior technologies.
13. Actually, most large-scale public investments in infrastructure industries such as highways, airways, and hydroelectric plants were justified largely in terms of their positive effects on economic development, i.e., their positive externalities.
14. In the case of the railroads, for example, the use of "checkerboard" land grants (alternating sections of 640 acres or one square mile) along the right-of-way was a very clever and successful mechanisms for internalizing many of the positive externalities created by railroad investment.
15. The dominance of Boeing in world aircraft markets, for example, is in part the result of the substantial United States public investment in airports and the promotion of airlines through a system of regulation which cross-subsidized service to small cities.
16. In assessing the degree of linkage and geographic scope of positive externalities, one should distinguish between effects on national firms and effects on the national economy. If there are substantial externalities from industry x to industry y, the scope of which is national, and the linkage is very tight, rapid development of industry x in the United States may or may not benefit United States firms in industry y. Alternatively, the strong linkages between x and y may induce relocation of foreign firms in industry y to locate in the United States in order to realize the benefits of those vertical externalities. For national economic development, it is the location of economic activity not the national identity of its corporate owner, that matters most (Reich 1990).
17. Railroads in the United States are privately owned, but were built with massive cash grants, land grants, loans, and loan guarantees.
18. With optical fiber, the costs of long distance transport continue to fall dramatically; as toll rates fall, interstate calling will presumably increase. In addition, services that appear "local" in character,

such as voice messaging, can often be provisioned more economically through centralized facilities (e.g., a switch in Boston serving the New England states).

References

Arthur, W. Brian. 1989. "Competing Technologies, Increasing Returns, and Lock-In by Historical Events." *The Economic Journal* 99:394 (March): 116-131.

Barr, Francois, and Michael Borrus. 1987. "From Public Access to Private Connections: Network Policy and National Advantage." BRIE Working Paper No. 28, University of California, Berkeley (September): 1-18.

Biehl, Dieter. 1982. *The Contribution of Infrastructure to Regional Development*. Commission of the European Communities.

Bernstein, Jeffrey, and M. Ishaq Nadiri. 1988. "Inter-industry R&D Spillovers, Rates of Return, and Production in High-Tech industries." National Bureau of Economic Research. Working paper No. 2554 (April)

Cawson, Alan 1987. "The Teletext Initiative in Britain: The Anatomy of Successful New-Corporatist Policy-making." Conference on New Technologies and Intermediaries, Stanford University (June).

Cohen, Stephen S., and John Zysman. 1987. *Manufacturing Matters*. New York: Basic Books.

Coopers and Lybrand. 1987. *State Policy & Telecommunication Economy in New York: Final Report*. New York State Office of Economic Development.

David, Paul. 1988. "Path-Dependence: Putting the Past into the Future of Economics." I.M.S.S.S. Technical Report (No. 533, November). Stanford University.

David, Paul A. 1969. "Transport Innovation and Economic Growth: Professor Vogel on and off the Rails." *The Economic History Review*, Second Series 22, No. 3, (December): 506- 525.

Dosi, Giovanni. 1988. "Sources, Procedures and Microeconomic Effects of Innovation." *Journal of Economic Literature* 26 (no. 3, September): 1120-1171.

Fishlow, Albert. 1965. *American Railroads and the Transformation of the Ante-Bellum Economy*. Cambridge: Harvard University Press.

Gassman, H.P. 1985. "Information Technology Policy in Europe and Japan." In *The Information Economy: Its Implications for Canadian Industrial Strategy*, edited by Calvin B. Gotlieb, 112-125. Ontario, Canada: Royal Society of Canada.

Gresser, Julian. 1984. *Partners in Prosperity*. New York: McGraw-Hill.

Harris, Robert G. 1988. *California Telecommunications Policy for the Twenty-First Century*. Sacramento: California Economic Development Corporation (June).

Harris, Robert G. 1989. "Telecommunications Policy in Japan: Lessons for the U.S." *California Management Review* 31 (no. 3, Spring): 113-131.

Harris, Robert G. 1990. "Divestiture and Regulatory Policy: Implications for Research, Development and Innovation in the U.S. Telecommunications Industry." *Telecommunications Policy* 14 (no. 2, April).

Hirschman, Albert O. 1958. *The Strategy of Economic Development*. New Haven and London: Yale University Press.

Japanese Ministry of Posts and Telecommunications. 1987; 1988; 1989. *White Paper: Communications in Japan* (Annual editions). Tokyo.

Japan Information Processing Development Center. 1987. *Informatization White Paper*. Tokyo (March).

Kantrow, Alan M. 1986. "Government Policy and the Competitive Effects of Innovation."

In *Competitiveness through Technology*, edited by Jerry Dermer, 3-10. Lexington: Lexington Books.

Krugman, Paul. 1983. "New Theories of Trade Among Industrialized Countries." *American Economic Review* 73 (no. 2, May): 343-347.

Krugman, Paul. 1987. "Is Free Trade Passe?" *Journal of Economic Perspectives* 1 (no. 2, Fall): 131-144.

Krugman, Paul. 1987. "Strategic Sectors and International Competition." In *U.S Trade Policies in a Changing World Economy*, edited by Robert M. Stern, 207-232. Cambridge: MIT Press.

Nelson, Richard. 1984. *High Tech Policies: A 5-Nation Comparison*. Washington, DC: American Enterprise Institute.

OECD. 1988. *The Telecommunications Industry: The Challenges of Structural Change*. OECD Series: Information, Computer and Communications Policy (No.14). Paris.

Patrick, Hugh. 1986. "Japanese High Technology Industrial Policy in Comparative Perspective." In *Japan's High Technology Industries*, edited by Hugh Patrick, 3-35. Seattle: University of Washington Press.

Pepper, Robert M. 1988. "Through the Looking Glass: Integrated Broadband Networks, Regulatory Policy and Institutional Change." Federal Communications Commission, OPP Working Paper Series (no. 24, November): 1-106.

Porter, Michael. 1989. "The Competitive Advantage of Nations." *Harvard Business Review* (March-April): 73-93.

Quinn, James. 1987. "The Impacts of Technology in the Services Sector." In *Technology and Global Industry: Companies and Nations in the World Economy*, edited by Bruce R. Guile and Harvey Brooks . Washington, DC: National Academy Press: 119-159.

Reich, Robert. 1990. "Who is Us?" *Harvard Business Review* (March-April).

Rosenberg, Nathan. 1982a. "Learning by Using." In *Inside the Black Box: Technology and Economics*, edited by Nathan Rosenberg, 120-140. Cambridge: Cambridge University Press.

Rosenberg, Nathan. 1982b. "Technological Interdependence in the American Economy." In *Inside the Black Box: Technology and Economics*, edited by Nathan Rosenberg, 55-80. Cambridge: Cambridge University Press.

Rothwell, Roy. 1986. "Technological Change and Reindustrialization: In Search of a Policy Framework." In *Competitiveness through Technology*, edited by Jerry Dermer, 97-122. Lexington: Lexington Books.

Rubinger, Bruce. 1986. "Competing through Technology: The Success Factors." In *Competitiveness through Technology*, edited by Jerry Dermer, 25-38. Lexington: Lexington Books.

Rugman, Alan M., and Alain Verbeke. 1989. "Strategic Trade Policy is not Good Strategy." San Francisco: Strategic Management Society Conference (October).

Schnoring, Thomas. 1989. "Research and Development in Telecommunications: An International Comparison." Airlie House, VA: Telecommunications Policy Research Conference (October).

Shin, Richard Tong-Jun. 1988. "Econometric Estimation of Telephone Costs for Local Exchange Companies: Implications for Economies of Scale and Scope and Regulatory Policy." Unpublished doctoral dissertation, University of California, Berkeley.

Shoosan and Jackson Inc. 1989. *The Impact of Regulation and Public Policy on Telecommunications Infrastructure and U.S. Competitiveness*. Washington, DC: Northeast-Midwest Institute, The Center for Regional Policy (April).

Teece, David J. 1987 "Profiting from Technological Innovation: Implications for Integration, Collaboration, Licensing and Public Policy." In *The Competitive Challenge*, edited by David J. Teece, 185-220. Cambridge: Ballinger.

Thimm, Alfred L. 1989. "Europe 1992—Opportunity or Threat for U.S. Business: The Case for Telecommunications." *California Management Review* 31 (no. 2, Winter): 54-75.

von Hippel, Eric. 1988. *The Sources of Innovation*. New York: Oxford University Press.

7

PRODUCTIVITY GROWTH AND TECHNOLOGICAL CHANGE IN THE UNITED STATES TELECOMMUNICATIONS EQUIPMENT MANUFACTURING INDUSTRIES

Show-Ling Jang
J.R. Norsworthy

Semiconductor technology lies at the heart of the revolution in information technology. While the official price index in the National Income and Product Accounts for computers has been revised to account for changes in the performance characteristics of computer systems (Cole, et al. 1986), no comparable modification has been made to the price of semiconductor devices. Yet semiconductor devices incorporated in telecommunication equipment have been largely responsible for the technological change that led to deregulation of the telecommunication services industry. The rapid rate of adoption of advanced telecommunication equipment and the decline in cost (without corresponding decline in quality) of telecommunication services are indirect qualitative evidence for embodied quality change in telecommunication equipment. Our empirical investigation is designed to develop quantitative evidence for quality change in semiconductor devices based on their use in telecommunication equipment. We have carried out a similar investigation for the contribution of semiconductor devices to productivity growth in computer equipment (Jang and Norsworthy 1988). In that case, however, the prior quality adjustment of computer industry output for improved performance left large unexplained total factor productivity growth.

There is also no comparable quality-adjusted price and quantity information for telecommunication equipment as there is for computer equipment. We are, therefore, drawing inferences about quality changes in semiconductors from the pattern of substitution of semiconductor devices for other inputs. Under these circumstances, we expect that our estimates of quality change in semiconductors will be lower than those that would be obtained with additional information measuring quality change in telecommunication equipment.[1]

The productivity growth of United States telecommunication equipment manufacturing industries (SIC 3661 and 3662) during 1967-86 is measured based on the data from the Census of Manufacturers and Annual Survey of Manufacturers, deflated by price indexes developed from the Producer Price Index program. Since the output data for these industries has not been adjusted for quality change comparable to that carried out for the computer industry, the measures of their productivity growth in this study is downward biased. However, it is a good demonstration of how the direct measurement of productivity growth can be conducted through a growth accounting approach and econometric model. The framework of this paper is as follows. We describe the characteristics of United States telecommunications equipment manufacturing industries in section 1. The econometric models are outlined in section 2. Estimated empirical results are analyzed in section 3. Section 4 reports the conclusions. Data sources, measurement, and concepts are described and discussed in detail in the appendix.

1. Characteristics of the United States Telecommunications Equipment Manufacturing Industries

Time series data for two four-digit industries, SIC 3661, telephone and telegraph apparatus, and SIC 3662, radio and TV communication equipment—which we designate as "other" telecommunication equipment, are the basis for this study. The telephone and telegraph equipment industry (SIC 3661) includes manufacturers of switching and switchboard equipment (SIC 36611) and telephone sets, teleprinters, modems, and other telephone and telegraph apparatus and parts in SIC 36612.

The incorporation of new equipment into communications networks, in response to the new digital technology and increased competition in the early 1980s, accounts for the increase in the shipments of telephone and telegraph equipment industry from $12.3 billion in 1980 to the peak $17.8 billion in 1985. The United States network is continuing its conversion from analog to digital systems. The slowing pace of network expansion and modernization has led to declines in shipments to $15.7 billion in 1986, because most of the conversion has been completed.

The radio and TV communications ("other" telecommunication equipment) industry (SIC 3662) is divided into seven categories: (1) communication equipment, except broadcast (SIC 36621); (2) broadcast, studio, and related equipment (SIC 36622); (3) alarm systems (SIC 36624); (4) search and detection, navigation, and guidance equipment (SIC 36625); (5) traffic control equipment (SIC 36626); (6) intercommunication equipment (SIC 36628); and (7) electronic systems and equipment, not elsewhere classified (SIC 36629). Search, detection, navigation, and guidance equipment is the dominant category in SIC 3662, accounting for about 60 percent of all product shipments in 1988. Demand for this equipment is primarily determined by large-scale government procurements for new military applications. Although many of these products were originally designed for military uses, a substantial and increasing number—including radar, sonar, air traffic control equipment, and electronic navigation—now have established markets in the civilian sector.

Telecommunication equipment except broadcast is the next largest category in SIC 3662, representing about 23 percent of total product shipments by the industry in 1988. This category includes fiber optic systems, mobile and cellular radio equipment, and facsimile equipment.[2]

Shipments of other telecommunication equipment, SIC 3662, have increased by a factor of four in the last decade from $13.2 billion in 1976 to $51.7 billion in 1986[3], driven by United States government purchases and rapid technological change.[4]

All of these equipment types in both industries incorporate microelectronic components—chiefly semiconductor devices—as switches, microprocessors, controllers, etc.

2. The Econometric Models

An earlier paper formulates econometric methods for measuring the quality change embodied in an input used in production (Jang and Norsworthy 1990). In this paper, we apply the approach to assess the contribution of semiconductor inputs in the two telecommunications equipment manufacturing industries. Output prices have simply been analyzed as given.[5]

Much of "other" telecommunications equipment (SIC 3662) goes to industries other than telecommunication services—to radio and television broadcasting, to defenseelectronics, and so forth. Once again, these products are not sold to conventional enterprises producing output forcompetitive markets; however, there is no basis at present to adjust the output prices. Because regulation of telecommunications services limited profits through an upperlimit on the rate of return per unit of capital, there probably was an incentive during most of the period studied to build in more product quality and to extend the service lives of the equipment to reduce maintenance costs, etc.For given equipment designs, it is probably reasonable to assume that the equipment was produced at minimum variable cost, the critical assumption for the variable cost function that is used here to model production.

The translog restricted-variable-cost function model introduced by Brown and Christensen (1981) is given by:

$$\ln C = a_o + \Sigma_i a_i \ln p_i + \tfrac{1}{2} \Sigma_i \Sigma_j a_{ij} \ln p_i \ln p_j + b_Y \ln y + b_K \ln k \\ + b_{KY} \ln k \ln y + \tfrac{1}{2} b_{YY} \ln^2 y + \tfrac{1}{2} b_{KK} \ln^2 k \\ + \Sigma_i c_{iY} \ln P_i \ln y + \Sigma_i c_{iK} \ln p_i \ln k \qquad (1)$$

where $i, j = l, n, m, s, v$ for the variable inputs: production worker labor (l), nonproduction labor (n), purchased materials inputs (m), semiconductor inputs (s), and purchased services (v).

p_i = price of variable input i,

y = deflated real gross output,

k = real capital input of structures and equipment, and
C = variable cost of production.

Norsworthy and Jang (1988) argue that the technology of production is best captured in a model that minimizes errors in the quantities of inputs used in production, rather than errors in the cost shares of the inputs. Thus, instead of estimating the cost share equations, we estimate the demand equations for the variable inputs.

Based on Shepard's Lemma, the cost shares for the translog variable cost function are then:

$$\frac{\partial \ln C}{\partial \ln p_i} = s_i = a_i + \Sigma_j a_{ij} \ln p_j + b_{iK} \ln k + b_{iY} \ln Y. \qquad (2)$$

Demand equations for variable inputs are then:

$$q_i = C \times \frac{s_i}{p_i} + e_i \quad i = l, n, m, s, v \qquad (3)$$

where s_i is written as in (2), and e_i is an additive error term.

Restrictions imposing symmetry and homogeneity of degree one of variable cost in prices of variable inputs are as follows:

$$\begin{aligned}
& \Sigma_i a_i = 1 && i = l, n, m, s, v \\
& \Sigma_j a_{ij} = \Sigma_i a_{ij} = 0 && \text{for all } i, j \\
& a_{ij} = a_{ji} && \text{for all } i, j \\
& \Sigma_i c_{iK} = 0 && \text{for all } i \\
& \Sigma_i c_{iY} = 0 && \text{for all } i \\
& b_{YY} + b_{KY} = 0 \\
& b_{KK} + b_{KY} = 0 \\
& c_{iK} = -c_{iY} && \text{for all } i
\end{aligned} \qquad (4)$$

The translog variable cost function is estimated jointly with the five variable input demand equations, using the full information maximum likelihood method (FIML) in the SORITEC econometrics package, separately for each industry, SIC 3661 and SIC 3662, covering the period 1967-86.

The translog variable cost model may be modified to incorporate unmeasured quality change in an input. There are several ways that the modification may be introduced. Here we assume that significant unmeasured quality change in semiconductor input is proportional to measured total factor productivity change in the semiconductor industry, after adjustment for economies of scale. That is, the real or quality adjusted quantity for semiconductor input is higher, due to the rapid technological change, and the real price of the semiconductor input (p_s^*) is expected to be lower than measured in the official statistics (p_s). Thus

$$p_s^* = \frac{p_s}{I^\alpha} \text{ for some } \alpha > 0, \qquad (5)$$

where I is the index of total factor productivity change in the semiconductor industry (SIC 3674). The index is lagged one (SIC 3662) or two (SIC 3661) years to permit time for the currently produced semiconductor devices to be incorporated into the production of telecommunications equipment. In logarithmic form, (5) is expressed as:

$$\ln p_s^* = \ln p_s - \alpha \ln I. \qquad (6)$$

Then the variable cost function in equation (1) can be rewritten, incorporating the modified expression shown in (6), and the parameter estimated as part of the cost function model. Estimates of a quality-adjusted price for semiconductor input may then be calculated after the estimation of the cost function and input demand equations.

Note that the quantity demanded of semiconductor input, q_s^*, must be adjusted to agree with the quality-adjusted price, p_s^* from equation (5). The FIML estimation procedure, however, cannot update q_s^* as shown in the demand equation for semiconductor input as part of the iterative process of determining parameter values. We therefore applied the following procedure:

1. For the initial value of α, compute q_s^* using equation (5).
2. Estimate α as part of the cost function model.
3. Re-compute q_s^* from (5) using the new value of α.
4. Re-estimate α in cost function model using the parameter values from the prior estimation.

Steps 3. and 4. were repeated until successive values of q_s^* for each year differed by less than 1 percent. This procedure converged in three iterations for SIC 3661 and four iterations for SIC 3662 from an initial value of $\alpha = 0.1$.

In this framework, we can also test the hypothesis that $\alpha = 0$, i.e., that there is no significant quality change beyond that reflected in the current official price index for semiconductors. The simplest test is based on the t-statistic for the parameter α. The significance of the contribution of the price adjustment to the estimated model as a whole may also be captured in a likelihood ratio test.

We do not expect the rates of quality augmentation inferred from the two telecommunication equipment industries to be the same. Lancaster's (1971) theory of demand based on characteristics of goods represents an individual product as a bundle of characteristics. For semiconductor inputs, for example, the speed, device density, and power requirements can be expected to yield different advantages over alternative devices in different kinds of communications equipment. Further, a considerable number of different devices are grouped together as output of the semiconductor industry, with correspondingly large differences in function and prices per unit. Thus, it is reasonable to expect that the effects of embodied technical change in manufacture of telephone and telegraph equipment (SIC 3661) may differ in value per unit from that in other communication equipment (SIC 3662).

Total factor productivity or output per unit of total factor input (unadjusted for economies of scale) can be computed as the difference between the annual rates of growth of the input price and output prices by the growth accounting approach. This difference can be computed as the difference between the weighted sum of changes in the logarithms of the input price and changes in the logarithms of input prices between two time periods t and t-1. Total factor productivity (TFP) growth can thus be measured as

$$TFP = \sum_{i=1}^{n} \overline{w}_i (\ln p_{i,t} - \ln p_{i,t-1}) - (\ln p_{Y,t} - \ln p_{Y,t-1}), \qquad (7)$$

where $\overline{w}_i = 0.5 \times (w_{it} + w_{i,t-1})$, $w_{i,t}$ is the value share of put i in total cost, and $i = k, l, n, m, s, v$. $p_{i,t}$ is the price of input i at the time period t, and p_{Yt} is the price of output in period t.

We also compute the scale-adjusted TFP growth ($dTFP$) by including the short term scale-adjustment factor from the estimation of cost function as follows:

$$dTFP_{adj} = dTFP - \left(1 - \frac{\frac{\partial \ln c}{\partial \ln y}}{1 - \frac{\partial \ln c}{\partial \ln k}}\right) \times d\ln y, \qquad (8)$$

where $\frac{\partial \ln c}{\partial \ln y}$ is the output elasticity, and $\frac{\partial \ln c}{\partial \ln k}$ is the shadow cost of capital. $\frac{\partial \ln c}{\partial \ln y}$ and $\frac{\partial \ln c}{\partial \ln k}$ are obtained from the estimated econometric model.

The expression contained in parentheses in (8) is the inverse of the scale elasticity of output derived by Brown and Christensen, altered to measure only the departure from constant returns.

3. Empirical Results

3.1. Estimation of the Variable Cost Function

We have carried out the cost function estimations outlined above for the telecommunications equipment manufacturing industries SIC 3661 and 3662. The results are shown in tables 3.1 and 3.2, respectively.

The coefficients of the estimated variable cost function model for the telephone and telegraph equipment industry (SIC 3661) shown in table 3.1 suggest that most of the model characteristics are satisfactory. With the exception of the demand for "materials" in industry 3662, the input demand functions are concave in their own prices, as the elasticities in table 3.4 show. The shadow cost of capital, b_K, however is effectively zero. It was necessary to constrain the coefficient to be nonpositive.

Table 3.1. Estimated Translog Variable Cost Function
U.S. Telephone and Telegraph Apparatus Industry (SIC 3661)

Coefficient Name	Estimated Value	Standard Error	T-statistic
AO	5.86490	0.126935E-02	4620.38
RC	0.993904	0.416678E-02	238.530
AN	0.181473	0.183097E-02	99.1128
AM	0.427731	0.625821E-02	68.3471
AS	0.479590E-01	0.172259E-02	27.8411
ALPHA	1.66012	0.181556E-02	91.4383
AV	0.223830	0.260925E-01	85.7831
ANM	-0.522747E-01	0.105519E-01	-4.95404
ANS	0.697437E-02	0.269996E-02	2.58314
ANV	0.989119E-01	0.706931E-02	13.9917
AMS	-0.220558E-01	0.348632E-02	-6.32639
AMV	-0.135627E-03	0.745245E-02	-0.181990E-01
ASV	-0.206089E-01	0.175585E-02	-11.7373
ANN	0.231291E-01	0.153492E-01	1.50686
AMM	0.459946E-01	0.130171E-01	3.53339
ASS	-0.630563E-02	0.163172E-02	-3.86442
AVV	-0.146525	0.118612E-01	-12.3533
BY	0.579204	0.274048E-01	-21.1351
BK	-0.206442E-03	0.516433E-04	-3.99746
BKY	-0.924551	0.262008E-02	-352.871
CNE	0.707162E-02	0.811752E-02	0.871155
CME	0.229647E-01	0.140146E-01	1.63863
CSE	0.175761E-01	0.524054E-02	3.35387
CVE	-0.183063E-01	0.430067E-02	-4.25661
RL	0.398672	0.380027E-01	10.4906
RN	-0.409541	0.658190E-02	-62.2223
RM	0.504577E-01	0.126469E-01	3.98974
RS	0.290422	0.130522E-01	22.2508
RV	-0.478562	0.119823E-01	-39.9391

Log of Likelihood Function = 187.71

Equation Name	R^2	Durbin-Watson
Cost Function	0.9962	1.5026
Input Demand Equations:		
Production Workers	0.8844	2.4896
Nonproduction Workers	0.8919	1.2246
Materials	0.9950	1.5358
Semiconductors	0.9978	1.8832
Purchased Services	0.9844	1.2706

Table 3.2. Estimated Translog Variable Cost Function
Other Communications Equipment Industry (SIC 3662)

Coefficient Name	Estimated Value	Standard Error	T-statistics
AO	5.65704	0.160513E-03	35234.6
RC	0.980776	0.102392E-02	957.867
AN	0.259727	0.112298E-02	231.284
AM	0.268593	0.252597E-02	106.332
AS	0.561726E-01	0.117123E-02	47.9603
ALPHA	5.29281	0.815953E-03	6486.66
AV	0.232043	0.755138E-03	307.286
ANM	-0.100187	0.167950E-02	-59.6529
ANS	0.122940E-01	0.783586E-03	15.6894
ANV	0.351788E-01	0.413056E-02	8.51673
AMS	-0.202469E-01	0.118063E-02	-17.1493
AMV	-0.321945E-01	0.395280E-02	-8.14473
ASV	-0.134477E-01	0.313199E-03	-42.9366
ANN	0.756121E-02	0.439080E-02	1.72206
AMM	0.224842	0.788187E-02	28.5265
ASS	0.746830E-02	0.525726E-03	14.2057
AVV	-0.250932E-01	0.495388E-02	-5.06536
BY	0.902255	0.210695E-02	428.228
BK	-0.622389E-01	0.940764E-04	-661.577
BKY	-0.360841	0.21691OE-03	-1663.55
CNE	0.316222E-01	0.917724E-02	3.44572
CME	0.991881E-01	0.105925E-01	9.36398
CSE	-0.728733E-01	0.220668E-02	-33.0240
CVE	0.476278E-01	0.181685E-02	26.2144
RL	-0.347380E-01	0.277151E-02	-12.5340
RN	0.461335E-01	0.123238E-02	37.4344
RM	0.208205	0.168418E-02	123.624
RS	-0.520197E-01	0.169805E-02	-30.6349
RV	-0.461699	0.567752E-03	-813.206

Log of Likelihood Function = 103.10

Equation Name	R^2	Durbin-Watson
Cost Function	0.9985	1.6578
Input Demand Functions:		
Production Worker	0.8215	0.6754
Nonproduction Worker Labor	0.9832	1.1954
Materials	0.9879	1.1599
Semiconductors	0.9966	1.2461
Purchased Services	0.9970	0.8586

As noted in the data appendix, the absence of financial data for AT&T from the industry aggregate makes the capital results less than complete. Because of the parameter constraints connecting the capital and output coefficients, this problem may also affect the estimate of economies of scale, which shows increasing returns to scale of about 80 percent. The Durbin-Watson statistics, after first-order autocorrelation correction, indicate little remaining bias in the estimated coefficients due to serial correlation of the residuals. The first-order autocorrelation coefficients RC, RL, RN, RM, RS, and RV are shown in the estimation results.

The estimate of the coefficient of the quality-adjusted index α is 1.66 with a large t-statistic, which shows that α is significantly different from zero and that technological change embodied in semiconductor input for the telephone and telegraph equipment industry (SIC 3661) proceeded at about 2.66 times the rate of measured TFP increase in the semiconductor industry itself. The (log of the) total factor productivity index for semiconductors was entered in the model for SIC 3661 with a two-year lag. Based on the t-statistic, the hypothesis that there is no unmeasured quality change in semiconductor devices used in the manufacture of telephone and telegraph equipment is rejected. The quality-adjusted price of semiconductors used in SIC 3661 computed from equation (5) is shown in table 3.3.

The results of estimating the variable cost function model for other communication equipment, SIC 3662, are shown in table 3.2. In this case, the capital coefficient, b_K, is negative as expected. The Durbin-Watson statistics, after adjustment for first order autocorrelation, indicate some problems of bias from autocorrelation. With the exception of materials, the input demand functions are concave in the input prices, and the estimate of α is 5.29, with a t-statistic of 3.45. The α coefficient is considerably higher than that found in SIC 3661. In this model, the total factor productivity index of semiconductors is lagged only one year. Based on the t-test, there is considerable unmeasured quality change inferred from the use of semiconductor devices in SIC 3662, and the hypothesis of no such change is rejected.

Table 3.3 shows the official price series from the producer price index (PPI) for semiconductor devices, as well as the prices adjusted for quality change, based on usage in SIC's 3661 and 3662, which are calculated from equation (5) after the estimation. The official PPI series shows very little increase—about seven percent—from 1968 to 1977, and about 14 percent from 1977 to 1986. Our price of semiconductor input, adjusted for unmeasured embodied quality change from use of semiconductors in telephone and telegraph equipment (SIC 3661), shows a decline of about 69 percent from 168.84 in 1968 to 100 in 1977 and a further decline of about one-half from 1977 to 1986.

Table 3.3 also shows a dramatic implied price-decline in semiconductor devices used in SIC 3662, based on adjustment for unmeasured quality change by the same approach. The adjusted price falls by a factor of about 17 from 1968 to 1977 and by a factor of about 5 from 1977 to 1986. From our empirical results, the unmeasured quality change implied by use of semiconductor device in telephone and telegraph equipment industry, SIC 3661, is much smaller than that implied by

Table 3.3. Comparison of Price Indexes

Year	Semiconductors			Communications			Computers[f]
	PPI[a]	Incorp. in SIC 3661[b]	Incorp. in IC 3662[c]	Transmission[d]	Switching[d]	Small Central Switches[e]	
1968	93.27	168.84	1726.41	47.93	80.46	—	—
1969	93.54	185.53	1268.80	36.69	64.37	—	309.11
1970	92.29	166.72	1003.93	59.17	114.94	—	276.46
1971	91.46	154.26	809.84	66.27	135.63	—	237.26
1972	89.99	142.37	427.54	61.54	110.34	—	204.36
1973	91.29	118.72	202.29	73.96	110.34	—	184.93
1974	99.75	101.95	192.49	94.08	120.69	—	145.77
1975	101.75	99.53	211.41	97.63	182.76	—	132.75
1976	100.06	99.73	208.94	110.65	106.90	—	115.72
1977	100.00	100.00	100.00	100.00	100.00	—	100.00
1978	99.16	78.70	75.12	112.43	65.52	—	84.78
1979	100.16	72.92	52.69	66.86	104.60	—	73.21
1980	107.21	69.52	29.13	68.05	121.84	—	58.84
1981	106.57	56.15	27.96	78.70	154.02	—	53.78
1982	103.29	53.84	25.29	—	—	100.00	50.08
1983	109.44	55.90	18.47	—	—	96.01	38.61
1984	113.15	51.42	18.05	—	—	82.26	34.30
1985	112.11	49.98	15.68	—	—	69.62	—
1986	113.72	48.66	20.55	—	—	—	—

Sources:
[a] Producer Price Index, Bureau of Labor Statistics.
[b], [c] Quality-adjusted price index of semiconductors incorporated in the telecommunications equipment industries, i.e., SIC 3661 and 3662. They are estimated in this study.
[d] Flamm, Kenneth, in R.W. Crandall and K. Flamm, eds., *Changing the Rules*, The Brookings Institution, 1989, p. 373-389. Data source is historical AT&T data.
[e] *op. cit.* Data are from Rural Electrification Administration of the U.S. Department of Agriculture.
[f] Implicit price deflators for computer which was constructed by combining the IBM composite indexes for computer processors, disk drives, printers, displays, and a regression index for IBM tape drives. See Cartwright, D. W., "Improved Deflation of Purchases of Computers,," *Survey of Current Business*, March 1986, p. 7-11, and Rosanne Cole et al., "Quality-Adjusted Price Indexes for Computer Processors and Selected Peripheral Equipment,," *Survey of Current Business*, Jan. 1986, p. 41-50.

their use in other telecommunications equipment, SIC 3662. Unmeasured quality change certainly exists in the outputs of telecommunication equipment industries due to the rapid technological change indicated by their use of semiconductor, but no quality-adjustment has been made yet to the official price index. Flamm (1989) measures incremental switching and transmission cost using historical AT&T data and data from the Rural Electrification Administration of the United States Department of Agriculture. The results listed in table 3.3[6] show that cost transmission increases more than two times during 1968-1977, but decreases more than 20% during 1977-1981. The cost of switching increases through time, but declines during 1976-78. The price of small central office switches decreased about 30% during 1982-85, which is more in agreement with the prices of other equipment using significant semiconductor inputs.

The price index of computers used in the GNP accounts (Cartwright 1986) is adjusted for the quality change using a hedonic approach by Cole et al. (1986) at IBM. It is shown in table 3.3. The price of computers declines by a factor of 3.09 from 1969 to 1977 and by another factor of 3 from 1977 to 1984. In comparison with this computer price index, our estimated price of semiconductor devices used in SIC 3661 declines much more slowly, but price declines much more dramatically for semiconductor devices used in SIC 3662. It is very likely that performance-adjusted prices of telecommunications equipment over the whole period would decline more like the pattern for small central office switches in the brief period 1982-85. Such a pattern would result in correspondingly higher growth of real output and productivity than the measures obtained from the official price statistics.

3.2. Short Run Input Substitution and Complementarity

Patterns of input substitution are affected, not only by input price changes, but also by changes in input quality and in the composition of output. Tables 3.1 and 3.5 show short-run Allen partial elasticities of substitution computed from the

Table 3.4. Short Run Allen Partial Elasticities of Substitutions: U.S. Telephone and Telegraph Apparatus

	Industry (SIC 3661)				
Periods	ELL	ENN	EMM	ESS	EVV
1967-73	-12.8296	-3.8690	-1.0908	-22.1232	-5.9942
1973-79	-13.1692	-3.9199	-1.0906	-22.7738	-5.8700
1979-86	-13.0641	-3.7934	-1.0774	-21.2283	-6.3092
1967-86	-13.0232	-3.8572	-1.0858	-21.9989	-6.0710
	ELN	ELM	ELS	ELV	ENM
1967-73	-2.8204	1.5938	8.6453	3.6122	0.3149
1973-79	-2.9323	1.6023	8.8646	3.6164	0.3066
1979-86	-2.7970	1.5969	8.4745	3.7256	0.3322
1967-86	-2.8471	1.5976	8.6516	3.6553	0.3187
	ENS	ENV	EMS	EMV	ESV
1967-73	1.7985	3.3748	-0.0585	0.9986	-0.8114
1973-79	1.8266	3.3720	-0.0851	0.9987	-0.8324
1979-86	1.7570	3.4051	-0.0142	0.9986	-0.8039
1967-86	1.7921	3.3851	-0.0506	0.9986	-0.8152

Table 3.5. Short Run Allen Partial Elasticities of Substitution Other Communication Equipment Manufacturing (SIC 3662)

Periods	ELL	ENN	EMM	ESS	EVV
1967-73	-5.5002	-2.7102	0.3609	-15.7722	-3.6335
1973-79	-5.0477	-2.8037	0.5802	-13.7548	-3.4728
1979-86	-5.3221	-2.7195	0.4864	-15.0984	-3.4578
1967-86	-5.2917	-2.7432	0.4764	-14.8868	-3.5180
	ELN	ELM	ELS	ELV	ENM
1967-73	1.9921	-0.5200	2.5978	1.8569	-0.4038
1973-79	1.9547	-0.5430	2.2809	1.7770	-0.5591
1979-86	1.9711	-0.5614	2.4668	1.8075	-0.4788
1967-86	1.9726	-0.5425	2.4494	1.8135	-0.4805
	ENS	ENV	EMS	EMV	ESV
1967-73	1.9252	1.5634	-0.4585	0.5048	-0.1116
1973-79	1.8159	1.5596	-0.3558	0.4807	0.0795
1979-86	1.8813	1.5451	-0.4595	0.4981	-0.0192
1967-86	1.8745	1.5554	-0.4264	0.4947	-0.0172

estimated variable cost functions for the two telecommunications equipment industries, SIC 3661 and 3662 respectively. It must be emphasized that these substitution elasticities are short run—they are based on the assumption that capital input is fixed, and thus that the elasticities of substitution between capital and the variable inputs are zero.

The own-price elasticities of substitution for all variable inputs in SIC 3661 are negative, as demand theory requires. That for production-worker labor, ELL, increases, while those for nonproduction labor, ENN; semiconductors, ESS; and services, EVV, decline through time. The decline is especially pronounced for services whose share in variable cost increases significantly through time.

Most pairs of inputs are substitutes in SIC 3661. A significant exception is nonproduction and production worker labor, which are complementary throughout the period examined; further, the degree of complementarity has increased through time. This pattern is typical of high-technology industries and is found in semiconductors (Jang and Norsworthy 1988a) and aircraft engines and airframes (Sung and Norsworthy 1989). Some degree of complementarity also occurs between nonproduction workers and materials and between semiconductors and services. Complementarity is increasing, although still small, in the former case.

In SIC 3662, the own-price elasticities of substitution are negative, with the exception of materials. The magnitudes of these elasticities are fairly stable through time. Before correction for serial correlation, all of the own-price elasticities showed trends. Most input pairs are substitutes; however materials inputs are complementary with both types of labor and with semiconductors, and semiconductors and services are very slightly complementary in the first and last periods.

3.3 Output, Productivity Growth, and Returns to Scale

The telephone and telegraph equipment industry experienced most rapid output growth in the 1967-73 period. Since no quality adjustment has been made on the output data that we use here, the measured output growth and productivity growth in this study, obviously, are understated. As table 3.6 shows, the growth fell almost by half in 1973-79 and nearly to zero in 1979-86. Total factor productivity growth rose almost 1 percent per year in 1967-73 and fell in the last two periods, before adjustment for scale effects. After scale adjustment, TFP rose slightly in the two later periods and declined by nearly two and one half percent annually in 1967-73. This adjustment of output per unit of total factor input appears to be perverse in 1973-79. While the scale adjustment was negative for five of the six years in that period, the large decline in output from 1974 to 1975 resulted in a positive scale adjustment that overwhelmed the effects of smaller negative adjustments during the period. The adjusted growth in total factor productivity is negative overall, at 0.65 percent per year. This may reflect changes in the output mix toward more resource-intensive products, rather than an actual productivity decline.

Table 3.6. Output and Total Factor Productivity Growth

Periods	Output Growth	TFP Growth	Returns to Scale	TFP Growth after Scale Adjustment	Shadow Cost of Capital
U.S. Telephone and Telegraph Apparatus Industry (SIC 3661)					
1967-73	0.0822	0.0090	1.7048	-0.0238	-0.0245
1973-79	0.0473	-0.0067	1.9625	0.0022	-0.0333
1979-86	0.0037	-0.0014	1.8404	0.0007	0.0629
1967-86	0.0423	0.0002	1.8361	-0.0065	0.0049
Other Telecommunications Equipment Industry (SIC 3662)					
1967-73	-0.0156	-0.0037	1.1863	-0.0008	-0.0203
1973-79	0.0766	0.0252	1.1777	0.0136	-0.0618
1979-86	0.0817	-0.0011	1.1829	-0.0137	-0.0353
1967-86	0.0494	0.0064	1.1823	-0.0010	-0.0389

The results for SIC 3661 show that the average cost elasticity of output is only .57, which indicates enormous economies of scale: about 1.84. As noted above, the R&D, design, and software costs for switches are very large, compared to the costs of fabrication, which would result in substantial economies of scale. These costs may well have resulted in unmeasured quality improvement in the switches as well, an issue not addressed in this paper. In the light of greatly reduced regulation, some of the scale economies from R&D, design, and software costs in the industry may decline, with slower (perhaps largely unmeasured) improvement in quality.

During the earlier periods, 1967-73 and 1973-79, when output was growing rapidly, the shadow cost of capital was negative, as economic theory predicts. In the most recent period, slow output growth, and perhaps, deregulation have resulted in a positive shadow cost, characteristic of an industry with substantial excess capacity. However, as noted above, the capital results are weak, due to omission of AT&T's financial data in computation of capital input. For SIC 3662, the "other" communication equipment industry, output declines during the 1967-73 period and rises rapidly thereafter. Total factor productivity declines in the first and last periods, but rises rapidly—at 2.5 percent per year—in 1973-79. After adjustment for the effects of scale economies, productivity declines in the last period as fast as it rises in 1973-79, so that overall productivity performance is almost flat. Scale economies in the industry are much lower than in telephone and telegraph equipment manufacturing, although they are still respectable at about 18 percent. The shadow cost of capital is negative throughout the period studied and is highest in 1973-79, when productivity growth was highest.

4. Conclusions and Implications for Future Research

In this paper, we have estimated variable cost function models for two telecommunications equipment manufacturing industries. In these models, unmeasured quality change in semiconductor inputs has been estimated for both industries, based on the assumption that unmeasured quality change in semiconductor devices is proportional to measured changes in total factor productivity growth in the semiconductor industry. Because there may be significant unmeasured quality change in telecommunications equipment itself, the estimates of implied quality change based on substitution patterns may be interpreted as lower bounds on actual quality change. Considerable differences are also found between the results for the two industries: the quality change implied by use of semiconductors in telephone and telegraph equipment, SIC 3661, is considerably lower than that implied by their use in other telecommunications equipment, SIC 3662. This evidence is not necessarily contradictory, however. The multiple characteristics of semiconductor devices are consistent with different rates of effective quality change in different uses. It is also likely that the advances in semiconductor devices probably enter the products of SIC 3662 with a shorter time lag than the products of SIC 3661.

Appendix. Data Sources, Measurement, and Concepts

The data used in this study are the historical time-series data at 4-digit SIC (Standard Industrial Classification) level for United States telephone and telegraph apparatus industry (SIC 3661) and radio and TV communication equipment industry (SIC 3662).

To estimate the econometric models, the information required is total cost (TC), variable cost (*VC*), price and quantity of output (*Y*), capital stock (*K*), production-worker labor (*L*), non-production worker labor (*N*), semiconductors (*S*), purchased services (*V*), and intermediate input (*M*). These measures are derived and constructed based on several data sources. The major sources are the *Census of Manufacturers* (CM), *Annual Survey of Manufactures* (ASM) of the Census Bureau; the Producer Price Index program of the Bureau of Labor Statistics (BLS), and *Survey of Current Business* and *The Detailed Input-Output Structure of the U.S. Economy*. Following is a detailed description of the sources and methodology used to create the input, output, and price data for these two industries.

A.1. Labor

The labor input is disaggregated into two components, production-worker labor (*L*) and nonproduction-worker labor (*N*). The number of nonproduction workers is computed by subtracting the number of production workers from the number of all employees given in the CM or ASM for each year; payroll for nonproduction workers is computed similarly. Supplemental labor costs are added into the payrolls of both production workers and nonproduction workers in proportion to their shares in total payroll. The augmented payroll of nonproduction workers divided by the number of nonproduction workers is the annual salary per nonproduction worker. Employment is used as the unit of measure because hours of nonproduction workers are typically not measured, or not measured well. The hours worked by production workers and their hourly wage rates based on the augmented payroll, which are derived from the CM and ASM, are used as the quantity and price of production workers respectively.

The production workers are defined by the Census of Manufacturing as workers (up through the line-supervisor level) closely associated with these production operations at the establishment. Employees above the working supervisor level are excluded from this item, and are classified as nonproduction employees, as are those engaged in factory supervision above the line-supevisor level.

A.2. Semiconductors

From a technological perspective, semiconductors are one of the most important materials in the manufacture of communications equipment industries. We separate the semiconductors (SIC 3674) from the intermediate materials, which include all of physical materials, and electric and gas utilities, shown in the CM and ASM. The ratio of the expenditure in purchased semiconductors to the total intermediate materials is taken from the I-O Tables in the Census years. These ratios are interpolated to get the percentage for each year. The price index for semiconductors comes from gross output deflators developed in the Bureau of Labor Statistics' (BLS) economic growth program.

A.3. Materials

Annual materials expenditures excluding semiconductors (and most purchased services) are taken directly from the CM and ASM. The real quantity of materials input is obtained by deflating the materials expenditure. We develop the aggregate price deflator for materials by

$$P_M = \sum_{i=1}^{n} W_i P_i$$

where $i=1,2,...,n$. Based on the detailed input-output table, all of physical materials and services purchased from the manufacturing sector and electric, gas, water and sanitary services are included. The prices (P_i) of these detailed materials are obtained from the producer price indexes of BLS. The weight (W_i) of each individual material in aggregate intermediate input in these two industries is computed from the input-output tables. First of all, we compute the weight from the input-output tables of 1958, 1963, 1967, 1972, and 1977. We then interpolate these weights to obtain the approximate weights for each year.

A.4. Purchased Services

The services provided by transportation, communications, wholesale and retail trade, finance, insurance and real estate, and government sectors, especially the computer services, have become more and more important in the production process, but the cost of materials measured in CM and ASM does not measure the cost of these purchased services.

The ratios of the purchased services expenditure to total cost are taken from the I-O tables during the Census years and then interpolated to the annual share. Using the approach discussed in A.3, we developed the price index of the purchased services by aggregating the detailed purchased services shown in the I-O tables.

A.5. Variable Costs after Adjustment for Holding Inventories

Besides the direct costs of variable input factors such as labor, semiconductors, materials, and purchased services discussed above, manufacturers must pay the costs of holding work-in-process inventories. These costs can be measured in terms of holding related variable inputs. We thus compute the total cost of holding the work-in-process inventories by multiplying the quantity of the inventories in current dollars by the rate of return in the industry. This cost is then distributed to the individual variable inputs by their shares in total variable cost. For example, the cost of holding raw materials inventories is added to total materials expenditures. Thus, the price of materials is increased by the cost per unit of materials input of holding work-in-process inventory. The cost of holding the work-in-progress inventory is thus treated as part of the costs of the variable inputs, with the cost allocated according to the shares in the variable cost of production.

A.6. Capital Stock (for both physical assets and financial assets)

The quantities of capital stocks of equipment and structures in these two industries was computed by the perpetual inventory method, with the depreciation rate derived for this study. The investment data series comes from the capital stock data base of the Office of Business Analysis (OBA). The rates of economic depreciation applied for different types of producers' durable equipment and for private nonresidential structures, from Hulten and Wykoff (1981), are used in many productivity studies. The depreciation rates are not specific to industries nor do they change through time. Depreciation rates for capital stock in these two telecommunications equipment industries are developed as follows.

First the shares of the different types of durable equipment and structures in the total expenditures on capital goods for this industry are computed, based on the capital flow tables for 1963, 1967, 1972 and 1977 from the associated input-output studies. These shares are interpolated between Census years. Using these shares as weights, we sum up the depreciation rates for all types of equipment and structures from Hulton and Wykoff (1981) to get more precise depreciation rates for these two elements of the capital stock for this industry. The depreciation rates vary through time because the weights change.

To compute the service prices of capital, equipment and structures, we use the Jorgenson, Gollop, and Fraumeni (1987) approach somewhat modified. Besides the equipment and structures, other assets (especially financial assets) are also important in most manufacturing industries. We compute the rate of return on capital assets, which includes equipment and structures as well as the other assets—financial assets and various types of inventories—by dividing total property income by the sum of nominal values of all assets at the end of the prior year. The values of equipment and structures are the products of their asset prices and quantities, respectively, which are derived by the perpetual inventory method using investment from the OBA capital data base. The value of financial assets is estimated by multiplying the ratio of financial assets to the physical assets in the industry by the value of the physical assets. The ratios are obtained from the financial statements in Compustat Database for SIC 3661. Balance sheets of nonfinancial corporate business from the Federal Reserve Board of Governors is used as a proxy for SIC 3662, for which Compustat lists no companies at all. A serious deficiency in coverage arises with the financial data for both industries, because AT&T, a major producer of both types of equipment, is not listed in either SIC 3661 or SIC 3662 in the Compustat database. The omission of AT&T's financial data amounts to assuming that the capital requirements for production of telecommunications equipment in that company are the same as for other producers.

A.7. Total Cost and Output

The sum of shipments and changes in inventories of finished goods in current prices, which come from CM and ASM, is the total cost, before adjustment, for the cost of holding financial assets and inventories. The cost of holding financial assets and inventories is measured by multiplying the amounts of financial assets and inventories by the rate of return in the industry. To get the true total cost for production, the costs of holding financial assets and finished goods are subtracted from the sum of shipments and changes in inventories. Implicitly, production of output is separated from production of shipments. The quantity of real output is the deflated value of total revenue. We deflate the output by using the appropriate BLS price index from the PPI.

The quantities and prices of variable inputs are normalized to price indexes with price equal to 1.00 in 1977, except total cost. Quantity indexes are then obtained by dividing expenditures on the input by the normalized price.

Notes

An earlier version of this paper was presented at the 64th annual WEA International Conference, Lake Tahoe, CA June 18-22, 1989. The authors are grateful for comments from Thomas Abbott, Michael Crew, Robert Dansby, and Jack Triplett.

1. The same methods, however, can be applied to a model of the telecommunication service industry to estimate quality change in telecommunication equipment.
2. See *1989 U.S. Industrial Outlook*, p. 27-2.
3. The shipments data come from the *Census of Manufacturers* (CM) and *Annual Survey of Manufacturers* (ASM).
4. Demand for high-technology military electronic equipment is expected to continue in the future. Long-term military projects such as the Defense Communications System, the Worldwide Military Command and Control System, and renewed commitment to the Strategic Defense Initiative (SDI) could make for significant growth in shipments, particularly for radar systems. In the civilian sector, industrial and commercial demand will continue for such products as microwave communications equipment, mobile and fixed radio equipment, etc. See 1989 Industrial Outlook.
5. This approach has been taken despite the tendency for rate-of-return regulation to distort efficiency incentives. Problems arising from this source are beyond the scope of this paper.
6. Flamm (1989) assumes that switching activity was proportional to total local calls plus ten times long-distance messages, and that transmission capacity is proportional to total circuit miles of telephone carrier installed in Bell System. The incremental cost of switching capacity is computed as annual change in the net book value of central office switching equipment. That of transmission is measured by annual change in the net book value of central office circuit and radio equipment.

References

Averch, H., and Johnson, L.L. 1962. "Behavior of the Firm Under Regulatory Constraint." *American Economic Review* LII (No. 5, December): 1052-1069.

Brown, R.S., and Christensen, L.R. 1981. "Estimating Elasticities of Substitution in a Model of Partial Static Equilibrium: An Application to U.S. Agriculture 1947 to 1974." In *Modeling and Measuring Natural Resources Substitution*, edited by Berndt and Fields.

Bureau of the Census, Department of Commerce, *1958, 1963, 1967, 1972, 1977, Census of Manufactures.*

Bureau of the Census, Department of Commerce, *Annual Survey of Manufactures.*

Bureau of Economic Analysis, U.S. Department of Commerce, *The Detailed Input-Output Structure of the U.S. Economy, 1963, 1967, 1972 and 1977.*

Cartwright, D.W. 1986. "Improved Deflation of Purchases of Computer." *Survey of Current Business* (March): 7-11.

Cole, R.E., Chen, Y.C., Barquin-Stollman, J., Dulberger, E.R., Helvacian, N., and Hodge, J.H. 1986. "Quality-Adjusted Price Indexes for Computer Processors and Selected Peripheral Equipment." *Survey of Current Business* (January) 66:41-50.

Crandall, Robert W. 1989. "The Role of the U.S. Local Operating Companies" In *Changing the Rules*: 114-146, edited by Crandall and Flamm.

Crandall, Robert W., and Flamm, Kenneth 1989, eds. *Changing the Rules: Technological Change, International Competition and Regulation in Communications*. The Brookings Institution, Washington, D.C.

Flamm, Kenneth 1989. "Technological Advance and Costs: Computers versus Communications." In *Changing The Rules*: 13-61, edited by Crandall and Flamm.

Huber, Peter W. 1987. *The Geodesic Network, 1987 Report on Competition in the Telephone Industry*, U.S. Department of Justice, Antitrust Division.

International Trade Administration, U.S. Department of Commerce, 1989. *1989 U.S. Industrial Outlook*: 27.1-29.6.

Jang, S. L. 1987. *Productivity Growth and Technical Change in the U.S. Semiconductor, Computer and Telecommunications Equipment Industries*. Ph.D. Dissertation, R.P.I., Troy, N.Y.

Jang, Show-Ling, and Norsworthy, J. R. 1988a. "Scale Economies, Learning Curves and Downstream Productivity Growth: A Study of Technology in the U.S. Microelectronics and Computer Industries." Technical Report 02-88, Center for Science and Technology Policy, School of Management, Rensselaer Polytechnic Institute.

Jang, Show-Ling, and Norsworthy, J. R. 1988b. "Productivity Growth: Technological Change and the Structure of Production in the U.S. Computer Industry." Technical Report 05-88, Center for Science and Technology Policy, School of Management, R.P.I.

Jang, Show-Ling, and Norsworthy, J. R. 1990. "Measurement Methods for Technological Change Embodied in Inputs." *Economics Letters* 32: 325-330.

Lancaster, K. 1971. *Consumer Demand: A New Approach*. Columbia University Press, New York.

McElroy, Marjorie, B. 1987. "Additive General Error Models for Production Cost, and Derived Demand or Shared Systems." *Journal of Political Economy*, (No. 4) 95:737-757.

Norsworthy, J. R., and Jang, Show-Ling 1988. "Quantity-Based Measurement of Technological Change in Economic Models." Working Paper 01-88, Center for Science and Technology Policy, R.P.I.

Norsworthy, J. R., and Jang, Show-Ling 1989a. "A New Framework for Measuring and Analyzing Productivity and Technology in Service Industries." Presented at the Conference of the Pacific Telecommunications Council, Honolulu, Hawaii, January 1989.

Rey, R.F., ed. 1983. *Engineering and Operations in the Bell System*, 2nd ed., Murray Hill, N.J.: AT&T Bell Labs.

Schindler, G.E., ed. 1982. *A History of Engineering and Science in the Bell System*, Murray Hill, N.J.: AT&T Bell Labs.

Sung, S., and Norsworthy, J. R. 1989. "A Quantitative Analysis of Technological Change and Dual-Use Technology: U.S. Aircraft Industry, 1961-85." Presented at the Annual Meeting of Western Economic Association, Lake Tahoe, CA, 1989.

Triplett, J. E. 1989. "Price and Technological Change in a Capital Good: A Survey of Research on Computers." In *Technology and Capital Formation*, edited by D. Jorgenson and R. Landau: MIT Press.

8

ENTRY AND WELFARE LOSS IN REGULATED INDUSTRIES

Timothy J. Brennan

The normative objectives of public utility regulation ("PUR") are to counteract the inefficiencies of monopoly and to ensure that the regulated products are made available in some broadly equitable fashion. The flaws of PUR include:

1. "Capture" theorists, students of "rent-seeking," and the economics of collective action all predict that the regulators, in practice, will act to benefit the relatively concentrated interests of the industries that they regulate, at the expense of the larger but more diffuse public interest.[1]

2. A well-intentioned regulator cannot process the information necessary to ensure efficient performance, especially recognizing the informational asymmetries between it and the firms it regulates.[2] One may expect the information problem to be more severe in industries with relatively rapid technological change and product innovation.[3]

3. Firms may have incentives to diversify and exploit the market power in their regulated markets, with harm to both regulated ratepayers and the performance in the markets the regulated firms enter.[4]

4. The tax and subsidy schemes inherent in regulatory cost allocation and pricing structures are inevitably inefficient, compared to the ideal "lump-sum" transfers.[5]

An appealing remedy to the flaws from public utility regulation is to open up regulated markets to entry. In theory, permitting entry would limit the incentive of incumbent firms to "capture" a regulator and eliminate rents to seek. Entrants could bring in the innovative processes and products to market more quickly, and the potential competition from these entrants would eliminate the need for a regulator to oversee the R&D efforts of the utility. The regulated firm could not profitably discriminate against unaffiliated firms in access to its services or cross-subsidize other operations by raising price in its regulated markets, if new entrants would offer the product at competitive prices. Finally, entry can render inefficient redistribution unsustainable, forcing the regulator to either make the redistribution both more efficient and more politically visible, or to eliminate the redistribution altogether (Brock, 1984).

Despite the appeal of the arguments for entry, advances in the theory of strategic behavior give good reason to be skeptical about the ability of entry to ensure efficient performance of natural monopoly markets. By now, these advances are fairly well known; Section 1 of this paper reviews the reasons to suspect that opening up the market to entry, continuously or through a franchise competition, is unlikely to either generate competitive results or eliminate the need for regulation of non-price product attributes. Less well-known is a small but growing literature suggesting that potential competition or successful entry may reduce welfare. Section 2 of this paper discusses arguments developed for unregulated oligopoly markets. Insights from the "successful entry" literature can be combined with optimal taxation considerations to examine possible welfare losses when a multiproduct regulated firm faces entry in some of its markets. Welfare can go down even where an entrant is more efficient than the regulated firm at serving the entered market if, as is likely the case, political considerations prevent the taxation of firms (entrants) to subsidize their (incumbent) competitors.[6] We develop a simple test regulators can use to see whether such entry should be discouraged or barred. Results are summarized and concluding observations made in Section 3.

1. Competing For the Market

For purposes of discussion, we will assume that public utility regulation is not so misplaced as to be imposed on an industry which would be subject to intense ongoing competition among a relatively large number of sellers. While such industries have been subject to rate and entry regulation—trucking comes to mind as an example—few (outside the industry and, possibly, its regulators) would disagree with the proposition that deregulation and entry would result in superior performance. The merits of permitting entry can only be at all contentious when the industry would be, at best, a fairly narrow oligopoly and, at worst, a monopoly.

Many authors have suggested that the major obstacles to competition are legal barriers to entry. Kahn, (1970, vol. 2, 116) for example, writes "The possibility of competitive entry is the principal limitation on monopoly power in a market economy.... No barrier to entry is more absolute than one imposed by the sovereign power of the state." Legal barriers to entry are often a part of the rate regulation process. Breyer (1982, 194) finds that "Virtually every form of classical regulation tends to *raise barriers to entry* into the regulated industry." [Italics in original] He notes, in particular, an association between cost-of-service regulation and legal requirements that entry be disallowed unless a commission finds that the new firms would serve the public interest.

This association, however, is no accident. As we will see below, the provision of traditionally regulated natural monopoly[7] services (as opposed to regulated non-monopoly services, such as trucks) involves a large, irreversible capital commitment by the regulated firm to the specific regulated market.[8] The size and irreversibility of this investment implies that a firm is unlikely to make it without some assurance that it will be able to recover enough revenue, in excess of variable cost, over the service life of the firm to cover the present value of the funds used to make the investment. A reasonable component of that assurance would be a guarantee that entry would not be permitted, at least until the firm had fully depreciated its investment.[9]

The irreversibility of the investment has a more important and direct consequence for the ability of entry to control price. In theory, an incumbent monopolist vulnerable to potential competition may have no incentive to charge prices sufficiently high to generate positive profits. The most recent restatement of this conjecture regarding the benefits of potential competition is contestability theory (Baumol, Panzar, and Willig 1982; Baumol 1983). In this theory, the vulnerability of the monopolist to entry springs from susceptibility to "hit-and-run" entry. If the monopolist sets a price high enough to generate supracompetitive profits, an entrant can undercut the monopolist and take away its business. Never knowing when it will wake up to find its customers gone, the monopolist's only choice is to maintain its prices sufficiently low to prevent this from happening.

Contestability has generated a considerable follow-on literature (surveyed in Schwartz (1986)), inspired by proponents' claims that it is a "revolution in the theory of industry structure," (Baumol 1983) and, more importantly, by its implication that one need not bother with either complex oligopoly game theory to understand concentrated markets or undertake economic regulation to control them. The controversy over contestability has centered on two key facets. Under perfect contestability, the entrant has to be able to enter and capture customers before the incumbent monopolist can change price—what we may call incumbent "response lag." The second is that entry must be costlessly reversible. In principle, this may be consistent with the considerable fixed costs seen in natural monopoly industries; the important criterion is whether costs of serving the market are "sunk."

If the incumbent can cut price in response to entry before the entrant can costlessly leave, then the entrant must decide whether the profits it can reap prior to the price reaction exceed the costs of exiting the market. If these expected profits of entry are negative, entry will not be forthcoming, and monopoly pricing need not be deterred. For sufficiently large price reaction lags and sufficiently small losses in sunk costs, potential entry will still force the incumbent to hold price below the monopoly level. Schwartz (1986) estimates values for the degree of sunk costs and price reaction lag necessary to get the incumbent monopolist to set pre-entry price below the monopoly level and concludes that the necessary levels of sunk costs are so low, or price reaction lags so long, that contestability is unlikely to inhibit monopoly pricing; in his terms, contestability theory is not "robust."[10] Ironically, he finds that contestability may apply, if anywhere, to markets in which regulators prevent incumbents from responding to price after entry. His conclusion suggests that there may be some merit in the oft-lamented policy of not permitting regulated firms to respond to competition. However, entry into regulated natural monopoly markets will typically involve enormous sunk costs. This implies that entrants will need to be sure that incumbent's can't react post-entry, but that in turn implies that incumbents may be so vulnerable to error in price forecasts or to technological change making entry profitable, that no one may be willing to be the first firm to provide a regulated service.

Even if contestability theory were to apply in regulated contexts, it may conflict with other goals of the regulator. One such example may be a policy against discrimination. If a firm with economies of scale in a contestable market can price discriminate, it will be forced to do so. Otherwise, an entrant could come in, undercut the incumbent's price to its current customers by some small $\varepsilon > 0$ and charge prices in excess of marginal cost to customers not served. Figure 1 illustrates the result.

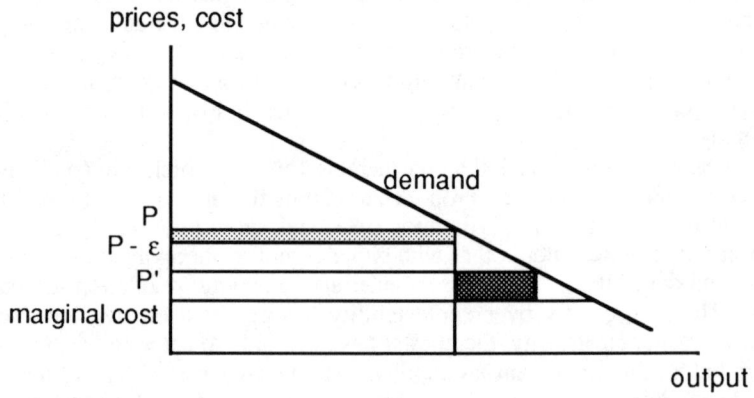

Assume P is the price that just covers a nondiscriminating monopolist's fixed costs.[11] The darkly shaded area is the gain a discriminating entrant could reap from charging a lower price P' to attract demand at reservation prices below P. The lightly shaded area represents the loss the entrant incurs to attract the incumbent's customers. This loss can be made arbitrarily small, implying that the discriminating entrant could, assuming contestability, profitably capture the market from a nondiscriminating monopolist. In general, a firm in a contestable market will be constrained by competition to maximize output, obtaining just enough revenue to cover costs. Price discrimination, if possible, will require nonlinear pricing schedules or charging different prices to different customers.[12] This may reduce welfare, if intermediate goods are involved and third-degree price discrimination is employed (Katz 1987); in any event, contestability-induced price discrimination may run counter to political or statutory goals of the regulator.

While there is some dispute regarding contestability of airline markets[13], it may be interesting to observe that airline pricing patterns may illustrate this price discrimination result. Suppose from travelers' perspectives that meaningful markets for airline services are generally narrow, e.g., flights between a specific pair of cities at a particular part of the day (morning, afternoon, evening). Between most cities at most times, a single airline can meet market demand; the market is a natural monopoly. In most airline flights, we observe considerable variation in the pricing of tickets, indicating price discrimination. In those few airline markets where demand is sufficiently great to be served efficiently by more than one airplane, however, the possibility of arbitrage renders price discrimination impossible. We observe this on the northeast "shuttle" routes, where pricing is uniform. The above argument shows that such pricing is consistent with contestability and need not indicate the ability to reap monopoly profits.

Moreover, absent price discrimination, contestability will not in and of itself justify elimination of regulation or quality or non-price parameters. Assume, for example, that a monopolist has to provide the same level of quality to all customers. Examples may include the fraction of space reserved for nonsmokers on airplanes, levels of electricity reliability, telephone line noise, or cable television service. Contestability, if it holds, would ensure that service at a given level of quality would be priced optimally, but will not ensure that the optimal level of quality will be found.

Suppose that there are two levels of quality, A and B. To make the model simple, assume that A and B can be provided at equal cost, but that type A consumers prefer A to B while type B consumers prefer B to A. (Airline smoking would fit this scenario.) Assume that there are n_i consumers of type i, each consumer buys one unit of the product, and let p_{ij} be the reservation price of a type i consumer for quality level j. Quality level A could be socially preferable, in that

$$n_a[p_{aa} - p_{ab}] > n_b[p_{bb} - p_{ba}].$$

Suppose that price discrimination is impossible, and the current monopolist is charging a uniform price p such that costs are just covered, i.e., if costs are $C(q)$,

$$p[n_a + n_b] = C(n_a + n_b).$$

To reflect the natural monopoly assumption, assume that average cost declines with output.

Now suppose the incumbent has chosen quality level B. An entrant offering quality level A cannot profitably charge p, since it will not attract type B customers away from the incumbent. Unless type A consumers prefer A to B by enough to be willing to support an A monopolist on their own, it will not be profitable for the A monopolist to enter. The change in prices must be less than the gain in benefits. In this model, assuming the A entrant would just be covering costs, this condition would be

$$\frac{C(n_a)}{n_a} - p < p_{aa} - p_{ab}.$$

Declining average cost implies the left hand expression is positive, implying inequality need not be satisfied even if A is the socially preferable level of quality. If transaction costs preclude negotiation among the A and B customers themselves to resolve the quality issue, *a la* the Coase theorem, regulation may be necessary to ensure optimal quality. On the one hand, it may be worth while to note that one can believe airlines are contestable while supporting anti-smoking rules. On the other hand, it is disturbing to note that contestability at its best absolves the regulator of natural monopoly of only the pricing issue. Entry even in the most optimistic of situations may not eliminate the need for regulation of other dimensions of operations.

An alternative solution, proposed by Demsetz (1968) was that holding a one-shot competition for the market could eliminate inefficient outcomes usually implied by natural monopoly production. Asking "Why must rivals share the market?," he envisioned replacing regulation with an auction in which prospective ex post monopolists would compete ex ante for the right to serve the market. Subsequent research has pointed out difficulties with Demsetz's solution to the regulation of natural monopoly, which spring from the fact that the monopoly franchise relationship will generally extend over a substantial period of time.[14] The duration of the relationship, specificity of assets, and likelihood of changing circumstances leads to the potential for ex post opportunism that cannot be completely covered by an ex ante franchise contract. Ongoing enforcement and adaptation of the contract weakens the distinction between franchising and regulation.[15]

2. Competing In the Market: Entry-Induced Inefficiencies

2.1. Entry Losses in Unregulated Markets

Before turning to the losses imposed by entry in regulated markets, we should consider the problems open entry may pose in unregulated markets. Many of these theories will contribute to our understanding of the potential losses entry can induce in regulated markets.[16] The idea that entry could be harmful is not new. Kahn (1970) and Breyer (1982) describe the history of the "destructive" or "excessive" competition notion. Kahn finds the theory potentially credible, but only if there is imperfect information on the part of corporate managers, who might inefficiently close down operations made unprofitable due to excess capacity in the market, or on the part of consumers, who might not be able prior to purchase to detect easily quality reductions brought on by price reductions in excess capacity periods. Despite these views on the possibility of market "imperfections" that make competition destructive, Kahn finds that regulation ostensibly on their behalf has been inappropriately applied, citing trucking and stock brokerage as prominent examples. Breyer is, if anything, even less kind to "excessive competition." He finds that it could refer to either the existence of natural monopoly pricing conditions, cyclical demand swings in high fixed costs industries, or predation. His conclusion that the "excessive competition" rationale does not apply to the industries for which it has been asserted should not be surprising. It would only be invoked to exclude entry, but if "excessive competition" was costly and foreseeable, such entry would probably not be forthcoming.

There is firmer ground, though, for inferring a welfare loss from entry. The first involves, specifically, potential entry. Spence (1977; 1979) and Dixit (1980) have set out the theory that an incumbent firm may expand its productive capacity to deter entry. The mechanism is that the entry decision depends upon the expected post-entry price. In a market with an incumbent monopolist, an entrant will likely be too large to expect to take the pre-entry price as given regardless of its entry. Thus, its expectations on post-entry price will be based on post-entry market conditions, such as demand, the nature of the competitive interaction (Bertrand, Cournot, etc.), and, importantly, the incumbent's marginal production cost. Since the expected post-entry price will generally be an increasing function of the incumbent's marginal cost, investments by the incumbent to reduce marginal cost can reduce that price, possibly below the level sufficient to attract entry. Excess capacity, specific to the market, is a means to that end.[17] Stiglitz (1981) had pointed out, as a corollary to the Spence-Dixit excess capacity theory, that potential competition may reduce welfare because it induces wasteful cost-reducing investment (R&D, in Stiglitz's example) solely to deter entry.

Another insight from research in the economics of R&D is that additional competition to acquire a patent may prove socially wasteful, if the time at which the research proves successful is not very sensitive to the number of independent research paths.[18] Public policy to exclude entry (or permit monopoly) to promote R&D activity is appropriately controversial, since conclusions are specific to assumptions regarding product market structure, spillovers, and, most of all, the nature of the R&D game (Reinganum 1989). Nevertheless, this simple example of a patent race illustrates a potentially more telling story against entry, and one closer to the regulated setting, most recently provided by Mankiw and Whinston (1986) and Schwartz (1989). Mankiw and Whinston point out that part of the profits of entry come not from the generation of additional consumer surplus, but from the opportunity to "steal" profits from one's competitors. There is no welfare gain attached to the latter, but the profits may induce resources to be allocated to entry. Schwartz also points to a second source of inefficiency, when entry reallocates output from a low marginal cost incumbent to a high marginal cost entrant.[19]

Reallocation of output leads to a more familiar class of circumstances in which entry can reduce welfare. If a monopolist requires the profits from price discrimination to cover its costs, and entry (or arbitrage) prevents price discrimination, the monopolist will drop out. The following example shows that entry in such circumstances can reduce welfare. Suppose the incumbent serves two groups of customers, A and B, charging prices p_a and p_b that maximize profits in the respective markets. We assume that the revenues from these markets are just covering the incumbent's costs. Competitive entry occurs in market A with marginal cost $p_a - \varepsilon$, driving price down to $p_a - \varepsilon$. The monopolist no longer finds it profitable to stay in, causing a welfare loss in B. If competition among the entrants reduces their profits to zero, and the monopolist was earning zero profits to begin with, then the entry will reduce welfare if the consumer's gain from the A market is exceeded by the consumer's loss in the B market.

Since exit occurs for any positive ε, the welfare loss in B is independent of ε as long as $\varepsilon > 0$, and since consumer welfare in A is a continuous and increasing function of ε, equal to 0 when ε is 0, then ε can be chosen sufficiently small so the losses in B outweigh the gains in A, resulting in a net welfare loss. This possibility was given a more sophisticated and game-theoretic foundation in the sustainability literature (Faulhaber 1975; Panzar and Willig 1977; Baseman 1981, Berg and Tschirhart 1988).

2.2. Entry Losses in Multiproduct Regulated Markets: A Welfare Test

The analyses of price discrimination, sustainability, and Mankiw and Whinston's and Schwartz's analysis of the costs of entry due to the opportunity for profits elsewhere apply to a special but common situation facing regulators—whether to permit entry into a regulated firm's markets. Here, I take "markets" to refer either to separate products or to separate groups of consumers who can be charged different prices for the same product. The source of the entry loss is related to arguments made in Braeutigam (1979) concerning the inability of regulators to achieve an optimum when a regulated firm faces competition from firms offering differentiated products. It is also tied closely to theories on the optimum size of the tax base (Starrett 1988, 135-40).

The story begins with the presumption that price is above marginal cost in a regulated firm's markets, e.g., to cover fixed[20] costs used in the production of both products or to carry out a redistributive scheme through interservice subsidies. A firm may find it profitable to enter one of the markets at the going price. If the entrant's cost of serving the market exceeds the incremental cost to the regulated firm, entry is inefficient and is induced purely by the price structure. This production inefficiency is well known and policies to address it have been offered (Brock and Evans 1983; Einhorn 1987). Less well known is the possibility that an entrant who can serve its market at lower cost than the regulated firm still may cause net losses in direct economic welfare, i.e., without imputing welfare benefits associated with distribution or favoring particular classes of customers. This is because the regulator has to adjust rates upward in other markets to maintain the same contribution to fixed costs as was contributed prior to entry, and the losses in welfare in those markets need not be made up by welfare gains in the entered markets.[21]

We can make this into more than a theoretical curiosity by offering the regulator a simple test that may be helpful in determining when entry should not be permitted. It should be noted, though, that the welfare loss here comes from the practical requirement that only a regulated firm's customers are expected to contribute to fixed costs. Hence, entry into a regulated firms markets essentially shrinks the "tax base" or set of markets from which cost recovery can be generated. In extreme cases, this entry into one market can cause exit from all the other markets, in a manner akin to the "price discrimination" case discussed in the previous section. Since this "tax base" reduction causes the welfare loss, the optimal policy is clear—require entrants to make the same contribution to the regulated firm's fixed costs as the regulated firm was prior to entry.

We can present these results with a model. Consider a regulated multiproduct firm. For product I, suppose there are potential or actual entrants with constant marginal cost ce_i, where ce_i is less than p_i, the price the regulated firm had been charging for I. Let cr_i be the regulated firm's average incremental cost for producing I. Assume that if the regulated firm is a more efficient I producer than the entrants, i.e., $cr_i \leq ce_i$, the regulated firm sets a "limit" price for I equal to ce_i. If the entrants are more efficient, i.e., $cr_i > ce_i$, the regulated firm reduces supply or exits market I, and the price of I just equals ce_i.

In either case, the actual or potential entrants earn zero profits. If $cr_i \leq ce_i$, the entrants do not enter; if $cr_i > ce_i$, they compete all profits away. Where the regulated firm is a more efficient producer, it still earns positive profits from the sale of I. Assume that the regulator allows the regulated firm to raise its prices in other markets by just enough to allow it to earn the same profits it was earning prior to entry, and that demand in other market is sufficiently strong to permit the firm to do so. In particular, if the regulated firm was earning zero profits prior to entry, it will earn zero profits after entry; costs are still being covered. If the entrants are earning zero profits, and the profits of the regulated firm do not change, the test of whether entry improves economic welfare is whether the gain in consumer surplus in markets where prices fall exceeds the loss in consumer surplus in other markets where prices rise to keep the regulated firm "whole". Using that result, we can reach the following conclusions:

Proposition 1. If a regulated firm had been setting prices to maximize consumer welfare, given that it was allowed to receive a given level of profits, and if entrants have constant marginal cost,
 (a) (potential) competition from less efficient producers reduces welfare, and
 (b) (actual) competition from more efficient producers may reduce welfare.[22]

We will assume that the entrants act competitively. If they do not, potential or actual competition will be less efficient, strengthening the conclusions.

Proof of (a): Let $p°$ be the vector of prices set prior to the potential competition, p^1 be the vector of prices occurring after the potential competition, and $\Pi°$ be the regulated firm's profits. If $S(p)$ is the consumer surplus at p, by definition $S(p°) > S(p)$ for all $p \neq p°$ such that $\Pi(p) = \Pi°$. Since $\Pi(p^1) = \Pi°$, $S(p°) > S(p^1)$.

Proof of (b): Let A be the set of goods for which more efficient entry occurs, i.e., where $cr_a > ce_a$ for all $a \in A$. Let

$$p^* = \text{argmax } \{S(p) | \Pi(p) = \Pi° \text{ and } p_a = cr_a \text{ for all } a \in A\}.$$

From (a), $S(p°) > S(p^*)$.

Let p^d be the vector of prices in which $p_a = cr_a - d$ for all $a \in A$, and $p_a = p^*_a$ for all $a \in \sim A$ (i.e., not in A). This is the price vector that would result if $ce_a = cr_a - d$. We cannot conclude that $S(p^d) < S(p°)$ directly from the argument in (a), since $\Pi(p^d)$ would be less than $\Pi°$ if the regulated firm had to supply markets in A at prices below incremental cost. However, if after entry the regulated firm does not have to supply goods A, $\Pi(p^d) = \Pi(p^*) = \Pi^\circ$. Since the aggregate consumer welfare function is continuous in prices, there exists a $\delta > 0$ such that $S(p\delta)$ is still less than $S(p^\circ)$, since $S(p^\circ) > S(p^*)$. Unless actual entrants are "sufficiently" more efficient than the regulated firm, even their entry will reduce welfare. |

The welfare loss occurs since the entrants' customers no longer have to make the same contribution toward the firm's costs that they made prior to entry, thus raising prices and reducing welfare in other markets. If the entrants' customers had to pay the same price over marginal cost that they paid while customers of the regulated firm, inefficient potential entry would never occur and actual entry would increase welfare for the usual reasons—by reducing production costs and prices. Political considerations, however, frequently require regulators to cover production costs only from customers of the regulated product.[23]

The results in Proposition 1 hold also because the regulator is assumed to be maximizing consumer welfare prior to entry, subject to a given level of profit. If entry makes the regulator more diligent or better able to maximize consumer welfare and control the regulated firms costs, this conclusion may not hold.[24] If $\Pi^\circ > 0$, actual or potential entry that led to a reduction in the regulated firm's profits could increase welfare. However, if $\Pi^\circ = 0$, the prices p° are "Ramsey" prices, and welfare cannot be increased, if the regulated firm is to be kept whole without subsidies from outside sources. Note that potential entry may keep a regulated firm from earning enough to cover its total costs in the remaining markets. If so, it would be forced out of business altogether, with consequent welfare losses in the other markets.

We can develop an approximate test to determine whether potential or actual entry increases or decreases welfare.

Proposition 2. An approximate test as to whether entry increases welfare is whether the ratio of the "average" price reduction in the markets with entry, to the "average" price increase in the non-entry markets, exceeds the ratio of the "average" output in the non-entry markets to the "average" output in the markets with entry.

Proof: The proof should clarify the meaning of Proposition 2.

As an approximation (an exact result if demand curves are linear), the change in consumer surplus ΔS from a change in prices Δp is

$$\Delta S = -\Delta p \left(\frac{Q^{before} + Q^{after}}{2} \right),$$

where the superscripts "before" and "after" refer respectively to before and after the change in prices. This is obvious from the following diagram, for decreases in price:

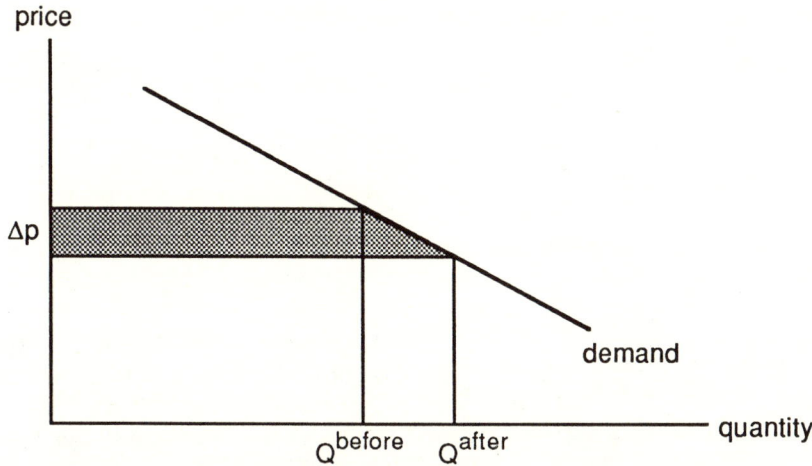

For increases in price, the location of the "before" and "after" quantities would be reversed, but the equation would remain valid.

To economize on notation, let

$$\overline{Q_\alpha} = \frac{Q_\alpha^{before} + Q_\alpha^{after}}{2}.$$

If, as assumed, profits do not change, entry is efficient if and only if the aggregate gain in consumer surplus in markets where price falls exceeds the loss in consumer surplus in markets where price rises. Using our approximation and notation, and taking price changes in absolute value terms to make comparisons easier, entry is efficient if and only if

$$\sum_{\alpha \in A} |\Delta p_\alpha| \overline{Q_\alpha} > \sum_{\beta \in \sim A} |\Delta p_\beta| \overline{Q_\beta}.$$

Define the following average of price changes, weighted by the quantity measures in markets A with price decreases and markets $\sim A$ with price increases, respectively as

$$\Delta p_A = \frac{\sum_{\alpha \in A} |\Delta p_\alpha| \overline{Q_\alpha}}{\overline{Q_A}} \text{ and } \Delta p_{\sim A} = \frac{\sum_{\beta \in \sim A} |\Delta p_\beta| \overline{Q_\beta}}{\overline{Q_{\sim A}}}, \text{ where}$$

$$\overline{Q_A} = \sum_{\alpha \in A} \overline{Q_\alpha} \text{ and } \overline{Q_{\sim A}} = \sum_{\beta \in \sim A} \overline{Q_\beta}.$$

The "efficiency of entry" condition can thus be restated as

$$\Delta p_A \overline{Q_A} > \Delta p_{\sim A} \overline{Q_{\sim A}}, \text{ or}$$

$$\frac{\Delta p_A}{\Delta p_{\sim A}} > \frac{\overline{Q_{\sim A}}}{\overline{Q_A}}.$$

This is what is meant by "ratios of averages" in the statement of the proposition. ∎

Proposition 2 is intuitively plausible. The larger is the price increase or the size of the markets in which entry has not occurred, the less likely that entry increases welfare. Note that if there are just two markets and entry occurs in just one of them, then, A and $\sim A$ are just single markets, the changes in price are simply the changes in price in those markets without any "averaging", and the quantities in the expression are just the averages of the pre- and post-entry quantities sold in those markets. Keep in mind, though, that all of these quantities except for the change in prices in A are endogenous, thus, one should be careful about applying this test.

3. Summary

Entry has been viewed as of great importance in ensuring competitive market performance, and it deservedly plays a major role as both a tool and goal of economic policy. Its virtues have tempted many to use it to fix the inefficiencies plaguing the regulation of natural monopoly industries. Any policy to regulate entry must be weighed against the possibility that it would invite unjustified entry restrictions, e.g., to protect incumbents in competitive markets. Nevertheless, policy analysts should exercise a modicum of caution before concluding that eliminating entry restrictions will cure the illness regulation either creates or is intended to correct. Ongoing competition for the market will often be ineffective, and even where it works, it may produce pricing or quality outcomes viewed as inferior by economic or distributive standards. Competition for the market could be held prior to entry, but changing circumstances and the potential for opportunism all suggest that franchising will not serve as a substitute for continuous regulatory oversight.

Despite the vacuity of the concept of "destructive competition," actual entry can cause welfare losses in a variety of ways. Potential entry may induce effective yet expensive investments by incumbents in entry deterrence, with little or no benefit to consumers. Entry based on the attempt to steal profits from incumbents may bring only meager benefits to consumers exceeded by costs of entry or reallocation of output from low-cost to high-cost firms. Entry in one market may reduce welfare overall if it drives an incumbent price-discriminating monopolist out of other markets—an example of a nonsustainable natural monopoly.

Applying these lessons to regulated industries, we see that entry can reduce welfare by forcing prices up in the markets that have not been entered. This effect essentially results from a shrinking of the set of commodities that the regulator can "tax" to cover the regulated firm's fixed costs. If political considerations prevent entry from being "taxed," it may be efficient to exclude entrants who can serve their markets at a cost below the incremental cost to the monopolist of serving those markets. A test is derived that indicates when there are welfare gains, assuming that entry is competitive and pre-entry prices were "second-best" efficient. While the test may have some practical import, it may be more effective as a guide to thinking more carefully about entry policies regulators might institute.

Notes

I'd like to thank Mary Fitzpatrick, Karen Palmer, Sharon Gifford, and Richard Simnett for helpful comments. They bear no responsibility for remaining errors.

1. The seminal article is Stigler (1971); see also Krueger (1974) and Peltzman (1976). A recent exception to this is Wittman (1989), who argues that economists should have as much faith in the efficacy of public democratic institutions as they have in private markets.

2. The leading article in this area is Hayek (1945). Formal economic analyses of the inefficiencies created by erroneous regulatory decisions began with Averch and Johnson (1982). Sophisticated recent work utilizing the economics of asymmetric information include Baron and Myerson (1982), Laffont and Tirole (1986), and Sappington and Sibley (1988). Farrell (1987) argues that an imperfect central authority (a "bumbling bureaucrat") may outperform private negotiators.

3. Lewis and Sappington (1989) consider how different regulatory methods and self-selection may be incorporated in a regulatory mechanism when the regulator does not know the expected effectiveness of a regulated firm's research efforts.

4. Deterring inefficient diversification was the rationale behind the divestiture of AT&T and subsequent restrictions on the activities of the divested local telephone companies (Brennan 1987; 1990a). Regulatory mechanisms that divorce price from reported costs reduce some, but not all, of the incentive for anticompetitive diversification (Haring and Kwerel 1987; Brennan 1989a; 1989b).

5. Posner (1971). Griffin (1982) estimated that the redistribution created through the subsidy of inelastic local calling by more elastic long-distance use created a welfare loss of just over one-and-a-half billion dollars in 1975. See Wenders (1987, Ch. 4) for an extensive survey of the welfare effects induced by redistributive pricing in regulated telephone service.

6. An examination of regulator conduct in the presence of entry is in Evans and Garber (1989). Barclay, Gegax, and Tschirhart (1989) find that legislated rules obliging electric utilities to purchase from cogenerators at an "avoided cost" basis can lead to inefficient expansion of generating capacity.

7. Sharkey (1982) provides definitions and analyses of natural monopoly cost functions.

8. The implications of this sunk investment for leaving the firm vulnerable to opportunism on the part of the regulator are discussed below.

9. See Brennan (1990b) for discussions of the role of depreciation and rate-of-return policy in ensuring investment recovery and in structuring the optimal time path of tariffs.

10. Schwartz also discusses cases of "hit-and-stay" entry, where the entrant finds it more profitable to remain in the market after the monopolist's price reaction than to recover the "non-sunk" part of its initial investment. In such cases, the threat of "hit-and-stay" entry may induce an incumbent to set a lower price.

Shepherd (1984) also surveys findings that contestability (or "ultra-free entry") is not empirically robust.

11. Economies of scale ensure that a price equal to average cost will exceed marginal cost.

12. The design of such pricing schedules was set out in Willig (1978), although not applied to contestability. There need be no unique pricing schedule that maximizes output subject to a revenue constraint, if price discrimination is possible.

13. For the affirmative, see Bailey (1981); on the negative, see empirical literature cited in Schwartz (1986).

14. Some of the arguments are surveyed in Crew and Kleindorfer (1986), Sherman (1989), and Crew and Zupan (1990).

15. The leading article presenting these flaws in franchising is Williamson (1976). Klein, Crawford, and Alchian (1978) set out the connections between asset specificity, opportunism, and long-term contracts.

16. I do not plan to address here the consequences of permitting regulated firms to diversify into unregulated markets. For discussions of this topic, see Brennan (1987; 1990a).

17. We have observed above that the inability of regulated incumbents to adjust price may increase the force of potential entry as a constraint on pre-entry prices. In effect, the market becomes more contestable.

18. Imperfect appropriability of the results of research may also lead to too little innovative activity in the presence of competitors who would gain from the spillover (Reinganum 1989).

19. Schwartz (1989) shows that a *costless* innovation can reduce welfare even if final product prices fall, if the innovator's post-innovation marginal costs exceed those of its competitors.

20. By "fixed," I mean the difference between total costs and the revenue that would be raised if prices equal marginal costs. If marginal costs increase with output, the difference will be less than fixed costs; if marginal costs decrease with output, this difference will be greater.

21. Phillips (1982) models the inefficiency that can follow when an incumbent is not allowed to match rates charged by competitors in the entered markets.

22. This possibility was initially suggested to me by Lawrence J. White.

23. While these considerations may create inefficiencies in this context, they may have a salutary origin. A political commitment not to have customers of firm A cover the costs of firm B may prevent inefficient taxes and subsidies. The long-term costs of weakening this commitment need to be compared with the short-term benefits of having a regulated firm's competitors contribute to that firm's costs.

24. Richard Simnett has pointed out that entry may provided information about when a market might be competitive. This information would be especially valuable when the regulator lacks the information or incentive to force the regulated firm to act efficiently in the public interest.

References

Averch, H., and L. Johnson. 1962. "Behavior of the Firm Under Regulatory Constraint." *American Economic Review* 52:1052-69.

Bailey, E. 1981. "Contestability and the Design of Regulatory and Antitrust Policy." *American Economic Review Papers and Proceedings* 71:178-83.

Barclay, P., D. Gegax and J. Tschirhart. 1989. "Industrial Cogeneration and Regulatory Policy." *Journal of Regulatory Economics* 1:225-40.

Baron, D., and R. Myerson. 1982. "Regulating a Monopolist with Unknown Costs." *Econometrica* 50:911-30.

Baseman, K. 1981. "Open Entry and Cross-Subsidization in Regulated Markets." In *Studies in Public Regulation*, edited by G. Fromm. Cambridge, MA: MIT Press.

Baumol, W. 1983. "Contestable Markets: An Uprising in the Theory of Industry Structure." *American Economic Review* 73:491-96.

Baumol, W., J. Panzar, and R. Willig. 1982. *Contestable Markets and the Theory of Industry Structure*. San Diego: Harcourt Brace Jovanovich.

Berg, S., and J. Tschirhart. 1988. *Natural Monopoly Regulation*. Cambridge: Cambridge University Press.

Braeutigam, R. 1979. "Optimal Pricing with Intermodal Competition." *American Economic Review* 69:38-49.
Brennan, T. 1987. "Why Regulated Firms Should Be Kept Out of Unregulated Markets: Understanding the Divestiture in U.S. v. AT&T." *Antitrust Bulletin* 32:741-93.
Brennan, T. 1989a. "Regulating by Capping Prices." *Journal of Regulatory Economics* 1:133-47.
Brennan, T. 1989b. "Divestiture Policy Considerations in an Information Services World." *Telecommunications Policy,* 13:243-54.
Brennan, T. 1990a. "Cross-Subsidization and Cost Misallocation by Regulated Monopolists." *Journal of Regulatory Economics* 2:37-51.
Brennan, T. 1990b. "General 'Indifference' Results Under Rate-of-Return Regulation." University of Maryland, Baltimore County.
Breyer, S. 1982. *Regulation and Its Reform.* Cambridge, MA: Harvard University Press.
Brock, G. 1984. "Bypass of the Local Exchange: A Quantitative Assessment." *OPP Working Paper Series* 12. Washington: Federal Communications Commission.
Brock, W., and D. Evans. 1983. "Creamskimming." In *Breaking Up Bell: Essays on Industrial Organization and Regulation,* edited by D. Evans. New York: North-Holland.
Crew, M., and P. Kleindorfer. 1986. *The Economics of Public Utility Regulation.* Cambridge, MA: MIT Press.
Crew, M., and M. Zupan. 1990. "Alternatives to Rate of Return Regulation Including Franchise Bidding as Deregulation," this volume.
Demsetz, H. 1968. "Why Regulate Utilities?" *Journal of Law and Economics* 11:55-65.
Dixit, A. 1980. "The Role of Investment in Entry Deterrence." *Economic Journal* 90:95-106.
Einhorn, M. 1987. "Optimality and Sustainability: Regulation and Intermodal Competition in Telecommunications." *Rand Journal of Economics* 18:550-63.
Evans, L., and S. Garber. 1989. "The Rational Regulator's Response to Enhanced Opportunities to 'Bypass' the Public Telephone Network." *Journal of Regulatory Economics* 1:271-92.
Farrell, J. 1987. "Information and the Coase Theorem." *Journal of Economic Perspectives* 1:113-29.
Faulhaber, G. 1975. "Cross-Subsidization: Pricing in Public Enterprise." *American Economic Review* 65:966-77.
Griffin. J. 1982. "The Welfare Implications of Externalities and Price Elasticities for Telecommunications Pricing." *Review of Economics and Statistics* 64:59-66.
Haring, J., and E. Kwerel. 1987. "Competition Policy in the Post-Equal Access Market." 2 *FCC Rcd* 5:1488-93.
Hayek, F. 1945. "The Use of Knowledge in Society." *American Economic Review* 35:519-30.
Kahn, A. 1970. *The Economics of Regulation.* Cambridge, MA: MIT Press.
Katz, M. 1987. "The Welfare Effects of Third-Degree Price Discrimination in Intermediate Goods Markets." *American Economic Review* 77:154-67.
Klein, B., R. Crawford, and A. Alchian. 1978. "Vertical Integration, Appropriable Rents and the Competitive Contracting Process." *Journal of Law and Economics* 21:297-326.
Krueger, A. 1974. "The Political Economy of the Rent Seeking Society." *American Economic Review* 64:291-303.

Laffont, J.-J., and J. Tirole. 1986. "Using Cost Observation to Regulate Firms." *Journal of Political Economy* 94:614-41.
Lewis, T., and D. Sappington. 1989. "Regulatory Options and Price-Cap Regulation." *Rand Journal of Economics* 20:405-16.
Mankiw, N. G., and M. Whinston. 1986. "Free Entry and Social Inefficiency." *Rand Journal of Economics* 17:48-58.
Panzar, J., and R. Willig. 1977. "Free Entry and the Sustainability of Natural Monopoly." *Bell Journal of Economics* 8:1-22.
Peltzman, S. 1976. "Toward a More General Theory of Regulation." *Journal of Law and Economics* 19:211-240.
Phillips, A. 1982. "The Impossibility of Competition in Telecommunications: Public Policy Gone Awry." In *Regulatory Reform and Public Utilities*, edited by M. Crew. Lexington, MA: Lexington Books.
Posner, R. 1971. "Taxation by Regulation." *Bell Journal of Economics and Management Science* 2:22-50.
Reinganum, J. 1989. "The Timing of Innovation: Research, Development, and Diffusion." In *Handbook of Industrial Organization*, edited by R. Willig and R. Schmalensee. New York: Elsevier Scientific Publishing.
Sappington, D., and D. Sibley. 1988. "Regulating Without Cost Information: The Incremental Surplus Subsidy Scheme." *International Economic Review* 29:297-306.
Schwartz, M. 1986. "The Nature and Scope of Contestability Theory." *Oxford Economic Papers (supp.)* 38:37-57.
Schwartz, M. 1989. "Investments in Oligopoly: Welfare Effects and Tests for Predation." *Oxford Economic Papers* 41:698-719.
Sharkey, W. 1982. *The Theory of Natural Monopoly*. Cambridge: Cambridge University Press.
Shepherd, W. 1984. "'Contestability' vs. Competition," *American Economic Review* 74:572-87.
Sherman, R. 1989. *The Regulation of Monopoly*. Cambridge: Cambridge University Press.
Spence, A. M. 1977. "Entry, Capacity, Investment, and Oligopolistic Pricing." *Bell Journal of Economics* 8:534-44.
Spence, A. M. 1979. "Investment Strategy and Growth in a New Market." *Bell Journal of Economics* 10:1-19.
Starrett, D. 1988. *Foundations of Public Economics*. Cambridge: Cambridge University Press.
Stigler, G. 1971. "The Theory of Economic Regulation." *Bell Journal of Economics and Management Science* 2:3-21.
Stiglitz, J. 1981. "Potential Competition May Reduce Welfare." *American Economic Review Papers and Proceedings* 71:184-89.
Wenders, J. 1987. *The Economics of Telecommunications*. Cambridge, MA: Ballinger.
Williamson, O. 1976. "Franchise Bidding for Natural Monopolies—in General and with Respect to CATV." *Bell Journal of Economics* 7:73-104.
Willig, R. 1978. "Pareto-Superior Nonlinear Outlay Schedules." *Bell Journal of Economics* 9:56-69.
Wittman, D. 1989. "Why Democracies Produce Efficient Results." *Journal of Political Economy* 97:1395-1424.

9

INFORMATION ECONOMICS AND NEW FORMS OF REGULATION

Michael A. Crew
Michael R. Frierman

The regulation of public utilities is currently undergoing some major changes. These are particularly in evidence in telecommunications, where technological change, competition, and entry are bringing about drastic rethinking in the way telecommunications are regulated. For AT&T Communications, price-cap regulation has now replaced traditional rate-of-return regulation in their interstate long-distance telecommunications business. Price-cap regulation is currently under active consideration for local exchange carriers (LECs), at least with regard to the revenues they receive by way of carrier access.[1] In addition, price caps for local telephone service have been proposed in some state commissions. Price caps then may be an idea whose time has come. If this is the case, then the likelihood is that price caps will be extended to the other traditional public utilities—electricity, gas, and water. Already in New Jersey, the Governor's Task Force on Market-Based Pricing has recommended price-cap regulation for electric utilities. In the event that price-cap regulation is applied to electric utilities, it may be only a matter of time before gas and water utilities become subject to price caps. Thus, the issue of price-cap regulation is relevant not just to telephone companies but also to gas, water, and electric utilities.

Although price-cap regulation is about to have significant effects in the way regulators and utilities operate, there are still a number of fundamental questions of economic efficiency that have not yet been resolved. Some of the current work of economic theorists on information economics is relevant to an understanding of the efficiency consequences of price-cap regulation and, ultimately, to a more precise form of comparative institutional assessment between rate-of-return (ROR) regulation and price-cap regulation. The purpose of this paper is to examine some of the implications of information economics for new forms of regulation, particularly price caps. By providing a rigorous analysis of incentives and by considering the nature of efficient contracts, principal-agent theory provides insights into some of the current issues in regulatory economics. It is relevant to the debate of price-cap versus ROR regulation. Price-cap regulation is often supported over ROR regulation on the grounds that it provides greater incentives for efficiency. Applying information economics to this problem indicates that this is not necessarily the case. By employing principal-agent theory and information economics, we are able to provide a more incisive approach to analyzing the efficiency of price caps versus ROR than heretofore.[2]

Section 1 will be by way of background, providing a comparison of price-cap and rate-of-return regulation. Section 2 provides a brief primer on the role of information economics in regulation. Section 3 will illustrate in relatively simplistic terms[3] how contributions from the information economics literature may be employed in assessing the efficiency of traditional ROR regulation and price-cap regulation. Section 4 discusses some of the implications of the analysis for regulatory policy and for future research.

1. Background and Review of the Issues

Traditionally, the concern of economists and lawyers with the regulation of monopoly was rather simplistic. Economists were concerned with the efficiency consequences of a monopoly price greater than marginal cost, while lawyers were concerned with the potential of monopoly for price gouging. Other considerations include the interaction between scale economies and marginal cost pricing and the resulting deficits that would ensue. For almost a century, rate-of-return regulation provided a compromise whose primary concern, at least ostensibly, was fairness, with concerns over the efficiency of regulation taking a back seat to such issues as price gouging and cross subsidies.

With changes in technology and the fuel price shocks of the 1970s, dissatisfaction with ROR regulation grew and attention turned to alternative forms of regulation. In particular, the notion of a price cap or an automatic adjustment attracted most interest and attention. An early example was the Michigan Bell price-cap scheme for the period 1980-1982,[4] followed by price-cap regulation of British Telecom following privatization in 1984. The form taken by the price cap was to set prices initially and then adjust them each year as a result of changes in the Retail Price Index, less a deduction for productivity. Essentially, the same policy was employed by the FCC in its price cap for AT&T's long-distance services.

Although price-cap regulation apparently has the blessing of both the companies and the regulators, it is not immediately apparent that it dominates ROR regulation in terms of its efficiency and equity characteristics. Accordingly, we will examine how it compares with ROR regulation in terms of efficiency and equity.

Recent developments in information economics, the new institutional economics, and public choice are very useful when it comes to comparing the efficiency of different regulatory forms. This paper concentrates on the role of information economics. It has long been known that regulation is not simply a matter of setting price equal to marginal cost in the tradition of neoclassical economics. Information problems surfaced at an early stage. Notably, the problem of how the pricing authority obtained marginal cost for pricing purposes was criticized in the early days by public choice theorists like Buchanan and Wiseman. However, in contrast to Wiseman who argued that nothing could be done, information economics provides a method of inducing firms to incorporate their true costs of production into their decisions.

Information economics employs the concept of asymmetric information. Regulation is considered to be a member of the set of problems known as principal and agent. In principal and agent problems, the principal hires the agent to act on his behalf because the agent has specialized knowledge or experience not readily available to the principal. Given that both the principal and the agent are economic men, it may be somewhat naive to assume that the agent will always act in the principal's interest if, for example, there is more money to be made by an alternative course of action. In particular, as emphasized in information economics, the agent will exploit to his advantage the information asymmetry between himself and the principal. For example, a physician may recommend therapy A over therapy B because he makes more money out of therapy A in the absence of constraints on his behavior. Information economics studies the nature of the constraints and the incentives systems that minimize the exploitation of information asymmetry by agents. Several methods are employed to deal with these problems. These are now illustrated. It is assumed throughout that the agent has an information advantage. In section 2, we will examine how such considerations apply to regulation. Before doing this, we will review the nature of ROR and price-cap regulation.

ROR regulation involves the regulator determining the amount of capital that the company has in the business and then applying a fair rate of return to this. In particular, the following simple formula illustrates the operation of ROR regulation.

$$R = E + (V - D)s \tag{1}$$

where R = Allowed Revenue (Revenue Requirements),
V = Value of the firm's cumulative investment (Rate Base),
D = Accumulated Depreciation,
s = Allowed rate of return on capital, and
E = Total expenses other than capital.

Thus the firm is allowed its cost plus a *capped* rate of return on its investment. In view of the factS that the firm gets its "costs" as determined by the regulator and that its profits are capped by the product of the rate of return times the rate base, its incentive to minimize total costs is attenuated. Indeed, because they earn a return on capital, they may have an incentive to provide an excessive amount of capital (Averch and Johnson 1962).

By contrast, price-cap regulation sets prices independently of the firm's costs or investment. It thus aims to set R as a function of something other than the firm's costs and capital invested. By decoupling the earning of revenue from the firm's costs, price-cap regulation seems to provide an incentive for the firm to minimize cost. Similarly, it provides an incentive toward dynamic economic efficiency. Thus, price caps seem to offer considerable advantage over ROR regulation, at least in the context of cost minimization and innovation. However, on closer inspection is this really the case? Price-cap regulation, while ostensibly being superior in efficiency terms to ROR regulation, may not have the desirable properties claimed for it by its supporters. For example, how is the initial price cap set? If the initial price cap is set based upon costs, then the firm has an incentive to overstate its costs to get a higher price. With the multiproduct firm, is the price cap based upon an index giving the firm flexibility to move individual prices up or down within the constraints of the index or are the prices that are set initially all adjusted by the same adjustment factor? Similarly, if the initial price is set based upon current rates, a number of problems arise. Current rates embody cross subsidies. Under current proposals, cuts in prices of greater than a certain amount do not count toward the index, and the amount an individual price may rise is capped at some multiple of the CPI. Another problem is what happens if the firm is successful in cutting its costs and as a result makes higher profits than anticipated? Does the regulator require the firm to take a price reduction? If this is a significant possibility, then there is a reduced incentive for the firm to minimize its costs and a consequent loss in dynamic efficiency. These are the kind of issues that will need to be analyzed when evaluating the efficiency incentives of price caps. We will now proceed in section 2 to illustrate how recent developments in the economic theory of information can be employed to analyze such regulatory problems.

2. Information Economics and Regulation: Truthful Revelation and Individual Rationality

Information economics recognizes that the agent will not reveal the asymmetric information to which he is privy unless he receives an incentive to do so. Thus, while it may be optimal for both parties to have the information so that they can adjust their behavior accordingly, the agent will not reveal the information in the absence of an incentive. One approach to the problem is to bribe the agent to reveal his information. Thus, if a scheme can be devised so that the agent has an incentive to reveal the information truthfully, then a more efficient outcome can be achieved. Designing incentive schemes which result in the agent revealing his information truthfully is a non-trivial task. Some payment schemes may end up with the agent pocketing the payments for the information and yet not revealing it truthfully or completely. For example, merely reducing proportionately the amount the agent is to receive because the principal knows that the agent has the ability to shirk still may not bring forth the amount of effort for which the principal is paying.

To understand better the way an incentive scheme must be designed to induce honest revelation of private information, we will consider a simple regulatory environment. Suppose that a monopoly firm can produce a single product whose costs of production are known only to the firm. In exchange for the production of this product, the regulator will compensate the firm (or allow the firm to be compensated) according to a contract. The firm is assumed to maximize its profits, which are simply the difference between the compensation and the cost of production.

Notice that, as described, the regulator is concerned only with the amount of compensation it must pay to the firm and the amount of output the firm produces. It is indifferent to the costs incurred by the firm. The regulator would prefer, for the same level of output, to pay less compensation. On the other hand, the firm would prefer higher compensation or lower levels of production. As the direction of preference over the relevant variables differ for the firm and the regulator, a potential conflict arises between the two over the level of output the firm should produce.

In an effort to eliminate this conflict, the regulator might attempt to make the firm's compensation depend on all available information. As the regulator can only observe the firm's level of output, the firm's compensation can be made to depend only on this. A piece work contract would be such a compensation scheme, for example.

Ideally, the regulator would like to make the compensation scheme depend on the costs of the firm. If the regulator could induce the firm to reveal honestly its knowledge of the costs of production, the regulator would be able to make a more informed decision. Of course, it is not in the firm's interest to reveal this information (for free), and so it would choose to produce a different amount than that intended by the regulator, given any feasible contract. This is an example of the *Adverse Selection Problem* in the principal agent model. (See Rees (1985) for example.)

It is possible however that, with the appropriate incentive, the firm could be induced to reveal its private information regarding its costs of production. The first step to obtaining the "optimal incentive contract" is to make use of the *Revelation Principle* (Dasgupta et al. 1979; Myerson 1979). This principle says that, of all possible contracts under consideration, the regulator need only consider direct, truthful mechanisms. That is, the regulator need only focus on compensation mechanisms which are composed simply of the relevant observable variables, i.e., direct, and which induce honest revelation, i.e., truthful.

To see how the Revelation Principal works, consider that the regulator must still condition the firm's compensation, call it ω, only on the observable output level, say x. However, in constructing the compensation scheme, the regulator takes into account the fact that when faced with the compensation $\bar{\omega}(x)$, the firm will choose its production level based on its private information regarding the costs of production, say θ. That is, the regulator knows that the firm will choose to produce that level of output which maximizes its profits, given the compensation scheme $\bar{\omega}(x)$ and with the knowledge of θ. Mathematically, the firm chooses x to maximize profits, $\bar{\omega}(x) - c(x;\theta)$, where θ is an index for the firm's cost function $c(x;\theta)$. Clearly, the firm's optimal choice in this problem will be a function of its information θ, say $\hat{x}(\theta)$, and so its compensation will be $\omega(\theta) = \bar{\omega}(\hat{x}(\theta))$.

Suppose instead of being offered the scheme $\bar{\omega}(x)$, the regulator allowed the firm to choose from the menu $(\omega(\theta), x(\theta))$, which maximized its profits. It would choose the pair which were associated with its actual, or true, value of θ. Thus, any compensation scheme based on observable variables, $\bar{\omega}(x)$, could be represented by the appropriate truth revealing mechanism $(\omega(\theta), x(\theta))$.

Now, the optimal mechanism must be designed in such a fashion (i.e., the design of $\bar{\omega}(x)$) that the firm in fact chooses the pair (ω, x) associated with the true value of θ. That is, the optimal incentive contract induces truthful revelation. By its choice of the pair (ω', x') from the menu (ω, x), the firm's true θ can be inferred. The restriction of contract design to truthful mechanisms, then, imposes an *Incentive Compatibility Constraint* on the regulator.

To describe the incentive compatibility constraint more exactly, define the firm's profits as $\pi(\omega, x; \theta)$, or incorporating the compensation scheme, $\pi(\omega(\theta), x(\theta); \theta)$. Suppose the firm were to chose a pair from the menu (ω, x) which implied a θ different from its known value $\hat{\theta}$. In this case, the firm would "report" θ and receive a profit equal to $\pi(\omega(\theta), x(\theta); \hat{\theta})$. We see then, that incentive compatibility requires that the contract be designed so that the firm's profits are maximized when it reports the true value of θ, namely $\hat{\theta}$. Hence, truthful revelation imposes the constraint that for all $\hat{\theta}, \theta$:

$$\pi(\omega(\hat{\theta}), x(\hat{\theta}); \hat{\theta}) \geq \pi(\omega(\theta), x(\theta); \hat{\theta}).$$

The main insight gained from incorporating this constraint into the regulator's problem is the observation that the firm must be paid a "rent" to induce it to reveal its information honestly (Baron and Myerson 1982). Suppose that there are only two possible cost functions the firm can have, so that for all x, $c(\cdot; \theta_1) < c(\cdot; \theta_2)$ (and $C(0, \theta_1) = C(0, \theta_2)$).[5] The regulator would naturally prefer to pay the firm its reservation level of profit given its type θ_1 or θ_2, say $\bar{\pi}(\theta_i)$, $i = 1,2$. If the regulator offered a menu which implied the firm could choose between a profit of $\bar{\pi}(\theta_1)$ or $\bar{\pi}(\theta_2)$, the firm would always choose the later, claiming it was a high cost firm. By following this strategy, the firm would in fact earn only $\bar{\pi}$ when $\theta = \theta_2$, but if $\theta = \theta_1$ the firm would earn a profit in excess of its reservation profit level.

To illustrate the problem confronting the regulator and the incentives faced by the firm, suppose that the firm's costs are given by the function:

$$c(\cdot; \theta_i) = FC_i + \left(\frac{\theta_i}{2}\right) x^2 \quad i = 1,2,$$

where $\theta_1 = 1$ and $\theta_2 = 2$. If the regulator knew whether the firm had high or low costs, it could provide the firm with the appropriate compensation schedule. For instance, it could request the firm produce from either of the two following schedules, depending on the firm's type:

Low Cost Schedule		High Cost Schedule	
x	ω	x	ω
1	.5	1	1
2	2	2	4
3	4.5	3	9

Each schedule provides the firm with zero profits (assuming for ease of exposition that fixed costs are zero). Of course the regulator does not know the firm's cost structure.

The regulator's dilemma arises from the fact that it cannot simultaneously induce honest reporting on the part of the firm *and* provide the firm with zero profits no matter what its cost structure. Suppose such a scheme were attempted. In any case, the regulator would establish a compensation scheme under which the high cost firm produced smaller amounts than the more efficient, low cost firm. Two such compensation schemes, one for low levels of production and one for high levels of production are given in the following schedules:[6]

	x	ω
θ_h	1	1
θ_l	2	2

or

	x	ω
θ_h	2	4
θ_l	3	4.5

If the firm were offered *either* of these schedules, it would always report its costs to be high. If it were in fact a high cost firm, it would earn zero profits under either schedule (and negative profits if it mimcked the low cost firm). However, if the firm were a low cost firm, it could make positive profits by mimicking a high cost firm. Under these conditions, the firm would make a profit of 0.5 when the low output schedule was offered and a profit of 2 when the high output schedule was offered.

To induce honest reporting when the firm is a low cost type, the regulator must rewarded low cost firms for such behavior. That is, the regulator must provide a rent to the low cost firm beyond its reservation profit level. This rent, however, must not be such that the high cost firm is induced to lie, claiming to be a low cost type. The optimal incentive scheme then is one for which the high cost firm receives only its reservation profit level, while the low cost firm receives profits in excess of its reservation level. Note, the low cost firm's rents can be seen to accrue from its monopoly over its private information. The greater the value of this information to the regulator, the greater the rent the firm will receive.

In the context of our example, consider the following compensation schedules (again, one each for low and high levels of production):

Schedule A		
	x	ω
θ_h	1	1
θ_l	2	3.5

or

Schedule B		
	x	ω
θ_h	2	4
θ_l	3	7

Under either schedule, a high cost firm would receive zero profits. In contrast to the previous schedules, under each of these schemes the low cost firm would receive a profit. The low cost firm would make a profit of 1.5 unit under schedule A and 2.5 unit under schedule B. Thus, the firm has an incentive to reveal its costs honestly when either of these compensation schemes are offered.

Of course the relationship between the regulator and the firm is a continuing one. With the insights gained in the preceding discussion, the impact of this aspect of the regulatory environment on the optimal contract can be analyzed. The new feature of the extension to a multi-period setting is the potential for the regulator to use information revealed by the firm in an opportunistic manner against the firm. If the firm were induced to reveal its costs at some point in time, the regulator could then potentially use that information later to provide only the reservation level of profit for that particular type of firm. Of course, if the regulator were somehow constrained so it could not use this newly acquired information, no further difficulties would develop. Hence, in a multi-period framework, the main issue of concern for determining an optimal contract is one of *commitment*.

To understand better the issue of commitment in a multi-period environment, it is important to be sure of the structure. In the two-period framework most often considered, the firm is assumed to know its type at the beginning of the first period. The firm's type, for example, whether its costs are high or low, is then assumed to remain the same across periods. In this setting, the firm's objective is to maximize the present value of its (two-period) profit stream. A contract in this environment then, specifies two compensation schemes, one for each period. The contract is offered to the firm at the beginning of the first period, and the firm decides to either accept or reject the contract.

Suppose the contract were constructed in a manner which induced the firm to reveal its information in the first period. The regulator could then use this information to adjust the compensation scheme the firm faces in the second period. However, there is a constraint on the extent to which the regulator can use this new information. For, in either period, the firm has the option to quit and produce nothing at all. The firm is always assumed to have the option to walk away from the relationship. Hence, the regulator can never propose a compensation schedule which implies that the firm receive a profit below its (discounted) reservation level (usually taken to be zero).

Suppose the regulator can fully commit at the beginning of the first period to a contract which stipulates payment in both periods. Then the optimal contract will be the same as the one described earlier, simply repeated in each period. This eliminates opportunistic behavior on the part of the regulator and ensures the low cost firm profits in each period. The regulator commits itself to not exploiting in the second period the information it gains in the first period.

Without the ability to provide a credible commitment to this behavior, it is not possible to induce the firm to reveal itself in the first period *and* produce in the second period. To see that this is so, suppose the contract offered the firm is composed of two compensation schemes, each like the one period compensation scheme described previously. In a single period setting, it was seen that the firm never found it in its interest to claim to be a higher cost firm than it actually was. Now however, the firm knows that no matter what contract the regulator offers in the first period, the regulator will have both the incentive and the opportunity to use any information gained in the first period to restructure the compensation scheme for the second period. The firm would (correctly) expect the regulator to exploit the information, so that the firm earned zero profits in the second period. Thus, the firm would have an incentive to overstate its costs. In order to negate this incentive, the regulatory must pay the firm in the first period the (discounted, present value of the) profits it would have otherwise received in the second period. Hence, the low cost firm must be paid an additional lump sum in the first period to prevent it from claiming that it is a high cost firm.

The lump-sum payment in period one, required to induce honest behavior by the low cost firm, now has an adverse effect on the high cost firm. The high cost firm would now find it profitable to claim to be a *lower* cost type than it actually was, and so receive the higher rents intended for that type firm.[7] In the second period, using its newly acquired information, the regulator would then attempt to impose zero profits on what it thought was a lower cost firm. However, this would result in negative profits for the, in fact, higher cost firm. As a result, the firm would simply choose not to participate in the second period. Hence, a firm would find it more profitable to pretend to be a lower cost firm than in fact it is. In this way, the firm has an incentive *not* to reveal its information honestly in the first period. Thus, if the firm has the alternative of not producing, and the regulator cannot commit itself, no contract can be constructed which would induce truthful revelation (Laffont and Tirole 1988).

It is precisely the ability of the firm to quit the industry (or reduce the quality of service) in the second period, thereby avoiding any penalty for lying in the first period, which leads to the inability to construct a truth revealing contract in the absence of commitment. However, caution must be taken when considering alternatives which require participation in the second period. Any alternative which requires the firm to produce when it would otherwise choose not to, allows for potential abuse by the regulator. Under these conditions, the regulator has the opportunity to drive the firm below its reservation profit level in the period in which it is required to produce. Any such requirement would then have to explicitly prohibit such abuse, in order to construct a contract which induces honest revelation. (See, for example, Baron and Besanko (1987).)

3. The Efficiency of ROR and Price Regulation

Let us now develop some of the implications of the theoretical framework in analyzing the efficiency of price cap and ROR regulation. One contribution is that essentially the same conditions for efficient regulation apply to price caps as to cost-of-service regulation. Without truthful revelation by the firm and commitment by the regulator, neither will be efficient. Moreover, neither price caps nor ROR regulation employ the kind of complex schemes for truthful revelation envisaged in the theory. As both are then going to be second-best compared to the efficiency standards of the theory, the question is which is likely to be less inefficient and whether the theory can contribute to efficiency.

Claims for the superior efficiency of price-cap regulation over ROR stem from the notion that ROR regulation, to the extent that it is a cost-driven system, does not provide incentives to minimize costs. By apparently decoupling price and cost, price caps provide an incentive for cost minimization. In addition, by providing automatic adjustments in price, the frequency of rate hearings is reduced, thereby offering a potential reduction in the transactions costs of regulation. However, using the arguments of section 2, it is not immediately clear that price caps provide significantly better incentives for efficiency than ROR regulation. Indeed, price cap regulation as currently envisaged is highly simplified relative to the theoretical compensation schemes designed to elicit truthful revelation. As for cost-based regulation, commitment on the part of the regulator and truthful revelation by the firm are required for efficiency of price-cap regulation. The reason why these are still required with price caps is that the decoupling of price and cost under price caps, at least as currently proposed, is by no means guaranteed.

As proposed in telecommunications at least and probably in electricity, there is a problem about setting the initial level of the price cap and the adjustment formula over time. Take the case of the proposal for LECs (which is very similar to the scheme in operation for AT&T and British Tel). This requires the setting of two principal parameters, the initial price level and the productivity deduction from the annual price adjustment.

Let us look first at the problem of setting the initial price level. It is not clear that the LECs' existing price structure is efficient and therefore would be the appropriate starting point for price based regulation. Traditionally, local service has been cross subsidized by toll service, both in the case of intraLATA toll provided by the LECs and interLATA toll provided by the interexchange carriers like AT&T.[8] Thus the likelihood is that the local service provided by the LECs is subsidized somewhat by their toll service. As their toll service faces competitive entry at these prices, the LECs would like to reduce toll rates while raising rates for local service. So if rates are capped at their present level and adjustments over time are limited to the CPI less a productivity deduction, there are likely to be few efficiency gains from more efficient pricing under price-cap regulation. On the other hand, if price-cap regulation is applied simply by means of a price index with complete freedom to change the prices within the overall index, then the regulator will fear that the company will set the local service price at the monopoly level and the toll prices at a predatory level, thereby exploiting its monopoly power. Thus a sort of compromise is proposed which allows the firm to reduce its "competitive" prices by any amount it wishes, but not to count the whole amount of this reduction in calculating effect on the price index.

While such an approach may provide some protection for the "monopoly" or captive customers, it does not encourage innovation and efficiency in pricing. For example, where a company currently has little or no local measured service (LMS), there seems to be a weak incentive to introduce LMS, because the introduction of LMS cannot increase the total revenue from the basket of local services beyond the (tight) limit imposed by the price cap. The incentive is further attenuated by the pricing mechanism for access charges. LECs charge the inter exchange carriers on a minute of use basis for access to their networks. While bypass can and does occur, it has not become a major problem because the monopoly at this level has been preserved by regulation. The LECs all have the same price structure. The charge is less at the originating end than it is at the terminating end.[9] The tariff does not vary by time of day. This and the subscriber line charges provide an important contribution from toll to local. The price-cap proposal provides no apparently stronger incentive to innovate than ROR regulation.

Another concern about the initial level of the price cap stems from some problems with regulatory accounting. In the case of the competitive firm, depreciation is entirely market determined. Therefore, in contrast to the regulated firm, depreciation plays no part in determining price. However, for the regulated firm the amount of depreciation is critically important in determining the amount of revenue that the regulated firm receives. As shown in equation (1), the amount of depreciation is a major input employed by the regulator in determining the firm's revenue. Indeed the regulator, by manipulating depreciation formulae, service lives, and the like, can have a dramatic effect on the revenue that the firm receives. Traditionally service lives of utility plant have been long, with regulators employing long lives in calculating depreciation. However, especially in telecommunications, in the presence of rapid technological change, primarily arising from the introduction of microelectronics and optical fiber, the actual service lives of telephone equipment have fallen dramatically, but the lives for depreciation purposes employed by regulators have fallen nowhere near as dramatically. Thus, there is reason to believe that the amount of deprecation currently being allowed by regulators may be insufficient. It could be inefficient in two respects. First, the market value of the LECs' plant and equipment may be seriously below its book value. Second, the amount currently being allowed may be less than the actual amount. While the setting of the initial level of the price caps provides an opportunity to raise the price level to recover the past depreciation deficiencies and current depreciation, there is little in the price-cap proposals to lead us to expect that this is going to happen. Moreover, the setting of depreciation provides the same kind of moral hazard problem examined earlier. The challenge is to get the company to reveal honestly its estimate of depreciation. Neither price-cap nor

ROR regulation provide the required incentive

Setting the level of the initial price cap is a non-trivial problem because of the problems of past cross subsidization and depreciation policies. One way around this problem would be if the regulator could get the LECs to reveal these amounts truthfully. The same problem of truthful revelation arises in setting the productivity deduction. It is presumably to the advantage of the firm to have the regulator believe that its productivity is lower than it really is. In this way, it can get a higher level of price adjustment over time. Thus, arriving at an efficient level for the price cap is extremely difficult in the absence of the truthful revelation of certain parameters by the firm. The challenge of information economics is to devise schemes for truthful revelation in practice.

Let us now look at some conditions that need to be present for the achievement of truthful revelation in practice. Clearly commitment on the part of the regulator is required and is recognized implicitly in the price cap proposals. Initially, the price caps are to cover a five-year period, after which time the parameters are reviewed by the regulators. It is by no means clear that such a commitment will be honored. In the case of British Tel, the original framework called for a three percent productivity deduction. This was raised in August 1989, at the end of the initial period, to four and a half percent. That the management of British Tel (BT) initiated the change does not lessen the need for commitment. Indeed BT's raising the issue itself may indicate the value that it placed on the commitment of the regulator, or possible recognition of the first-mover advantages in the game between it and the regulator. BT's profit growth had been very strong, and the company presumably felt vulnerable to charges of profiteering. In addition, the fact that 51% of the stock is still held by the British Government might have raised its sensitivity in this dimension. From the regulator's point of view, presumably there were advantages to agreeing to the revised deduction with BT. A sophisticated regulator aware of the need for truthful revelation might recognize that BT's productivity were indeed significantly better than the increased deduction allowed. However, if he is also aware of the importance of asymmetric information, the resultant need to bribe the firm to reveal its true level of productivity, and the importance of commitment to the integrity of the process, he might find the BT offer cheap at the price. It not only signals higher productivity but also preserves the notion of commitment, since it was BT and not the regulator that proposed the change.

The lesson of British Tel is one that United States utilities should not just ignore. From both the regulator's and the firm's point of view, significant effort is worth expending on preserving commitment, because the ex post alternatives to ex ante truthful revelation are not attractive. Because utilities do not normally have available to them the alternative of free exit if the regulator reneges, they have to employ alternative means of responding. One approach is to lower service quality. The regulator is aware of this possibility and may employ a number of approaches ex post to deal with it. He may monitor performance or audit the firm's records. For example, the contract may specify performance standards and require the company to keep records of performance standards. However, ex post control devices like auditing and monitoring are limited in their potential for achieving efficiency.

Monitoring is frequently used by principals in an attempt to ascertain agents' output ex post. In employment, for example, monitoring is frequently used in an attempt to prevent shirking on the part of the employee. One problem with monitoring is that it cannot guarantee performance. Some aspects of job performance can easily be monitored, for example, the time the employee starts work or leaves work, but others, for example, the quality of the employee's work, cannot. Thus monitoring, by concentrating on what can be measured, will induce excessive quantities of those attributes that can be easily measured, while bringing forth insufficient quantities of those attributes that are difficult to measure. Thus, depending on the extent to which quality of service and performance standards are easy to measure, it may be possible for a firm to vary quality in response to lack of commitment by the regulator.

How do these considerations apply in the case of regulated companies? Service standards may not be that easy for the regulator to measure. The agent, the utility, clearly has information advantages relative to the principal, the commission. It has superior information regarding demand and costs. In the absence of incentives to minimize cost, it does not do so, and the regulator is limited in the extent to which he can employ monitoring and auditing to enforce cost minimizing behavior and service standards.

There are some significant problems with implementing the current price-cap proposals. They are relatively blunt instruments that do not elicit truthful revelation and therefore provide only a limited obvious spur to efficiency. Because of this, price caps have to retain the ex post instruments of monitoring and auditing and, as a result, retain some of the problems of ROR regulation. How is it then that the LECs are embracing them?[10] Perhaps they believe that the added flexibility provided by price caps is very important. In addition, they believe that they can be more efficient. They have shed thousands of managers since Divestiture. They may believe that with improvements in technology they can shed more management and labor to achieve significantly more than the 3% productivity growth needed to break even.

They may have been influenced by the success of AT&T under price caps. However, AT&T faces a very different situation. Toll prices have been historically high, presumably, as a result of the cross subsidy to toll. Competitors, while not necessarily having lower costs or providing better service, were able, because of regulatory imposed delays, to under cut AT&T and erode its market share and profitability. By introducing price caps, AT&T is able to be more flexible and much quicker in its response to competitors. Clearly the same considerations do not apply to anywhere near the same extent to the LECs.

Another reason sometimes cited by proponents of price caps is that they have lower regulatory transactions costs than ROR regulation. One lesson of this analysis is that this is not necessarily the case, because of the limited role of truthful revelation and therefore efficiency ex ante in price caps and the reliance, like ROR regulation, on the ex post devices of monitoring and auditing. Although the nature of the monitoring and auditing will change under price caps, it will still be important. For example, there may be an incentive to try to show a lower rate of productivity than that actually achieved. Thus the type of monitoring and auditing will change significantly under price caps. The regulator will no longer be interested in the value of the rate base or whether costs were as stated by the company, but he will be extremely interested in measuring service quality and productivity growth. Whether there will be lower transactions costs as a result is not clear. Reduced frequency of hearings may reduce transactions cost. However, monitoring quality and productivity may be more expensive than monitoring the rate base and other expenses. Price caps may substitute continuous monitoring for periodic monitoring, and may substitute economists for lawyers and accountants, which would be an unambiguous improvement!

4. Summary and Implications for Future Research and Policy

The contribution of information economics to regulation arise from its notions of truthful revelation and commitment. Cost-based regulation, like ROR regulation, requires the company to provide truthful revelation of its costs, since the regulator rewards the company based upon its level of cost. The basic problem was to provide the firm with a sufficient incentive to reveal its true costs, so that the regulator could base his price on them. The message is that to induce efficiency requires that the regulator reward the firm. This apparently goes against the grain for politicians. Information economics spells out the tradeoffs loud and clear. The tradeoff is between efficiency and equity. Achieving more fairness requires a loss in efficiency. Additional efficiency can only be induced if the firm gets its share of the gain. Information economics pins down asymmetric information as the source of the firm's power and the need for it to receive a rent if it is to cooperate.

The challenge is to devise regulatory schemes that meet the criterion of inducing efficient operation by honest revelation of costs, while minimizing the rents to information paid to the firm. As we have argued, price caps do not meet the exacting standards implied by the theory. However, the theory does offer some insights. As the above discussion indicates, there are some reforms to price caps, particularly in the role of commitment, in the spirit of the theory that offer prospects of greater efficiency.

Thus, while we would argue that price caps in their present form, do not represent a significant breakthrough in improving the efficiency of regulation,[11] we are not against replacing ROR with price caps. We would like to see addressed the problems we raised, such as cross subsidy, compliance on quality standards, and capital recovery. In addition, we would like to see continued work in applying principal-agent theory and information economics to regulatory problems. They offer not only an incisive analysis of the problem but the potential for further advances in the future.

Notes

We would like to thank our discussants, Joseph C. Schuh and Dennis Weller, for helpful comments.

1. The Federal Communications Commission is considering price caps for the access charges on interstate calls. The California Public Utility Commission is now operating a price-cap scheme for telephone companies for intrastate revenues.
2. Without the benefit of the contribution of information economics and principal agent theory, Crew and Kleindorfer (1986) provide a simple transactions-costs-based comparative institutional analysis of various regulatory schemes.
3. The approach attempts to be readable by employing only minimal algebra and does not attempt to employ the rigor associated with information economics.
4. Our undertanding of the Michigan experiment owes much to a presentation by Howard Face at Rutgers Advanced Workshop in Regulation and Public Utility Economics, April 19, 1985.
5. When there is no production, the two cost functions provide for the same fixed costs.
6. Note the regulator is only interested in truthful revelation of the firm's costs. The regulator initially decides whether he wants low or high output. Depending on what output he desires, he offers one of the schedules. (Two schedules are provided to illustrate the notion that the regulator—once he has decided on an output level—can achieve truthful revelation for that output level.)
7. Our example can be used to illustrate this point. Suppose the discount rate were zero. Using schedule A, the regulator must pay the firm 5 (3.5 + 1.5) in period one to induce honest behavior by the low cost firm. However, if the high cost firm claims it has low costs, it would produce 2 units and receive a payment of 5. While the firm loses 0.5 on the production, this is offset by the lump-sum payment of 1.5 for a profit of 1.
8. Estimates on the extent of the subsidy vary. However, since Divestiture, with the introduction of non-trivial subscriber line charges of at least \$3.50, there has been some reduction in the amount of the cross subsidy provided from inter LATA toll usage.
9. Simnett (1989) provides a good description of the tariff and discussion of the issues. The current tariffs vary from company to company. For example, GTE charges \$0.01 for originating minutes and \$0.024421 for terminating minutes.
10. Recently Pacific Bell agreed a price-cap proposal with the California Public Utilities Commission, which goes further than any other plan in adopting price caps for local service. New York Telephone, on the other hand, has recently extricated itself from its rate stability plan. The New York experience underlines our contention that price caps are no panacea.
11. In the case of AT&T, we have not disputed that there may have been efficiency gains from price caps. However, as noted above, AT&T faces a different situation, including much more vigorous competition.

References

Averch, H., and L.L. Johnson. 1962. "Behavior of the Firm Under Regulatory Constraint." *American Economic Review* 52:1052-69.

Baron, David P., and David Besanko. 1987. "Commitment and Fairness in a Dynamic Regulatory Relationship." *Review of Economic Studies* 65: 413-436.

Baron, David P., and Roger B. Myerson. 1982. "Regulating a Monopolist with Unknown Costs." *Econometrica* 50 (no. 4, July): 911-30.

Crew, Michael A., and Paul R. Kleindorfer. 1986. *The Economics of Public Utility Regulation*. London: Macmillan.

Dasgupta, P.S., P.J. Hammond, and E.S. Maskin. 1979. "The Implementation of Social Choice Rules: Some Results on Incentive Compatability." *Review of Economic Studies* 49:185-216.

Laffont, Jean-Jacques, and Jean Tirole. 1988. "The Dynamics of Incentive Contracts." *Econometrica* 56 (no. 5, September): 1153-1175.

Myerson, R.B. 1979. "Incentive Compatability and the Bargaining Problem. *Econometrica* 47:61-74.
Rees, Ray. 1985. "The Theory of Principal and Agent, Part I." *Bulletin of Economic Research* 37(1): 3-26.
Simnett, Richard E. 1989. "Contestable Markets and Telecommunications." In *Deregulation and Diversification of Utilities*, edited by M.A. Crew. Boston: Kluwer Academic Publishers.

10

FRANCHISE BIDDING FOR PUBLIC UTILITIES REVISITED

Michael A. Crew
Mark A. Zupan

1. Introduction and Background

Analogous to the reforms sweeping through Eastern Europe, important changes have been taking place in Western utility industries. Competition has been occurring in telecommunications and gas and is beginning to take place in electricity. Price-cap regulation is beginning to be employed in telecommunications. Privatization and calls for privatization are on the rise. Such changes are all raising serious questions about the life expectancy of rate-of-return (ROR) regulation and whether, in the traditional set-up and implementation of public policy towards utilities, too little consideration has been given to market-oriented solutions to natural monopoly problems.

The problems with ROR regulation in promoting efficiency stem from its abandonment of market incentives. The discipline of the product market is replaced with price setting by a regulator. The capital markets' discipline, which occurs when assets are bid away from an inefficient user, is also severely attenuated. Commissions very rarely remove or even threaten to remove an incumbent utility. Indeed, the command and control mechanisms available to regulatory commissions are exceedingly weak compared to market incentives.

Franchise bidding (FB) attempts to bring back some market incentives by encouraging competition in the awarding of a franchise and allowing incumbents to be displaced at renewal. A powerful case for FB as a means of controlling natural monopoly was made two decades ago by Demsetz (1968). Where parties are required to bid for the right to a franchise and where the bid is awarded to the party offering the lowest price, FB offers the prospect of control of monopoly pricing and minimum cost operation. To the extent that it institutionalizes "regulatory lag"

(Joskow 1974), furthermore, FB promises dynamic efficiency advantages by providing strong incentives to innovate and/or reduce costs—especially if the property rights to the franchise are transferrable. Finally, the credible threat of non-renewal provides a further spur to efficiency.

Most analyses subsequent to Demsetz's arrived at an almost entirely opposite conclusion with regard to the potential efficacy of FB. Indeed, in the wake of the theoretical arguments and case studies presented by Goldberg (1976), Peacock and Rowley (1972), and Williamson (1976), among others, FB was largely left for dead by economists. Schmalensee (1979, 73) concludes that because of potential problems FB "is hardly a breakthrough in natural monopoly control technology." Such problems include imperfect competition at the time of a franchise award, producer "capture" of the regulatory process, the pursuit by franchisors of nonprice concessions at the expense of lower prices for general service, and difficulties in enforcing the spirit of a contract once it is struck and when it comes up for renewal—especially if the incumbent firm has distinct advantages over potential rivals and is prone to opportunism.

Notwithstanding the important problems with FB noted by the literature either through a priori argument or through the presentation of a case study of failure, systematic empirical evidence has recently been presented which suggests that Schmalensee's gloomy conclusion may not be entirely warranted (Prager 1986; 1989; Zupan 1989c; 1989d). The systematic evidence indicates that, at least for the case of cable television (CATV), FB can be employed successfully to prevent monopoly pricing, promote innovation and cost minimization, and deter opportunistic behavior by operators.

In view of the recognized inefficiencies of ROR regulation, the significant changes currently occurring in public utility regulation, and the favorable systematic evidence concerning the efficacy of FB in the case of CATV, we think that the time is ripe to reexamine FB as a means of utility regulation. Accordingly, this paper summarizes the lessons learned from the application of FB in the case of CATV and reviews the extent to which those lessons would apply were FB to be extended to utilities in general.

2. A Benefit-Cost Analysis of FB in the Case of CATV

In the case of cable television, franchising falls by and large in the regulatory domain of the municipality (Webb 1983). Local policymakers set franchising in motion by issuing a Request for Proposals (RFP). The RFP serves as a preliminary "wish list" by specifying—albeit vaguely at times (cf., Williamson (1976))—a city's minimum requirements and desired services.

On average, cable franchise competitions draw 4 to 5 applicants (Prager 1986). In their submitted applications, the contestants promise, although never in complete contingent claims fashion, a construction deadline, basic and pay tier programming and rates, and certain nonprice concessions. The nonprice concessions are primarily fixed-cost in nature and include: direct endowments; community programming;

institutional networks (I-nets) linking various public facilities in a city; excess channel capacity; and franchise fees levied as a percentage of operating revenues.

Of the applications obtained, local politicians weed out clearly inferior bids and conduct hearings on the remainder. Surviving bidders are allowed to amend their original proposals. Competition among remaining applicants ensures that the quality of the final winning proposal is at least as high as the quality of the best initially-submitted proposal. The winning bidder is generally awarded an exclusive, renewable contract—typically for a period of 15 years.

Once awarded, franchise contracts require ongoing contact and negotiation between cities and operators (Williamson 1976). The winning bidder does not disappear after winning the franchise and resurface 15 years later when it is time to refranchise. Rather, because of the incompleteness of the contracts, there are many details to be ironed out along the way and numerous unanticipated events to be mutually dealt with and resolved. The day-to-day ironing out may in fact be quite desirable due to the costs of contractually defining ahead of time parties' obligations under all possible states of nature that may attain (Posner 1986).

2.1. The Benefits Associated with FB

The recent evidence indicates that FB, as it has been applied in the CATV case, has at least four positive features: competition is "healthy" at the time of initial bidding; reputational concerns and the monopsony power possessed by city-buyers, among other factors, motivate firms to deliver on their promises during contract execution and limit opportunistic behavior by firms at the time of franchise renewal; rates are constrained below monopoly levels (at least when and where federal legislation has permitted local franchisors to control rates); and there are strong incentives to minimize costs and to innovate.

2.1.1. Healthy Initial Bidding Competition

Prager (1986) analyzes the experiences of 92 of 104 Massachusetts communities which undertook the cable-franchising process during the period 1973-1981. She finds that the number of applicants per community ranged from 1 to 17, with a mean of 5.2, and concludes that (pp. 23-24):

> Three or four applicants is a sufficient number to generate a healthy degree of competition at the franchising stage, and to ensure that the specifications set forth in the [RFP]...(which are generally quite demanding) will be met or exceeded by at least one firm. Overall, the Massachusetts experience suggests that franchise bidding satisfies the first requirement for effectiveness—an adequate degree of competition at the bidding stage.

2.1.2. Effective Restraints Against Opportunism

Although competition may be healthy at the time of initial bidding, it is infirm after a franchise is awarded and a system begins operating. Incumbent firms possess considerable advantages over potential rivals due to the idiosyncratic investments involved in a cable franchise relationship (Williamson 1976). The quasi-rents (Klein, Crawford, and Alchian 1978) associated with such investments provide an operator with the temptation to "hold up" (Goldberg 1976) a city for favorable changes in the terms of a relationship once the operator gets a foot in the door. And rate increases or scalebacks in nonprice concessions are among the favorable changes cable operators could extort from their city-partners.

The extent to which incumbency advantages foster bad behavior on the part of operators, however, appears to be limited. The results of systematic, empirical scrutiny indicate that operators are typically well-behaved (Prager 1986; 1989; Zupan 1989c; 1989d). Reneging on promises during a contract is infrequent and, when it occurs, it appears to be due primarily to unforeseen changes in demand or cost. The advantages of incumbency, furthermore, are typically not milked by operators at the time of franchise renewal; the deals obtained from incumbent operators by cities conferring renewals are as good as the deals obtained from rookie firms by similarly-situated cities concurrently awarding initial franchise contracts.

Among the defense mechanisms which appear to ensure that bad behavior by franchised operators is the exception rather than the rule are reputational constraints (Klein and Leffler 1981) and the potential for vertical integration (Joskow 1985; Klein, Crawford, and Alchian 1978) by cities into the distribution of local CATV services (i.e., municipal ownership). The ability of operators to exploit the advantages of incumbency also appears to be circumscribed by the countervailing power of cities to do likewise; i.e., while their irreversible investments place existing firms in a superior position vis-a-vis potential entrants, the sunk costs have value only to the city in which they are sunk. The monopsony power an incumbent city can bring to bear on an incumbent operator may be quite substantial.

2.1.3. Prices Below Monopoly Levels

Several pieces of evidence suggest that FB, at least when and where there are no proscriptions over the control of rates, can be successfully employed to prevent monopoly pricing. First, the jump in cable stock prices subsequent to the passage of the Cable Act of 1984 implies that FB was at least somewhat successful in limiting basic tier rates (Jaffe and Kanter 1989). The federal legislation freed most operators of local control over basic rates effective December 29, 1986.

Second, the observed change in total revenues in systems raising their rates suggests that local authorities were at least partially effective in controlling basic, as well as pay, rates prior to federal rate decontrol. Since the revenue from basic and pay services generally increased in response to a hike in basic and pay tier prices, respectively, this implies cable firms were constrained to operate along the inelastic portions of their demand curves (Zupan 1989c). Only an effectively price-regulated firm would operate along such a region of the demand curve.[1]

Finally, cross-sectional econometric analysis of the basic and lead pay tier prices charged in October 1984 by operators whose systems came onstream during the early 1980s suggests that FB can restrain prices below monopoly levels (Zupan 1989c). Everything else held constant, for example, rates are lower in systems that were subject to formal rate control in the fall of 1984 than in systems that were not.

The rates charged by operators in the fall of 1984 are also a negative function of the number of bidders initially competing for the franchise.

2.1.4. Strong Incentives to Minimize Costs and to Innovate

Although FB appears to be effective at preventing monopoly pricing, the econometric evidence also implies that operator profits are not constrained to equal zero (Zupan 1989c). Moreover, a review of the trade press indicates that cities rarely request a contract renegotiation. When market conditions turn out to be better than anticipated at the time of franchising, operators generally get to retain the unexpected windfall. Contract renegotiations are typically initiated by operators confronting market conditions that are less favorable than anticipated at the time of franchising. Cities, on the other hand, rely primarily on renewals to ensure that the terms of trade in their franchise accords are "at market" (Zupan 1989b).

The fact that cities rarely attempt to renegotiate franchise contracts when market conditions turn out to be better than expected suggests that FB is a "flexible" regulatory mechanism, providing operators relatively strong incentives to minimize costs and innovate. The gains associated with any cost savings or innovation redounds directly to the operator—at least until the time of the next franchise renewal. By contrast, effective rate-of-return regulation that rigidly constrains the regulated firm's profits to consistently equal zero provides little incentive for the firm to minimize costs or to innovate.

2.2. The Costs Associated with FB

While the findings summarized in the preceding subsection suggest that there are attractive advantages associated with FB in the case of CATV, the recent empirical evidence also indicates that there are two important problems connected with FB. The two drawbacks are: an apparent overemphasis by local policymakers on nonprice concessions when awarding contracts; and delays in wiring, primarily in certain large cities, due to the lengthiness of the initial bid solicitation and evaluation process.

2.2.1. An Overemphasis on Nonprice Concessions

Of the various possible impediments to the promotion of efficiency through FB, the pursuit of nonprice concessions by policymakers appears to be the most significant obstruction in the case of CATV. No matter how potent a city's defenses against operator opportunism and no matter how perfect the competition at the time of initial bidding, the lowest level to which prices can be held ultimately depends on the costs associated with building and operating a cable system. If nonprice concessions raise costs (particularly if they needlessly raise costs—i.e., if they are bells and whistles that provide little in the way of economic benefits) and yet prove desirable to local policymakers, the efficiency-enhancing potential of FB is curtailed.

That franchise award decisions may be based partly on the nonprice concessions offered by competing bidders has been well-noted (Posner 1972; Shew 1984). Econometric estimation based on a random sample of systems coming onstream in the early 1980s reveals that nonprice concessions significantly increase the costs of building and running a cable system. Nonprice concessions account for 26 percent of building costs and 11 percent of operating expenses (Zupan 1989a). Most of the concessions, furthermore, appear to provide only limited economic benefits.[2]

By raising costs, nonprice concessions also translate into higher prices for cable consumers. Based on econometric analysis, for every dollar spent (per home passed by cable) on nonprice concessions, basic rates are $0.35 higher, all else held constant (Zupan 1989c).

2.2.2. Delays in Decision-Making

While the franchise selection process typically takes no more than one or two years to complete, a recent United States Department of Commerce report (1988, 27) notes that there sometimes have been long delays, particularly in certain large metropolitan areas:

> For example, the franchise selection process in one section of Los Angeles consumed more than five years, amid allegations that council members were delaying their decision in order to collect campaign contributions from the various bidders. Similar delays occurred in Washington, DC, and Baltimore before franchises were awarded. Philadelphia endured four separate franchising processes since 1966 before it finally selected a franchisee in 1984.

Where cities take a long time to solicit and evaluate franchise bids there may be substantial welfare costs. Consumers of basic service must do without such service during the delay. The beneficiaries from nonprice concessions also do not benefit until the award is made. The costs to a city and its citizens of a lengthy delay during franchise selection may significantly outweigh any benefits (e.g., obtaining a bid promising lower prices and/or greater nonprice concessions) from the delay.

3. Why Is FB not Employed to Regulate Utilities?

Is it because of the disadvantages associated with FB that ROR regulation has generally been employed to control utilities? We think not. For one thing, although there are significant costs associated with lengthy delays in the franchise selection process, such delays are uncommon. In addition, while the nonprice concessions pursued by local policymakers appear to provide only limited economic benefits, it would seem unlikely that ROR regulation has been adopted to restrict the pursuit of such concessions.

What then might explain why FB has not typically been employed to regulate utilities? We raise four possibilities. First, most utilities, such as telephone and electricity service, are probably considered to be more of a necessity than cable service is. The potential for monopoly pricing is of greater concern to telephone and electricity customers than to cable consumers. As a result, direct regulation, tighter control, is justified more easily for local telephone/electricity monopolies, while a more flexible, market-oriented regulatory technology is employed in the case of CATV.

Second, compared to CATV, most utility services probably are perceived to be more standardized commodities, less susceptible to technological change. The potential of a flexible regulatory mechanism that provides sufficient incentives to minimize costs and to innovate may thus not have appeared to be as strong in cases such as local telephone and electricity provision as it is in the case of CATV.

Third, FB is particularly effective when reputational concerns matter to franchisees. Where a bad name implies lost future business from existing and/or new customers, franchisees will be deterred from opportunistic behavior. In the case of certain utilities, such as telephone service, however, there has been, until recently, only one potential provider of services. With reputational considerations being diminished, FB becomes a less effective means for regulating natural monopolies.

Fourth, since FB implies the creation and maintenance of a market for natural monopolies it also implies the possibility of turnover in suppliers.[3] The difficulties that may be involved in the transfer of idiosyncratic assets, especially when the idiosyncratic assets are as sizable as they are in the case of utilities, have been well-detailed by Williamson (1976), among others.

4. How Could FB be Applied to Utilities?: A Proposal

Are the preceding justifications sufficient to imply that FB could not be successfully applied to present-day utilities? Several reasons suggest not. First, recent technological and legal changes have significantly enhanced the competitiveness and/or potential competitiveness of most utility markets (e.g., telephone, electricity, natural gas). The elements of natural monopoly that appear to remain are primarily at the local distribution/exchange level (cf., Broadman and Kalt (1989); Joskow and Schmalensee (1983); MacAvoy, Spulber, and Stangle (1989); Noll (1987); and Noll and Owen (1988)).

Even where elements of natural monopoly remain, there is now often more than one potential supplier, as a result of new technology. In the case of the emerging integrated broadband network (IBN) technology, for example, the list of possible suppliers includes the various Regional Bell Operating Companies spun off from AT&T in 1984 and some of the larger multiple system operator (MSO) cable firms. In natural gas or electricity distribution, potential suppliers for any one state or region could include both the existing distributor and distributors serving other states.

It would appear, therefore, that competition for some present-day utility markets could be healthy enough to implement FB in a fashion similar to that which is utilized in the case of CATV. Rather than forsaking market forces and relying on negotiation between regulators and a sole, insulated provider, competition between potential suppliers and reputational concerns thus could be harnessed to determine distribution company, because it is larger than the typical investment in a local CATV distribution company, might attract fewer potential suppliers—perhaps due to capital market imperfections—and thus provide any one supplier greater leverage over consumers and their regulatory representatives. A larger overall investment, however, also implies that any given supplier has more at stake in the relationship once the investment is made and is thus subject to greater monopsony power from consumers and the policymakers representing those consumers.

Fourth, while difficulties in transferring assets are bound to occur if FB is implemented, the CATV experience suggests that these difficulties may not be as severe as intimated by Williamson (1976). In 1987, for example, roughly 15 percent of all basic CATV service subscribers nationwide changed company hands due to system sales (Zupan 1989c). Any difficulties that do occur in transferring assets, furthermore, fundamentally reflect an advantage of FB over traditional ROR regulation rather than a disadvantage. Specifically, by enhancing the transferability of the property rights to utility assets, FB is likely to offer significant efficiency advantages over ROR regulation, which effectively insulates the existing supplier from direct competition and/or takeover. Pointing to the difficulties that may occur in valuing and transferring assets as a reason for not applying FB to utility markets is akin to arguing that corporate takeovers should not be allowed due to similar potential asset valuation/transfer problems in private markets—despite the evidence that takeovers or the mere threat of takeovers have significant, positive efficiency consequences (Jensen 1988).

Given all of the foregoing considerations, how might one implement FB in the case of utilities? As in the CATV case, it would be necessary for the regulator to provide an RFP. The RFP would specify service quality, minimum services to be provided, and arrangements for compensating the franchisee for inflation. The bidders would bid the prices at which they would be prepared to provide service as specified in the RFP. In addition, the bidder might indicate, along the lines of the current price-cap proposals, how much he was prepared to "give back" by way of productivity gains over time. Or, perhaps, as in the CATV case, the "give back" would be left unspecified and be determined at the time of franchise renewal. Once the regulatory commission had accepted the bid it would not go out of business. It would have responsibility of enforcing and administering the contract. Thus, it might have powers to enforce penalties in the event of failure to provide services agreed upon in the RFP and ultimately the right to condemn the franchise.

Such a scheme clearly differs from existing ROR regulation, but at first sight at least it looks a lot like price cap proposals either in operation for AT&T or under consideration for the local exchange carriers. The attraction of a price cap is that it decouples cost and price and therefore does not attenuate the objective of cost minimization, a serious deficiency of cost-of-service regulation. Another problem of ROR regulation has been that it has encouraged cross subsidies. In telecommunications, rates for local service have been traditionally below cost, while rates for toll service have been well above cost. Similarly, residential electric service may be cross subsidized by commercial and perhaps industrial service. For the

AT&T price-cap scheme, this does not present a major problem, because prices for long-distance services did not involve significant cross subsidies, and the price-cap scheme provided an opportunity for healthy competition with other carriers and resultant downward pressure on prices. For local exchange carriers there is, however, a major problem. Using existing price levels to set the initial prices in the price cap will continue existing inefficiencies. Residential service would continue to be priced below cost and capped. Toll and other service would be subject to downward price pressure from competition. So while local companies might gain in terms of the greater operating flexibility in competitive markets provided by the price cap, the major problem of perpetuating inefficient pricing structures would be unresolved.

Getting regulators, under the present system, to allow large increases in residential rates would be difficult. Just because they were introducing price caps might not seem a compelling enough argument to allow this kind of increase. So, for price-cap proposals currently under consideration, the prospect of obtaining initially efficient prices is not good. Adoption of FB might offer the prospect of a break in the continuing cycle of cross subsidy. With competitive bidding there would be a tendency for each bidder to price each product in relation to costs. Bidders would presumably not find the prospect of providing local service below cost attractive where the other services are subject to increased competition. Thus, competition in the bidding process would drive prices toward cost along the lines argued by the original exponents of FB, such as Demsetz.[6]

FB may have the attraction of providing the efficiency-enhancing benefits of price caps and in addition breaking the long cycle of cross subsidy. The question is whether it is practical for existing utilities. Most telephone and electric companies are huge in relation to CATV companies. Is it feasible to see large telephone and electric companies lose major chunks of their business? Are the transactions costs of transfer and compensation prohibitive in these cases? Would the problems of interconnection with the ousted company's other franchises be significant?

Let us review some of the costs and benefits associated with the loss by an incumbent telephone utility to a rival bidder. The situation has some of the features of a hostile takeover of the company's stock. In the case of a stock market takeover, the issue of compensation for the assets transferred is resolved in the market by the price paid by the bidder. Under FB, regulators may have to play a central role in deciding the price at which the losing franchisee's assets are sold for.

For labor and management, there is not a major difference between stock market takeover and takeover of an incumbent by a winning franchisee. The bidder decides how much of the existing labor and management he wishes to employ The bidder might decide to cut back on the workforce considerably, renegotiate union contracts, become non-union, and reduce management. FB thus provides the opportunity for a major cost-reducing restructuring that under price caps may only be gradual.

While FB may offer the prospect of considerable benefits in terms of X-efficiency, the problem of compensation for the assets transferred still remains. Experience, however, with CATV renewals has been that assets have often—and with relatively little friction—been transferred on a negotiated basis between the old and new franchisee (Zupan 1989d).

Whether this would occur with the much larger and much more entrenched assets of telephone and electric companies is not clear. Whether other companies would think it worth the risk of bidding against such giants is another important issue. If the process worked as smoothly as in the case of CATV, then there would appear to be considerable gains from introducing FB. If it did not and the result was costly litigation, then FB might result in a significant increase in the perceived and actual risks of the utilities business with a consequent increase in the cost of capital. Whether this added risk and transactions costs would exceed the benefits from FB is the question. The promised gains in efficiency are likely to be substantial. As we have argued, FB promises gains in X-efficiency. In addition, there are likely to be significant gains in allocative efficiency to the extent that the X-efficiency gains get translated into lower prices and that FB brings greater competitive pressures to bear on cross-subsidies.

We have just outlined the features of a generic scheme for the introduction of FB as an alterative to ROR regulation. For individual utility industries some refinements would be necessary. Let us look at each of the industries in turn.

4.1. Telecommunications

In view of the technological change that is taking place in this industry and its similarity with CATV, it would seem that telecommunications offers the greatest potential benefits from the replacement of existing ROR regulation by a form of regulation involving FB. IBNs are a case in point. Employing a single, digital fiber optic conduit, IBNs appear to be capable of providing a wide array of voice, data, and video services currently supplied by either local telcos or CATV operators.[7] IBNs also are likely to diplay economies of scale, as well as economies of scope, at the local exchange/distribution level.[8] Thus with the introduction of IBNs, the scheme outlined above may be applicable to local telecommunications.

Let us try to envisage how FB might operate for telcos and others in the case of IBNs.[9] Let us assume that the restrictions on provision of information services now imposed upon telcos are lifted.[10] Telcos will then wish to introduce IBNs on a gradual basis. Presumably they will start with the areas which they consider the most promising and then proceed to other areas. Having made the decision to go with an IBN, the telco has decided to scrap much of its existing investment. This has the effect of eliminating some of the difficulties in transfer of existing transaction-specific investments from the incumbent franchisee to the winning franchisee. A major potential objection to FB is eliminated.

There are going to be other problems with IBNs. If the telco knows that the franchise is going to be up for grabs when it announces its intention to set up an IBN, it may prefer to try to soldier on with existing technology and such protection as is offered by ROR regulation. This is likely to be the case as long as it has capital that is unrecovered. To encourage telcos to adopt new technologies and to be vigorous competitors under FB, some immediate steps may need to be taken to increase existing depreciation rates and therefore diminish the incentive that telcos may have to retain obsolete technologies and regulatory regimes.[11]

If problems of capital recovery and asset transfer are eliminated, are there any further problems in the application of FB to IBNs? One problem for a winning franchisee concerns interconnection with telco networks. For inter LATA traffic, existing arrangements cover this problem. The IBN's inter LATA traffic is carried by a longdistance carrier who pays whatever the tariff when or if he connects to the local telco's network. For traffic directly between the contiguous telco and the IBN, arrangements similar to those existing now between telcos would apply. Institutions currently in place that govern the relationships between telcos would apparently be adequate to accommodate FB with the introduction of IBNs.

With the technological changes taking place, competition is a reality whether or not FB replaces existing ROR regulation. In the wake of these changes, FB offers the potential to harness better the forces of competition for the pursuit of efficiency than does ROR regulation. FB may provide the dual benefits of increasing competition, and therefore the pressure for efficiency on telcos, and at the same time freeing telcos to respond to competition and to enter new markets. There appear to be potential gains in allocative efficiencies and X-efficiency and, by allowing telcos the freedom to enter other markets, there is increased potential for them to take advantage of scope economies. By spurring technological change, FB might also spur competition, not just at the bidding stage, but in the actual supply of IBN services. Thus, the franchises may in the future not need to be the exclusive franchise currently associated with CATV companies.

4.2. Electricity

The generic scheme might have to be modified in the case of electricity to take into account fluctuations in fuel prices, as these make up a large proportion of an electric utility's costs and are largely beyond the company's control. Although fuel adjustment formulas may lead to inefficiencies under ROR regulation (Baron and Taggart 1980), their effects under a system of FB and price caps may not contribute to inefficiency so much, since other prices will be adjusted for the general increase in price levels. While the details have to be worked out, and they are beyond the scope of this paper, the allowance of automatic fuel price increases is unlikely to have a major negative impact on FB for electric utilities.[12]

Of more concern is the problem that there is currently no technological innovation of the significance of IBNs that would eliminate the potential problem of asset transfer in the case of electric utilities. With the introduction of more competition in generation and the possibility of greater interconnection between companies, it is possible that more competition and therefore the application of FB can be achieved. This seems some way off in electric utilities, at least at the distribution level. Generation franchises are de facto here with the introduction of bidding schemes.[13]

4.3. Gas, Water, and Sewer

In these industries asset transfer is likely to be the most important issue to consider in applying FB. With water there may be a potential role for FB in restructuring the industry and modernizing the infrastructure. Currently many small water systems are in a bad state of repair.[14] Under ROR regulation, there is little incentive for existing privately-owned water companies to purchase them because they have little or no rate base and therefore potential for little or no earnings under ROR regulation. The main feasible alternative currently is public takeover. FB might provide an efficient alternative in this case, because the asset transfer problem has been virtually eliminated.

5. Summary and Conclusion

Based on recent, systematic evidence from local CATV markets, FB appears to be successful at: ensuring effective competition at the time of initial bidding; promoting promise-keeping during contract execution and deterring opportunistic behavior at the time of franchise renewal; providing incentives for regulated firms to innovate and to minimize costs; and restraining prices below monopoly levels—provided that there are no proscriptions against the regulation of rates by franchising authorities. While FB is not without its drawbacks and is not currently employed to regulate utilities, the CATV evidence suggests that it may deserve a second look. At least relative to traditional ROR regulation, which has relied primarily on negotiations between regulators and sole suppliers insulated from competition to promote efficiency, FB offers a means of harnessing better the invisible hand of market forces to assist in the pursuit of efficiency in utility markets.

Notes

In addition to our discussants, Michael Riccardelli and Dennis Weller, we would like to thank Richard Simnett for comments.

1. Although federal law has consistently proscribed the local regulation of pay rates, operators may exercise pricing restraint due to healthy competition at the time of initial bidding and/or the fear that "overly aggressive" pay pricing behavior after a contract is granted will invite some form of retaliation by a city and its policymakers. (See Olmstead and Rhode (1986) for an example of the role that fear of regulation, rather than regulation itself, may play in restraining pricing behavior by suppliers.)
2. See Zupan (1989c).
3. In contrast, ROR regulation essentially gives up on the possibility of asset transfer.
4. See Zupan (1989c).
5. Under price-cap regulation, regulators may, of course, rely on industry-wide performance to determine the terms of trade and changes in those terms of trade. (See Hillman and Braeutigam (1989).)
6. Although, given the preferences displayed by local authorities for nonprice concessions in CATV, we do not mean to imply that FB will entirely eliminate cross subsidy if it is expanded more broadly to utilities. FB will merely serve to insure that prices track costs better and that, if policy makers wish to promote cross subsidies, the costs associated with these goals will be more transparent.
7. See Zupan (1989e).
8. See Zupan (1989e).
9. Technological changes may make competition more feasible. However, before real competition

is feasible, telcos need to be released from the existing restrictions and allowed to offer information and other services, such as some of those currently provided by CATV companies. If they are not freed from current restrictions, the benefits for them to installing IBNs and the benefits to society from IBNs will be reduced.

10. Without this, their incentive to install IBNs will be attenuated. See Harris (1990) on the negative competitive consequence for the United State economy relative to other nations that may result if such restrictions are not lifted.

11. Capital recovery issues are beyond the scope of this paper. For a discussion of depreciation and capital recovery under technological change and regulation see Crew and Kleindorfer (1990).

12. To a certain extent, many FB contracts in CATV had automatic cost pass through features prior to rate decontrol, i.e., the basic tier price was allowed to rise by the rate of increase in the CPI.

13. Rothkopf, Teisberg, and Kahn (1990) provide extensive discussion of the role of bidding for generation in electric utilities.

14. This is true particularly for many small private systems.

References

Baron, David, and Robert Taggart. 1980. "Regulatory Pricing Procedures and Economic Incentives." In *Issues in Public-Utility Pricing and Regulation*, edited by M.A. Crew. Lexington, MA: Lexington Books.

Broadman, Harry G., and Joseph P. Kalt. 1989. "How Natural is Monopoly? The Case of Bypass in Natural Gas Distribution Markets," *Yale Journal on Regulation* 6 (no. 2, Summer) :181-208.

Brown, Lorenzo, Michael Einhorn, and Ingo Vogelsang. 1989. "Incentive Regulation: A Research Report," Office of Economic Policy, Federal Energy Regulatory Commission, Technical Report 89-3(November).

Crew, Michael A., and Paul R. Kleindorfer. 1987. "Productivity Incentives and Rate-of-Return Regulation." In *Regulating Utilities in an Era of Deregulation*, edited by M.A. Crew. London: Macmillan.

Demsetz, Harold E. 1968. "Why Regulate Public Utilities?," *Journal of Law and Economics* 11 (no. 1, April): 55-65.

Goldberg, Victor P. 1976. "Regulation and Administered Contracts," *Bell Journal of Economics and Management Science* 7 (no.2, Autumn): 426-448.

Harris, Robert G. 1990. "R&D in U.S. and Japaneses Telecommunications." In *Competition and the Regulation of Utilities*, edited by M.A. Crew. Boston: Kluwer (forthcoming).

Hillman, Jordan J. and Ronald R. Braeutigam. 1989. *Price Level Regulation for Diversified Public Utilities: An Assessment*. Boston: Kluwer Academic Publishers.

Jaffe, Adam B. and David M. Kanter. 1989. "Market Power of Local Television Franchises: Evidence From the Effects of Deregulation," unpublished working paper, Department of Economics, Harvard University, (July).

Jensen, Michael C. 1988. "Takeovers: Their Causes and Consequences," *Journal of Economic Perspectives* 2 (no. 1, Winter): 21-48.

Joskow, Paul L. 1974. "Inflation and Environmental Concern: Structural Change in the Process of Public Utility Regulation," *Journal of Law and Economics* 17 (no. 2, October): 291-327.

Joskow, Paul L. 1985. "Vertical Integration and Long-Term Contracts: The Case of Coal-Burning Electric Generating Plants," *Journal of Law Economics and Organization* 1 (no. 1, Spring): 33-80.

Joskow, Paul L. and Richard Schmalensee. 1983. *Markets for Power: An Analysis of Electric Utility Deregulation*. Cambridge, MA: MIT Press.

Klein, Benjamin, Robert Crawford, and Armen Alchian. 1978. "Vertical Integration, Appropriable Rents, and the Competitive Contracting Process," *Journal of Law and Economics* 21 (no. 3, October): 297-326.

Klein, Benjamin and Keith Leffler. 1981. "The Role of Market Forces in Assuring Contractual Performance," *Journal of Political Economy* 89 (no. 4, December): 615-641.

Knoeber, Charles R. 1989. "A Real Game of Chicken: Contracts, Tournaments, and the Production of Broilers," *Journal of Law, Economics, and Organization* 5 (no. 2, Fall): 271-292.

MacAvoy, Paul W, Daniel F. Spulber, and Bruce E. Stangle. 1989. "Is Competitive Entry Free? Bypass and Partial Deregulation in Natural Gas Markets," *Yale Journal on Regulation* 6 (no. 2, Summer): 209-248.

Noll, Roger G. 1987. "The Twisted Pair: Regulation and Competition in Telecommunications," *Regulation* 3/4: 15-22.

Noll, Roger G. and Bruce M. Owen. 1988. "U.S. v. AT&T: The Economic Issues," in *The Antitrust Revolution*, John Kwoka, Jr. and Lawrence White eds. Glenview, IL: Scott, Foresman.

Olmstead, Alan L. and Paul Rhode. 1985. "Rationing Without Government: The West Coast Gas Famine of 1920," *American Economic Review* 75 (no. 5, December): 1044-1056.

Peacock, Alan T., and Charles K. Rowley. 1972. "Welfare Economics and the Public Regulation of Natural Monopoly." *Journal of Public Economics* (June): 227-244.

Posner, Richard A. 1972. "The Appropriate Scope of Regulation in the Cable Television Industry," *Bell Journal of Economics* 3 (no. 1, Spring): 211-240.

Posner, Richard A. 1986. *Economic Analysis of Law*. 2nd. ed., Boston: Little, Brown and Company.

Prager, Robin A. 1986. "Firm Behavior in Franchise Monopoly Markets: The Case of Cable Television," unpublished Ph.D. dissertation, M.I.T.

Prager, Robin A. 1989. "Franchise Bidding for Natural Monopoly: The Case of Cable Television in Massachusetts." *Journal of Regulatory Economics* 1 (no. 2, June): 115-132.

Rothkopf, Michael J., Thomas J. Teisberg, and Edward P. Kahn. 1990. "Why are Vickrey Auctions Rare?" *Journal of Political Economy* 98:94-109.

Schmalensee, Richard. 1979., *The Control of Natural Monopolies*, Lexington, Massachusetts: D.C. Heath and Company.

Shew, William B. 1984. *Costs of Cable Television Franchise Requirements*, White Plains, New York: National Economic Research Associates.

Webb, G. Kent. 1983. *The Economics of Cable Television*, Lexington, MA: Lexington Books.

Williamson, Oliver. 1976. "Franchise Bidding for Natural Monopolies—in General and with Respect to CATV," *Bell Journal of Economics and Management Science* 7 (no. 1, Spring): 73-104.

Zupan, Mark A. 1989a. "Nonprice Concessions and the Effect of Franchise Bidding Schemes on Cable Company Costs." *Applied Economics* 21 (no. 3, March): 305-324.

Zupan, Mark A. 1989b. "A Test for Regulatory Lag and the Role Played by Periodic Contract Renewals in Mitigating Such Lag in Local Cable Franchise Relationships." *Journal of Regulatory Economics* (no. 1, March): 1-20.

Zupan, Mark A. 1989c. "The Efficacy of Franchise Bidding Schemes in the Case of CATV: Some Systematic Evidence." *Journal of Law and Economics* 32 (no. 2, part 1, October): 401-456.

Zupan, Mark A. 1989d. "Cable Franchise Renewals: Do Incumbent Firms Behave Opportunistically?" *Rand Journal of Economics* 20 (no. 4, Winter): 473-484.

Zupan, Mark A. 1989e. "Should Franchise Bidding Schemes be Employed to Regulate Integrated Broadband Networks?" Working Paper, USC School of Business, (February).

11

PRIVATIZATION OF ELECTRICITY IN THE UNITED STATES
Douglas A. Houston

1. Introduction

Advances in generation, transmission, and computerized switching technologies suggest that the power industry could be moved toward market-defined structures and behaviors, supplanting numerous aspects of public utility regulation. Yet state and federal regulators have responded erratically to these underlying changes, often delivering policies at cross purposes. Such inconsistency is unfortunate but understandable, given the divergent interests at stake and the paucity of evidence on key issues. The ongoing regulatory revisionism—that some would describe as an evolution—carries with it a high cost. Participants in the industry cannot clearly picture the future power industry, given the garbled messages from regulators, and consequently invest cautiously, retarding the very market developments considered most promising.

One way to speed the adjustment process is to provide a radically different example of a power market, one not hobbled by a maze of continuing regulation. Such a perspective can be achieved by privatizing and deregulating the United States power agencies. These are the Tennessee Valley Authority (TVA) and the five Power Marketing Administrations (PMAs).[1] Their privatization could serve as a revolutionary (as opposed to evolutionary) model, providing much needed evidence about power markets that would inform those who would more broadly reform or deregulate this industry. This paper frames such a privatization proposal and examines its impact.

At the crux of the issues about the direction of change in the industry—and the appropriate role for federal power--is an old debate and a new one. Public power in the United States was originally defended as a means to assure comprehensive regional power planning (Shapiro 1989, 102). More recently, concern has focused on the technological and managerial demands placed on a large power system to perform multiple, integrative tasks. As a transmission network expands, closer horizontal relationships may become more important for efficient power production, transmission, and distribution. Following this line of thinking, critics of privatization argue that changing the federal public power statutes and moving toward further disintegration in the industry is foolhardy at a time when technological efficiency mandates more cooperation and integration. They argue that regional planning, a goal astutely built into the laws behind federal power, should remain.

As with most arguments, there is another side. Marketing is a budding phenomenon in the power industry, and numerous efficiency-based arguments have been made in support of even further market development and deregulation (Smith 1987). Further, concluding that broad and comprehensive planning and control makes sense does not preclude competitive, unregulated marketing of power—as long as transmission issues can be adequately addressed through voluntary, joint actions by independent participants in the industry. The burgeoning debate on how market oriented behavior will deal with transmission remains unsettled. It is an important issue in privatizing federal public power that is taken up in this paper.

By way of a preface, the following points make up the key elements of a proposal for a privatization of electric power that is elaborated in this paper: (1) The sale of federally owned electric power assets (excluding dams) to private parties; (2) The formation of independent power-producing firms where this is feasible; (3) Accomplishing (2) through public stock offerings with discount purchase options for employees and managers; (4) Creation of an open-access transmission grid in the TVA region that would be jointly owned by its users. (Elsewhere, federal power transmission assets would be sold with open access as a condition of sale.) (5) A write-off by the government of all nuclear assets that cannot be sold; and (6) Legal exclusion of public utility regulation from newly-privatized power markets, whose remaining regulatory oversight would be the task of the Federal Energy Regulatory Commission (FERC). These six points make up the skeleton of a privatization policy. It does not presume complete knowledge of how competitive power markets will function in the future. This information will never be available in the real world, nor is it necessary to make useful policy. Indeed, one can expect that considerable further evolution will occur. The proposed policy, however, would start in motion the forces of competition.

The paper is ordered as follows. The next section briefly explores the political dimensions of electric power privatization in the United States. Then, the specific components of a federal power privatization for the United States are developed, and this is followed by a section placing privatization within the context of three industry scenarios.

2. Power Privatization: Political Context

In mature industries, such as electric power, interest groups have clear expectations about how things work within the well-developed institutions at hand. However paltry the benefits received from this system, at least a measure of stability is derived from its continuance. Radically altering established procedures, even if seemingly beneficial in time, also will be perceived as destructive of that stability and, for that reason, will face interest group resistance. Yet even widespread support for the status quo can be undone if groups anticipate significant losses from the continuation of the regulatory regime or significant advantages from switching. In a strategic sense, any interest group would seriously consider the possibilities of working to gain radical change, such as privatization with deregulation, when this new state offers much higher expected net gains. Additionally, the mere introduction of such a proposal clouds the future, creating less assurance about outcomes within any imagined future state, including the existing one. In other words, the risk-return trade-offs are pervasively affected, and this could lead risk-averse interest groups to explore radical change, if only to diversify their portfolios of political options (Houston 1987). Although privatization of federal power in the United States will be difficult to initiate, once the concept is clearly delineated, support can mount quickly. Dramatic breaks in seemingly inviolable public policy then become feasible.

Realistically, the sweeping British privatization currently underway is unlikely to parallel any future American federal power privatization, given the interest group domination of decision-making in the United States. Any American privatization would be less dramatic in scope, more piecemeal in implementation, more diverse in institutional features confronted, and, undoubtedly, more politically contentious. Advantages from privatization, federal debt reduction (perhaps in the range of $10-$20 billion) and gains from more efficient production, distribution, and pricing of electric power, are scattered among millions of people. For the typical citizen, the gains are small, probably insufficient to build a pro-privatization political constituency. On the other hand, the perceived losses borne by more narrowly-defined interest groups are sufficient motivation for them to act in opposition. Only when these latter interest groups believe that continuation of federal power entails large future liabilities or that privatization offers large future benefits would a major privatization become politically feasible. In particular, both consumers of federal power and employees of the providing agencies have large stakes in the future of the power organizations, and either could prevent a privatization. Thus, the proposal presented in this paper suggests ways to target benefits to these two key interest groups.

One way is to bribe key recalcitrant players. By making "side payments," the United States government (i.e., taxpayers) would bear substantial costs. Yet the gain in interest group support from doing so also may be substantial, and costs borne by taxpayers may be viewed as an investment in making the industry more productive. For example, a nuclear plant write-off would eliminate consumers' fears that future prices will embody these sunk, nuclear-related costs; share discounts to workers can turn employees and managers into owners of new firms with strong incentives to make them succeed. And, with privatization, a federal power organization that could not generate sufficient revenue to cover its costs would no longer be a federal bailout candidate. All in all, the investment by taxpayers in a privatized industry may yield substantial long-term returns.

A major justification for federal power privatization is that it can demonstrate empirically, to other sectors of the power market, the effects of extensive competition. This argument is made more compelling today due to the difficulty of altering the extensive regulation of the investor-owned sector. The demands of interest groups, acting within and upon complex, overlapping authorities of state and federal regulations, have greatly inhibited movement toward competition among public utilities. By contrast, the federal government alone controls the superstructure of the TVA and the PMAs, and action to restructure these authorities can occur more readily. Thus, broadly reforming the industry may begin with a demonstration of open, competitive power markets formed from what is now public power. The TVA's privatization and deregulation would be a particularly useful case study because it contains both potential power-producer firms and an integrated transmission system. If a radical privatization succeeds, then traditional assumptions about the value of regulation and the limitations of competition would be questioned. Also, market participants adjacent to the newly privatized system would be likely to call for voluntary exchange with producers and consumers within the privatized TVA region. The combination of these two forces might greatly alter the political support for the status quo. While privatization of federal power is often seen as a minor step in a slow revision of the electric power industry, the process, when coupled with deregulation, instead may be a powerful force for change.

3. The General Elements of a Federal Power Privatization

3.1. The Federal Power Entities

Federal power is represented by three structurally distinct elements: the Tennessee Valley Authority (TVA); the Power Marketing Administrations (PMAs) (Alaska, Bonneville, Southeastern, Southwestern, and Western Area Administrations); and the Rural Electrification Administration (REA). The latter is beyond the scope of this study. Statistics on the TVA and the PMAs are contained in table 1.

The TVA is a federally owned corporation, created by the TVA Act of 1933. Many purposes were established statutorily for the Authority other than power generation, but the TVA made electric power service its dominant mission by the end of World War II. Unlike the PMAs, TVA not only markets power but also produces it. Essentially it is a generation-transmission utility (the biggest in the United States), controlled by a Board of Directors, with reporting responsibility to Congress.

The PMAs act primarily as agents for the federal government, marketing power generated from dams. The largest PMA is Bonneville Power Administration (BPA), created in 1936 as a temporary agency for regional hydroelectric development; today it brokers power from over 30 federal hydroelectric projects and operates one of the nation's largest transmission systems. During the mid 70s, BPA began underwriting the expansion of investor-owned thermal (nuclear) plants,

Table 1. Selected Statistics of PMAs & TVA, 1987	APA	BPA	SEPA	SWPA	WAPA	TVA	TOTAL	PMA & TVA as % of TOTAL, US
Total gigawatt hour sales (YR)	330	68,984	6,486	5,807	40,911	108,546	231,064	9.3%
% Total Sales that are for resale	99.1%	67.3%	100%	100%	83.7%	84.6%	80.1%	
Revenues for YR (millions $)	8	1,520	118	86	599	5,200	7,531	
Avg. price per KWH (¢ per KWH)								
- industrial	6.0	2.3	—	—	5.0	6.8	4.3	
- resale	2.4	2.2	—	—	1.5	4.4	3.1	
overall[a]	2.5	2.2	1.8	1.5	1.5	4.8	3.3	
Net Generation of Electricity (gigawatt hours)						94,606[b]	205,363	8.0%
Accounting Valuations (millions $) of:								
Total Production Plant	79	—	—	—	—	12,190	12,269	
Transmission Plant	30	2,834	—	81	3,395	1,877	8,217	
General Plant	4	293	—	3	58	641	999	
Total In-service Plant	113	3,127	—	85	3,453	14,708	21,486	
CWIP	3	201	—	—	449	8,777	9,430	

Note: Totals may not equal sum of components because of independent rounding.
[a] Excludes some other sales categories
[b] Based on 1986 TVA Annual Report
APA - Alaska Power Administration
BPA - Bonneville Power Administration
SEPA - Southeastern Power Administration
SWPA - Southwestern Power Administration
WAPA - Western Area Power Administration
TVA - Tennessee Valley Authority

using the now infamous "net billing" arrangements. Although the 1937 Bonneville Project Act clearly disallows the organization from building or owning generating facilities, the BPA contravened the law through the swapping of its own hydrogenerated power (at very low rates) for the more expensive future thermal output from organizations established to construct nuclear plants. Losses were passed on to BPA consumers. In doing this "net billing," BPA became responsible for a portion of construction costs and incurred liabilities to certain ("preference") utilities (Shapiro 1989, 24-26). Thus, BPA owns long-term contracts for power which, in essence, give them ownership standing in nuclear power. The residual risks of ownership, however, are distributed, by law, back upon BPA consumers.

The TVA's mix of generating plants (in terms of net generation of power) is heavily weighted to coal-fired steam plants, with less than 10 percent of capacity now coming from hydroelectric sources. Aggressive marketing of power in the 1940s and 1950s led the Authority to construct steam plants because hydroelectric opportunities were exploited. Then, in the early 1960s, a massive nuclear program was unveiled to meet expected escalation of demand, a demand linked to ongoing subsidization of electricity prices. But the nuclear power program was devastated by a variety of technical and managerial problems, and only recently has the TVA begun to restart plants. Nuclear power now accounts for less than 10 percent of TVA power generation. Much of the $8.7 billion of construction-work-in-progress (see table 1) is made up of nuclear plants that are unlikely to be completed.

3.2. Overview of Proposal

Government and utility industry analysts typically predict that: the industry will become more disaggregated (vertically); wholesale power marketing functions will expand; and public utility regulators (who must attempt to respond to market-driven changes) will exercise less control. These trends, moreover, are anticipated to continue, even without explicit regulatory reform or deregulation (Martinson and Loria 1987, 19-24; Congress of the United States, Office of Technology Assessment 1989, 35-58). Further, regional market distinctions are becoming less meaningful as technological considerations suggest that transmission grids could be expanded efficiently. All these factors make unlikely a return to a tranquil world of narrowly (and legalistically) defined markets, overseen by regulatory commissions. All industry scenarios examined in this paper are predicated upon continuing pressures for more competition throughout the industry.

Policy issues involved in privatization of federal power are presented and discussed below. In any complex, speculative story (which privatization certainly is), the need for context is great. Thus, the probable effects of privatization are discussed in a following section, which evaluates privatization within three distinct industry scenarios.

3.3. Treatment of Power Generation Assets in Privatization

A suggested initial policy is to separate generating assets from other assets before sale. The objective for fossil fuel facilities would be to form new, stand-alone generating firms, and careful packaging of these generating assets would encourage entry into the production sector. For privatization of hydroelectric facilities, the proposed principle is to sell only the aspects of a dam's operations connected with power. Other uses of the dams would remain under federal ownership and control.

Realistically, a broad range of capacity and plant mix might be compatible with an efficient stand-alone generation organization. Undoubtedly, the structure of an efficient power generation firm would not be obvious at the time of privatization. Thus, uncertainty is inherent in packaging and selling generation assets, but buyers could reconfigure assets in response to information they gather about the marketing and regulatory environment. Buyers generally can complement any asset mix, if needed, through acquisitions or by construction. In the case of the TVA, several fully formed production firms might be assembled for sale from that corporation's array of generating units which includes approximately 6 million kilowatts of hydroelectric capacity, 17.6 million kilowatts of steam plant capacity, and 2.5 million kilowatts installed in gas turbine facilities (Tennessee Valley Authority 1986, 29).

In selling generating assets into a competitive marketplace, a crucial issue is the type of commitments required of producers. For example, producers could be obligated to maintain reserve capacity for their own customers or the customers tied into an entire transmission system. This requirement could evolve even under private ownership in an unregulated market. If one conjectures that multiple, interrelated tasks will be demanded of each producer (Pierce 1986, 1221-1224), then the likelihood of independent power producers (IPPs) being significant players in a power market is remote.

As mentioned, in this proposal the dams from which hydroelectric power is generated would not be sold. By law, these facilities serve multiple purposes related to flood control, fisheries, and irrigation, as well as power production (Conkin 1983, 32). Growing concern about environmental damage from the operation of dams could increase political demands to limit uses, thereby weakening any private property rights established in them. Thus, in this proposal for privatization, most of the dams' uses would be retained by the federal government, and only the power production capacities sold. Still, this unbundling of power production cannot fully resolve uncertainty on the part of a private buyer about how his power rights will be treated in the future. The federal government could elevate other conflicting uses over power production—unless constrained from doing so. An asset sale, therefore, probably would require a contract specifying the detailed conditions of use and remedies for damages. Although long-term leasing of hydroelectric capacity might reduce the time span over which a firm is exposed to such attenuation of rights risks, leasing would do nothing to alter the political circumstances that cause the uncertainty and leases would have to be renegotiated periodically. In general, leasing is a limited and fragile form of privatization, and selling the hydroelectric assets outright is preferable.

Favoritism has been common in the history of operations of hydroelectric facilities by the federal government. The BPA, for example, has "preference" users, mostly small, rural enclaves, that are allowed to buy "cheap" hydroelectric power at well below market price, while other customers have had to queue up for what was left. Preference pricing provides vast subsidies to the recipients and distorts the efficient allocation of electricity from its most valued uses. This rationing scheme also has bred resentment and strong political counterattacks by other user interests, such as large industrial firms, desiring to receive "cheap" hydroelectric power themselves. In searching for the means to achieve "justice" among its strident users, the BPA has entered into schemes to increase power capacity (even though these may overstep its statutory authority), while continuing to set prices uneconomically (Shapiro 1989, 21-45).

Political resistance to privatization of hydroelectric power will come from currently favored users who stand to lose billions of dollars from the elimination of these pricing practices of the PMAs. Because gaining pricing efficiency is a major advantage anticipated from privatizing, policies that would institutionalize a favored status for many users would be illogical. For example, placing selective price caps on privatized power would merely substitute regulation for federal ownership as a means to attain political ends. Still, politically powerful users cannot be ignored, and some incentives must be provided to them or else privatization can be derailed. One approach would be to provide favored customers with a one-time payment from proceeds of the hydroelectric asset sales. Alternatively, the targeted groups may be permitted to acquire ownership in hydroelectric facilities at a sale price considerably below the expectation of market value. Thereafter, the owners either could operate or sell the assets. Either way, the influence of users over these resources would be deflected from political to private power marketing. A significant objective in devising methods to privatize the hydroelectric assets of the federal government will be to avoid institutionalizing commitments to any group.

3.4. Disposal of Nuclear Power Plants

Selling nuclear power units presents unique problems. The BPA has acquired the generating capacity of five nuclear power projects and is obligated to pay all or part of project budgets plus debt service costs, whether or not the projects are completed. Three of these projects have been delayed indefinitely (Bonneville Power Administration 1986, 44-46). Under law, the BPA must cover all its expenses and therefore passes on the costs of these obligations to all customers (Shapiro 1989, 25-26).

Only the TVA directly owns nuclear stations. Its nuclear program, as of November 1989, consists of two operating units at Sequoyah, with perhaps another unit at Browns Ferry to be restarted within the year. Eight units were cancelled in the early 80's due to a lack of consumer demand; three completed plants remain closed due to safety-related problems; three units are in various states of completion; and a last unit is deferred. These nuclear assets are valued on the TVA balance sheet at over $16 billion. Attempts to start any of the idled plants will face political pressure from environmental interests and groups worried about nuclear safety, such as the Tennessee Valley Coalition. The latter is a public interest group closely watching the TVA's attempts to forge ahead with nuclear production. Realistically, only a few of the TVA's closed nuclear units are likely to gain Nuclear Regulatory Commission (NRC) certification, regardless of who owns them.

For the TVA, each nuclear station unit represents a unique puzzle. Can it be certified or recertified, at what cost, and in what time frame? Because the answers vary by unit, each should be separately offered for sale. In some cases, no market may exist because ownership represents unacceptable risks connected with certification, operation, decommissioning, and removal of spent fuels. In these privatization "failures," the government would remain as caretaker, but the privatization objective also would remain. Thus, the government's role with respect to such nuclear "lemons" would be either to alter the safety characteristics of the plants so that they can be sold or, failing that, to dismantle them, accepting the losses. Unacceptable alternative solutions, given the goal of advancing power markets, would be subsidizing the sale of the assets, or masking negative market values of plants by bundling them with more marketable units, possibly non-nuclear ones.

Perhaps the path of least resistance for the federal government would be neither to privatize nor to decommission (itself a complex and politically volatile issue) the nuclear operations. Instead, strong pressure may be applied by nuclear power supporters to get as many plants in operation as possible under federal ownership, with the underlying presumption that a federal authority can avoid many of the difficulties encountered by investor-owned utilities that operate nuclear plants. Expectation of favoritism or subsidy, however, is not an efficiency defense for continued government ownership and operations of plants. If the costs associated with providing nuclear power vary merely on the basis of government ownership over private ownership, then the problem is an inconsistency in legal treatment. Changes in law and regulation to more accurately reflect the full social cost of nuclear power are called for, but this institutional difficulty should not be the rationale for halting privatization.

More generally, eliminating existing subsidies in public power provision is one important reason behind the privatization movement; without their elimination, private markets cannot as easily form or function. Keeping the federal government fully out of the power-selling business is necessary to avoid a backsliding dependency upon subsidies—either because a government business is under duress or because of interest group demands for "cheap" power. Thus, the drafting of privatization legislation should never provide for a residual organization to provide an operating base for market "lemons." Disposal or sale of assets should be the limit of government participation in the production market.

The BPA's involvement in nuclear power through power contracts also cannot be ended easily, given the nonperformance of most of the underlying asset base and the ongoing litigation surrounding the nuclear units. Thus, attempts to sell off the contracted capacity may prove fruitless. Nevertheless, BPA should be a willing seller. Unlike the case of the TVA, where an army of employees is dedicated to nuclear production, the BPA has no such nuclear specialization and, consequently, little allegiance to nuclear power. Getting BPA out of nuclear power is hardly controversial, but may prove infeasible; thus, nuclear privatization in the Pacific Northwest may amount to little more than a large write-off to be borne by taxpayers and consumers. By contrast, privatization of nuclear units owned by the TVA is quite feasible—but extremely controversial—with the TVA itself voraciously defending the Authority's role in promoting nuclear power.

3.5. Transmission and the Access Issues

Resolving questions about who will use the electricity transmission lines—and under what conditions—is the linchpin in the industry's evolution in the 1990s. Before proposing how transmission assets should be treated in a federal power privatization, we will discuss the general role of transmission in the industry.

The transmission access debate can be billed, roughly, as a battle of "haves" versus "have nots," each side trying to establish convincing arguments—with very little empirical support. On one side are most of the major utilities, owning their own transmission lines, moving power to their captive customers. Their unrelenting view, and that of their trade association, the Edison Electric Institute, is that limited access to transmission is needed to assure highly reliable service to risk averse customers. Opening the transmission system, beyond the scope of voluntary pooling agreements among utilities and bulk power sales among consenting utilities, is argued to undermine the reliability objective (Rosso 1989). Today, with few exceptions, the public utility law accepts the right of utilities to restrict access (Weiss and Spiewak 1989, 43-48).

On the other side of the debate are a variety of potential users of transmission services—including IPPs, cogenerators, large power users, and some utilities experiencing either chronic capacity excess or shortfall. These entities frequently argue that competitive gains could be made by allowing (forcing) power to pass through transmission systems owned by third parties (i.e., those who are neither the buyer nor seller of the power). To them, a transmission system owned by a third party or parties is a bottleneck to competitive marketing. These defenders of opening transmission systems also typically argue the merits of greater competition over the many well-noted inefficiencies of the public utility regulation. In sum, the argument is typically set as a choice between system reliability (with utilities and their industry association describing the vast technical complexity of operating a power system) (Transmission Access Technical Task Force 1988; 1989) versus competitive marketing of power (with non-utilities praising the potential gains from market transactions over a transmission system accessible on demand). Viewed in this way, the argument centers upon the relative competitive gains, versus the reliability costs from mandating entry requirements.

This trade-off argument is incomplete and therefore misleading. Another way to express the issue is: How might the industry evolve, unburdened of its regulatory constraints on organizational structures? Or, could such market-defined organizations encourage valuable competitive forces and, at the same time, overcome the complex issues of control and coordination? Clearly, for effective competition to emerge, transmission coordination and planning problems must be resolved; agents within an effective competitive process cannot, logically, ignore the issues. The questions evoke speculation. Joskow and Schmalensee (1983, 109-138) have argued, persuasively to many, that the coordination problems are so great that a large monopolistic force must remain at the center of the industry.

Yet another view is that scale economies are a necessary but insufficient condition for monopoly power (Demsetz 1968; Smith 1987, 26). The development of a broad, closely coordinated and planned electric power system need not mean inevitable monopolization, with derivative demands for detailed regulation. The crux of the argument is that the anticipation of monopolization of vital resources presents clear risks to any independent firms should they persist in operating in such an environment. Therefore, it also presents powerful motivation for such firms to search for institutional and transactional forms that mitigate that risk. A great benefit to allowing open markets in power is that information on these matters, otherwise unknowable, would be generated through the entrepreneurial search behavior of participants in the industry. By contrast, the typical public policy solution to such a problem is to presume the correct path can be discerned a priori (Hazlett 1985, 21).

In the face of scale and scope economies to both vertical and horizontal integration, relatively small individual firms (e.g., independent power generators and distributors) still can make sense. The efficiently managed firm in the power industry, for all other purposes, may be smaller than the size of a technically efficient system or grid (Hughes 1962). With multiple firms, then, the remaining policy issues are twofold: (1) Can these participants develop the means to coordinate and plan so that the system-wide gains from multi-firm competition (over monopoly and/or public utility regulation) outweigh the added costs of these coordination arrangements? (2) Can the participants prevent the coordinating institution from itself eventually establishing a monopolistic presence? The answers to these questions are not clear, and gaining more understanding about an open market evolution in the electric power industry is vital. Such information is unlikely to come from the investor-owned sector, where regulators preclude most market experiments. A federal power privatization, therefore, might play an important role in unearthing some answers to the seeming riddles of transmission access.

3.6. A Transmission Privatization Proposal

Some observers fear that the owners of massive transmission grids could monopolize the industry, denying movement toward greater competitiveness among generation firms. But the extension of control by a transmission organization might instead enhance competitive exchange. Antitrust law and continuing oversight by FERC can be applied to maintain open-access provisions that would be established in the privatization statutes. More important than legal or regulatory protection, the broadening of the market, so that more producers can contract with more consumers, alters the incentives of any producer regarding transmission ownership. George Stigler (1968) has argued that the gains from vertically integrating a business are diminished by the broadening of the market at any level of activity. Today, much of the reluctance of investor-owned utilities to open transmission access further may be based on a fear of losing monopoly control over their franchised territories. But, with exclusive franchising removed, so too is the motivation to defend a transmission system once dedicated to captive customers.

An industry composed of numerous independent bits and pieces of transmission lines (as indeed, the industry is today) inhibits the greater market reach necessary for success in competitive markets. However, with expectations that less control over consumers and less authority to restrict transmission access will be exercised, a utility should be willing to exchange some ownership in its limited regional transmission assets in return for ownership rights in adjoining transmission system assets. Gradually, in an emerging competitive power market, such overlapping ownership of transmission might evolve into regional, jointly owned systems.

Privatization of federal transmission assets can accelerate this movement. The TVA transmission assets could form a stand-alone system, with ownership extended to all major regional users. This would include newly spun-off generators, distribution consumers, and industrial users. TVA now operates within the Southeastern Electric Reliability Council (SERC), with major interconnections to the Southern Company, also a single, integrated system (Federal Energy Regulatory Commission 1981, 89-90). Even closer coordination between the two should be encouraged, with the objective of allowing broader regional interconnections of users and suppliers. For the PMAs, transmission assets could be sold to major regional users, with legally stipulated open access provisions for nonowners. Further, cross-ownership of transmission among adjoining transmission systems could be encouraged.

The impact of these initiatives depends largely on how public policy toward adjoining public utility transmission access proceeds. Yet, even with little movement toward broader access, the small step of using the TVA and the PMAs as testing grounds for open access through joint ownership could prove very useful. It permits a competitive "yardstick" with which to measure the effectiveness of the existing industry structure.

The joint-ownership approach to transmission privatization seemingly would treat a transmission system as a common carrier, analogous to a canal that transports other people's "loads." By contrast, the transmission systems today are more like railroads, owning both the rails and the freight (Veljanovski 1987, 149). An electrical transmission system, however, differs considerably from a canal because the reliability of the overall system is affected by loads placed anywhere on the grid (Weiss and Spiewak 1989, 49-63). These technical problems are significant and complex, but can be usefully categorized as: capacity, control, coordination, and contractual issues. Utilities frequently argue that the encroachment of intruders (IPPs and retail accounts) would damage any utility's ability to deal with these complex issues (Rosso 1989, 18-26). Yet the view expressed by a 1987 NERC document ("Reference Considerations for Integrating Non-Utility Generating Units with the Bulk Electricity Systems") is that third-party generators do not offer insurmountable problems to transmission system reliability if they follow the same operating guidelines as utilities. Further, reliability to a system can be improved by bringing more diverse generators into play as transmission systems are broadened.

Perhaps contractual linkages will be the greatest stumbling block to operating an effective transmission system. If a contract for power is only between a generator firm and a distributor, then some systems costs may not be considered fully. For example, the demands for backup supply and dispatching in a system could fall back on the transmission owner to perform, or simply might not be performed as well. If the back-up owner were a utility, then the costs of indiscriminately handling loads would be borne by captive customers (in higher price or reduced reliability). However, in a system of joint ownership by users, these costs would be borne by all who are using the system to complete power contracts. Thus, under joint-ownership of transmission, it seems reasonable to expect power contracts to be formed among three parties: generator, consumer, and the transmission grid. In these contracts, detailed specifications of rights and obligations could be made. Significant control may be ceded to the transmission system management in order to effectively maintain system reliability and stability.

The prospects for developing these complex contracts in a market environment is improved because the participants in a power sale will also be, in most cases, participating owners in the transmission grid. As noted, the transmission owners would, in this proposal, be required to allow user access in a nondiscriminatory manner, subject to maintaining system integrity. Whether the industry would move toward such joint-ownership of transmission without prodding is questionable, given the need for major federal legislation to change the public utility statutes. Thus, the privatizing of the federal power entities can play a significant role of testing, in a limited fashion, the operation of a privately (but jointly) owned transmission system.[2]

3.7. Policy Toward Customers and Employees

Consumers who have previously been contractually dependent upon a federal power producer must be explicitly considered during privatization. The federal government has subsidized the PMAs and the TVA, allowing electricity prices to fall well below competitive levels in their respective regions. Blocks of shares in the PMAs and TVA might be offered for sale at a substantial discount to favored consumer groups in order to acquire much needed support for privatization. This approach has been applied by the British in numerous privatizations (Ascher 1987). The objective is to place consumers in a position under privatization where they will perceive themselves to be as well off or better off than under government ownership.

The magnitude of the needed payoff to consumers to get this support may be shrinking. Subsidies to the PMAs are being reduced by the Bush Administration (Executive Office of the President of the United States 1990, 141-142), and the nuclear woes of the TVA create a long-term liability for the system's consumers. Although TVA chairman Marvin Runyon has promised a three-year moratorium on raising prices, the billions of dollars in unrecovered investments in nuclear plants may eventually be recovered from consumers. In sum, the lack of a bright future for consumers of both the TVA and the PMAs makes privatization more attractive to them and reduces the size of side payments needed to win their support for privatization.

In the case of the TVA, blocks of discounted shares in the privatized GENCOs might be most effectively targeted for employees and management. During several of its past privatization efforts, the British have used successfully this share-offering approach to develop a strong advocacy from previously resistant unions. Unlike the PMAs, the TVA has a large payroll, and many unionized employees whose allegiance to the Authority is strong. And also, unlike the PMAs, the TVA has such grave financial difficulties that the price risks that consumers are exposed to may be sufficient to win their support without added ownership enticements.

For the cases of both the TVA and PMAs, all existing contracts with cooperatives, cities, and distributors would be assigned to the purchasers as part of the conditions of sale. Standards of service would be at least as high as those maintained by the federal producers. Thus, the consumers should never find themselves at risk of being cut off from reliable power supply. Distributors, however, should then be offered the right to recontract for power. With advance notification, these retail accounts could seek either "spot" power or long-term power contracts elsewhere, replacing the old supply relationship in total. In a power market with multiple suppliers, this recontracting option provides a means of lowering electricity bills and therefore can assist in winning local consumer support for privatization, especially when expectations of higher prices under continued federal supply presents a significant risk to the user. A critical element in making this option valuable is to assure transmission access.

3.8. Eliminating Price Regulation at the Wholesale Level

The selling of federal power historically has involved considerable subsidization. Explanations for such government pricing (Peltzman 1971; De Alessi 1975) are predicated on bureaucrats' enhancing political support. Whatever the causes, prolonged subsidization will inhibit competitive market development. The privatization described in this paper would eliminate price subsidizes. On the other hand, replacing government pricing with public utility, cost-plus pricing would be a poor bargain. Because privatization aims to stimulate competitive pricing, price regulation should cease when contracts for power are made. Buyers of power then would have added responsibility under contracting to use care in setting service conditions, a role now taken on by regulators.

Remaining price regulation of the newly privatized transmission services also should avoid public utility pricing principles. Because all substantial transmission users would also be its joint owners, establishing the conditions for access may not be as contentious an issue as many observers predict. It is likely that the transmission owners would set standards of access that would apply to users universally. To further buttress the openness of the transmission grid, FERC could be extended authority to deny what they consider to be non-economic exclusions or discriminatory pricing. If FERC believed that price regulation were needed, then forms other than rate base pricing should be considered.

A movement to privatize federal power generation and transmission assets and to apply market pricing principles may run head-on into public utility regulatory objectives. The clash could be greatest in the areas surrounding privatized federal assets that continue to operate under public utility regimes. As an example, consider a public utility adjacent to a privatized TVA that wished to sell power to a consumer (large industrial user or distributor) within the old federal power region. With privatization and deregulation, such a transaction now would be acceptable. On the other hand, the conditions of such a sale, including price, are normally subject to the authority of state public utility commission (PUC) (presuming it is intrastate). Therefore, to stimulate the interaction of the fringe public utilities with the newly privatized organizations, federal jurisdiction over the conditions of sales of all power from privatized power sites and over privatized transmission lines would be advantageous.

Yet, clearly, the surrounding state regulators still could constrain many opportunities to use the privatized-deregulated market more widely. If a public utility contractually diverts power away from franchise consumers, this could be challenged by a PUC. Additionally, joint ownership of transmission would not be welcomed because such agreements would undermine the delineation of assets necessary for asset base regulation. On the other hand, PUCs would not be uniformly hostile to attempts by utilities within their jurisdictions to expand marketing of power. If a utility has excess capacity, a ready market within the TVA region could reduce revenue requirements (and prices charged) to captive customers of that utility. In general, federal privatizations could provide examples of market innovations from which cautious PUCs can learn.

3.9. Environmental Interests

Critics cite a poor record on environmental issues as a consequence of federal power provision. Environmentalists have pointed to the detrimental effects from below-market pricing by the PMAs (Campbell 1986, 30). This pricing policy is in direct conflict with stated energy conservation goals established by the federal government.[3] The inexorable expansions of the range of power activities of the PMAs and the TVA over several decades (often posited to be a result of their attempts to satisfy their constituencies growing needs) have pushed environmental concerns far down on the list of government priorities. By curbing federal promotional pricing practices, privatization is consistent with energy conservation objectives. Emphasizing this prospect can win support from environmental groups that otherwise may have little ideological reason to do so. Additionally, selling the hydroelectric capacity of federal dams will eliminate the means to subsidize users of that power, and therefore will remove much of the pressure that users now apply to the federal bureaucracies. Privatization of power, therefore, can help put other goals related to the operation of the dams higher on the political agenda, a point which environmentalists have not missed.

The numerous safety problems associated with the TVA's nuclear program may be caused, in part, by a management willing to take on large risks to keep the "abundant" power flowing to users who form the bedrock political support for the Authority. A TVA privatization which places nuclear units back into private use could (as with the hydroelectric concerns) take pressure off federal bureaucrats to produce subsidized power for various constituencies. In the case of the BPA, administrators have had similar incentives to subsidize power users, leading to their disastrous involvement in nuclear power. These avenues for managerial digression would be closed with privatization, a point also not lost on opponents of nuclear power.

The TVA also has numerous fossil fuel-burning facilities whose environmental record is poor. Again, the problem plausibly can be linked to the bureaucratic drive to expand subsidized power as a means of gaining interest group support. Major confrontations between the TVA and the states in the Southeast over pollution from coal-fired plants were common in the 1970s. At that time, none of the TVA's coal-burning plants were in compliance with the environmental laws of the states in which they operated. Clearly, the added cost of pollution cleanup would have pressed consumer prices upward, endangering the political support from consumer advocates of the TVA. Thus, the Authority fought hard to weaken the environmental law provisions affecting the TVA. By turning the assets over to private ownership, the full force of environmental law would apply.

One cannot, however, dismiss the powerful political support that can be mounted to counter potential privatization advocates, such as environmentalists. In particular, BPA, whose role in regional planning has been extended over the years so that it has begun to resemble the TVA, has loyal backers. Legislators will not be weaned easily from the allure (or the pork-barrel potential) of the BPA. A 1985 Reagan Administration proposal to "defederalize" the BPA by 1988 (U.S. Department of Energy 1986) was met by furious dissent. Indeed, this Reagan proposal triggered a remarkable response—a congressional resolution stating that federal funds could not be used to study the privatization of PMAs.

How can the political opposition be overcome? One way, as suggested earlier, would be to make preference users into claimants on the value realized from the sale of hydroelectric capacity. The effect could be to dampen quickly the derivative enthusiasm of legislators for PMAs. Additionally, explaining that privatization will be a means to opening access to the PMA transmission grids will create new political supporters among those users and suppliers who anticipate gains from market developments. In general, the thorough and careful marketing of federal power privatization proposals can dispel unfounded fears of the consequences from privatization and clarify the costs of continuation of the PMAs. The wooing and winning of the environmentalists, however, may be the essential piece in the public choice puzzle. The Reagan proposal on the BPA was seen by many powerful environmental groups as destructive to environment and wildlife. But, as described previously, one of the likely features of privatization of hydroelectric power is that environmental interests would gain standing.

In sum, the expansionary practices of the PMAs and the TVA have roots in the politically articulated demands of power users. These pressures prevent federal producers from responding quickly or fully to other demands that have weaker political positions. Environmental interests, in particular, have not yet emerged to counter the power user interests. These user interests have dominated environmental ones with respect to the uses of federal dams, the safe construction and operation of nuclear power plants, and responsiveness to air and water pollution laws. The federal agencies have had the assignable wealth needed to practice massive subsidization because they obtain financial capital at well-below market rates, and sell power from hydroelectric sites at far below market value. In a privatized environment the subsidies (and the political marketplace built around efforts to collect them) would dry up.

4. The Effects of Federal Power Privatization Under Alternative Scenarios About the Industry

The privatization of the PMAs and the TVA that is described in this paper also involves regional deregulations of power. In the case of the TVA, the changes would create a regional microcosm of an open-power market, keyed to a more accessible transmission system. What would be the likely effects of these efforts on the industry's evolution? A useful way to examine federal power privatization is to place it within varying industry contexts. We will therefore analyze privatization under alternative industry structures. Table 2 contains three scenarios suggested in part by the Office of Technological Assessment (OTA) in their 1989 study, "Electric Power: Wheeling and Dealing."[4]

Scenario 1: Strengthening the Regulatory Bargain

Since the traditional system remains intact in this approach, the federal privatization would have little direct effect outside the privatized region. In the cases of PMAs, hydroelectric assets probably would be acquired by utilities or IPPs; thus, privatized assets would become enmeshed in public utility regulation. Joint ownership provisions and open access to the PMAs' transmission lines also may have little impact, other than facilitating bulk sales among utilities. One major impact would be in the BPA area, where the intertie lines to Oregon and California are 80 percent owned by BPA. Use of the transmission lines would be determined by a new joint ownership organization that, with the privatization, would include all major utilities and IPPs in the Pacific states, from California to Washington.

Table 2. Alternative Scenarios

Scenario 1 Strengthening the Regulatory Bargain	Scenario 2 Competition for New Bulk Power Supplies	Scenario 3 Transmission Services in a Disaggregated Industry Structure
• Industry consists of a mix of vertically integrated utilities, IOUs, public power, cooperatives, privatized federal power authorities, self-generators, QFs, and IPPs.	• Existing mix of generating entities expanded by IPPs and unregulated utility generating subsidiaries.	• Ownership and control of existing integrated utility industry is disaggregated into separate generation, transmission, and distribution segments.
• Existing regulatory structure with State preapproval of new generating projects and periodic prudence reviews during planning and construction.	• Existing regulatory structure with market-based rates for new competitive generation. Utilities use all source procurement for new bulk power needs. Contracts awarded to lowest cost supplier with consideration for nonprice factors.	• New Federal and State regulatory system. Price and entry regulation of generation replaced with competitive markets. Distribution utilities' services and retail prices remain regulated. Transmission prices reviewed by FERC.
• Negotiated transmission access arrangements.	• Transmission access provided by utilities as a bidding condition, or by privately negotiated arrangements, or under new Federal public interest wheeling authority (no retail wheeling).	• Transmission sector operates under joint ownership of user, providing nondiscriminatory access to all wholesale and retail customers. Denial of access subject to system efficiency defense; FERC and antitrust laws control.
• Traditional system coordination and control by integrated utilities or control centers.	• Traditional system coordination and control by integrated utilities or control centers. Unbundled bulk power dispatch, control, and transmission services provided through contracts.	• Bulk system planning and coordination by transmission firm. Generators identify, plan, and build new generation in response to market signals. Transmission company assumes responsibility for reliability of bulk system operations. Responsibility for estimating demand and securing adequate power supplies rests with distribution utilities. Bulk power dispatch, control, and transmission services provided through contracts; the services may or may not be unbundled.
• Prices set by regulatory proceedings and cost of service. Transmission prices and wholesale rates set by FERC (including approval of negotiated IPP power purchases). State oversight of retail rates and PURPA implementation.	• Retail and transmission prices set by regulatory proceedings. Wholesale power prices set through competitive procurement except for cost-base plants built by utility as last resort supplier. State and Federal regulators oversee terms and conditions of wholesale sales.	• Bulk power prices set by market. Transmission prices set by market, with FERC oversight and review. Retail prices are set by regulatory proceedings. Some State and Federal oversight of competitiveness of generation markets.
• Federal PMAs and the TVA privatized. Their transmission systems opened and ownership in transmission shared among users (both consumers and suppliers). All generation (previously federally owned) can be marketed, to the extent feasible. All distributors previously served by federal agencies can contract for service.	• Federal PMAs and the TVA privatized. Their transmission systems opened and ownership in transmission shared among users (both consumers and suppliers). All generation (previously federally owned) can be marketed, to the extent feasible. All distributors previously served by federal agencies can contract for service.	• Federal PMAs and the TVA privatized. Their transmission systems privatized and ownership in transmission systems shared among users (both consumers and suppliers). All generation (previously federally owned) can be marketed, to the extent feasible. All distributors previously served by federal agencies can contract for service.

Because only the privatized lines would have joint ownership status, numerous exclusionary problems in adjacent transmission lines may preclude significant extensions of the grid. Joint ownership should, nonetheless, provide an encouragement to marketing bulk power, and the existence of significant imbalances between power supply and demand among utilities in the region may stimulate vigorous negotiation for use of these utility-owned lines.

In the Southeast, a privatized TVA initially would be composed of: a large, jointly owned transmission system, several new stand-alone GENCOs, and 160 independent distributors and other large industrial consumers. Here, more resounding effects on the surrounding utility environment are possible. The TVA has the flexibility today to plan and operate its bulk power facilities as a single integrated system; under privatization the jointly owned transmission system also could function as a single integrated yet competitive system.

Wholesale marketing may grow. Currently, the TVA has 500 kv interconnects with the Southern Company subsidiaries to the southeast, the Middle South Utilities to the southwest, American Electric Power Company to the north, and the Illinois-Missouri Power Pool to the west. It has other interconnects at lower voltages with other individual utilities in the region (Federal Energy Regulatory Commission 1981, 85). More could rapidly be built with the undoing of federal law prohibiting TVA transactions beyond its old territories. In particular, the VACAR pool utilities to the east may enter the market in this way.

Any of the new independent producers or customers from the old TVA region would be free to negotiate with any of these outside organizations. At issue, then, is the extent to which utilities adjoining the TVA would engage in direct power sales and the extent to which they would negotiate contracts for the use of transmission services for third parties outside of the TVA area. The pace of change in the selling and buying of wholesale power may be rapid, reflecting the continuation of this trend among utilities in the 1980s. Recently, sales from investor-owned utilities (IOUs) have buttressed TVA capacity. These bulk sales undoubtedly would continue for some time, albeit with privatized power organizations.

But it is unlikely that we would see a further integration of transmission system activities such as a combination with the Southern Companies or Middle South Utilities. Doing so would jeopardize the system of regulation applied to these utilities and challenge the authority of state regulators on numerous issues. In many ways, the successful operation of the TVA privatized system would act as an irritant to nearby franchised utilities and their regulators. For example, dissatisfied captive distribution customers of these utilities may push regulators vigorously to be allowed to bargain with suppliers in the TVA region. Conversely, IPPs and Qualifying Facilities (QFs) within utility territories could demand wheeling privileges to retail buyers within the TVA region. Such pressure may eventually lead to the regulatory changes that will move the industry beyond the configuration shown in Scenario 1.

Scenario 2: Competition for New Bulk Power Supplies

The major changes from scenario 1 to scenario 2 are: (1) new generating capacity would be deregulated and utilities forced to acquire new capacity outside the utility framework; (2) wheeling is established for non-retail accounts; (3) transmission and retail prices remain regulated, but wholesale prices are unregulated in most instances. This approach to deregulation of new generating capacity sets up a two-tiered accounting and pricing system with current federal and state pricing regulation remaining for only the "old" capacity. This OTA proposal is similar to one presented by FERC, but differs in mandating bidding on new capacity and guaranteeing access.

Within this scenario, the privatization of federal power entities can rapidly impact the industry. Any wholesale account can request wheeling across all transmission lines so that, for example, a TVA area generator could contract with a utility, a utility's unregulated subsidiary, or an IPP. Retail accounts, however, remain captive and therefore are unable to competitively search for power supplies. On the other hand, utilities would be likely to contract to sell power to the privatized distribution organizations and large industrial consumers within the old TVA.

In sum, scenario 2 delineates new conditions, applicable across the industry, that will accelerate bulk sales transactions, but will not bring retail consumers into the market. Thus, retail price regulation would remain. A TVA privatization introduces a competing vision of the industry, one with broader disaggregation, deeper competitive penetration, and joint ownership of transmission. A privatized-deregulated TVA would provide a yardstick by which to compare the effectiveness of reform elsewhere. The PMA deregulations, because of the limited extent of transmission and power production capacity privatized, will be unlikely to present much of a counter case.

Scenario 3: Joint Ownership Transmission Services in a Disaggregated Industry Structure

This industry-wide scenario mirrors much of the privatization of the federal power entities proposed in this paper. The entire industry would be placed in a "revolutionary" mode, opening the door to further ownership integration of transmission grids and to expansion of marketing as the participants dictate. These developments raise questions of monopolization or cartelization. If monopolization becomes an issue, then federal regulators and antitrust enforcers could become more aggressive. This regulatory role, if excessively intrusive, may sacrifice some or all of the possible gains from private market evolution of institutional structure and practice. Yet, without such legal "teeth" to respond to perceptions of anticompetitive behavior, Scenario 3 would be unlikely to gain broad political support.

5. Conclusion

Over the past 15 years, many proposals to substantially reform or deregulate the system of public utility regulation in the United States have been made. Yet, little comprehensive, pro-competitive change has been accomplished. Change is slowed, in part, because of resistance by powerful industry participants, whose interests are served by the continuation of the existing regulatory system. Additionally, the complicated nature of this regulatory process makes change costly. By contrast, privatization and deregulation of federal power assets is a more politically achievable change because the institutional superstructure is in the hands of the federal government. While interest group pressures are also at work with federal power authorities, the magnitude of the public choice reform problem (obtaining sufficient political support to act) is far less than in the public utility sector. In sum, federal power privatization is a feasible policy option.

What has been presented as privatization here also incorporated significant elements of deregulation and a sweeping reorganization of the transmission assets. This approach is premised on the grounds that, without such restructuring, effective privatization could not occur. Because privatization implies private control of use and sale of resources, simply turning power production over to public utility-regulated firms would do little, if anything, to further that objective. A privatization-deregulation, on the other hand, can produce a valuable competitive yardstick by which we can measure the rest of the industry's performance. The TVA's privatization, in particular, could provide an unusual opportunity to develop a market alternative to regulation that, to date, has been missing in the United States.

Notes

My thanks to Carl Pechman and to Charlotte Twight for their helpful comments.

1. Although the PMAs were targeted for privatization in the 1989 federal budget, little action has been taken to implement this proposal, and the TVA still remains a non-candidate.

2. The federal government can encourage opening and broadening the transmission markets in another power industry sector where it has significant direct control: the Rural Electrification Administration's (REA's) cooperative system. The highly subsidized REA cooperatives, through their joint ownership of G&Ts (generating and transmission organizations) have amassed considerable generating and transmission assets over the past two decades. The Bush administration seeks to severely limit large capital subsidies from the federal government (Budget of the United States Government FY 1990, 5:43-44). By giving or withholding support selectively, the government can motivate these G&Ts to develop sharing arrangements with adjoining private utilities. To some extent, the G&Ts are doing this now. For example, Public Service of Indiana and the Wabash Valley G&T have an agreement to share transmission facilities. Municipal power groups also have gained rights to public utility transmission service, the most significant example being the integration in 1976 of the transmission systems of Georgia Power and the Municipal Electric Authority of Georgia.

3. $656 million dollars were spent by the federal government alone over FY 1988 and 1989 to support energy conservation goals.

4. One significant difference from the OTA study is that the third scenario in table 2 involves joint ownership of transmission services. This replaces the common carriage obligations in the OTA report. Few technological appraisals of common carrier status suggest that it could be efficient—or even institutionally stable.

References

Ascher, Kate. 1987. *The Politics of Privatization*. London: Macmillion Ltd.
Bonneville Power Administration. 1986. "Federal Columbia River Power Systems, Statements of Revenues and Expenses for the year ended Sept 30 1986 and 1985." *Annual Report*, U.S. Dept. of Energy.
Campbell, David C. 1986. "Federal Power Sales Makes Environmental Sense." *Wall Street Journal* (March 4):30.
Congress of the United States, Office of Technology Assessment. 1989. *Electric Power Wheeling and Dealing: Technological Considerations for Increasing Competition*.
Congress of the United States, Office of Technology Assessment. 1989. *Electric Power Wheeling and Dealing: Technological Considerations for Increasing Competition, Summary*.
Conkin, Paul K. 1983. "Intellectual and Political Roots." In *TVA: Fifty Years of Grass-roots Bureaucracy*, edited by Erwin C. Hargrove and Paul K. Conkin. University of Illinois Press.
Couto, Richard A. 1983. "New Seeds at the Grass Roots: The Politics of the TVA Power Program since World War II." In *TVA: Fifty Years of Grass-roots Bureaucracy*, edited by Erwin C. Hargrove and Paul K. Conkin. University of Illinois Press.
De Alessi, Louis. 1975. "Some Effects of Ownership on the Wholesale prices of Electric Power." *Economic Inquiry* 13:526-538.
Demsetz, Harold. 1968. "Why Regulate Utilities?" *Journal of Law and Economics* (April):55-65.
Executive office of the President of the United States. 1990. *Budget of the United States Government*. Washington: U.S. Government Printing Office.
Executive office of the President of the United States. 1990. *Major Policy Initiatives*. Washington: U.S. Government Printing Office.
Federal Energy Regulatory Commission. 1981. *Power Pooling in the United States*. Office of Electric Power Regulation (December).
Hazlett, Thomas. 1985. "The Curious Evolution of Natural Monopoly Theory." In *Unnatural Monopolies: The Case for Deregulating Public Utilities*, edited by Robert W. Poole, Jr. The Reason Foundation.
Hellman, Richard. 1972. *Government Competition in Electric Utility Industry*. New York: Praeger Publishers.
Houston, Douglas A. 1987. "The Mixed Interest in Deregulation." *Land Economics* 63 (no. 4, November):403-405.
Houston, Douglas A. 1988. "Privatization of the Tennessee Valley Authority." In *Federal Privatization Project*. The Reason Foundation.
Hughes, William R. 1962. "Short-Run Efficiency and the Organization of the Electric Power Industry." *Quarterly Journal of Economics* 76:592-612.
Joskow, Paul, and Richard Schmalensee. 1983. *Markets for Power*. Cambridge, MA: MIT Press.
Martinson, Linda, and Loria W. Thomas. 1987. "The Transitional Bulk Power Market." *Public Utilities Fortnightly* (November 26):19-24.
Peltzman, Sam. 1971. "Pricing in Public and Private Enterprises: Electric Utilities in the United States." *Journal of Law and Economics* 109-147.
Pierce, Richard J. 1986. "A Proposal to Deregulate the Market for Bulk Power." *Virginia Law Review* 72:1183-1235.

Rosso, David J. 1989. "Transmission Access - A Crucial Issue for an Industry." *Public Utilities Fortnightly* (February 16):18-26.

Secretary of State for Energy. 1988. *Privatising Electricity*. London: Her Majesty's Stationery Office.

Shapiro, David L. 1989. *Generating Failure: Public Power Policy in the Northwest*. Cato Institute: University Press of America, Inc.

Smith, V.L. 1984. "Market Contestability in the Presence of Sunk (Entry) Costs." *Journal of Economics* 15:69.

Smith, V.L. 1987. "Currents of Competition in Electricity Markets." *Regulation* 2:23-29.

Stigler, George. 1968. *The Organization of Labor is Limited by the Extent of the Market*. The Organization of the Industry Homewood, IL: Irwin.

Tennessee Valley Authority. 1986. *Annual Report*, Vol. 2.

Tennessee Valley Authority. 1987. *Annual Report*.

Transmission Access Technical Task Force. 1988. *Engineering and Reliability Effects of Increased Wheeling and Transmission Access*. Transmission Issues Monograph, no 2. Edison Electric Institute (November).

Transmission Access Technical Task Force. 1989. *"Customer Wheeling": A Fiction, Contrary to the Public Interest*. Transmission Issues Monograph, no 3. Edison Electric Institute (April).

Veljanovski, Cento. 1987. *Selling the State: Privatization in Britain*. London: Weidenfeld and Nicolson.

Weiss, Larry and Scott Spiewak, eds. 1989. *The Wheeling and Transmission Manual*. Wheeling and Transmission Monthly Publications.